AN UNCOMMON BOOKMAN

Ronnie Adams

An Uncommon Bookman

Essays in Memory of
J R R Adams

Edited by
John Gray and Wesley McCann

The Linen Hall Library
Belfast

Published by
The Linen Hall Library
17 Donegall Square North
Belfast BT1 5GD
Northern Ireland

© The Linen Hall Library
Published 1996

ISBN 1 900921 00 6

Printed by the Universities Press

Acknowledgements

The editors would like to thank the contributors for so willingly providing a text of real substance, and advance subscribers for helping to ensure the viability of the project. Financial support from the Belfast Society and the Cultural Traditions Group has also been essential to the enterprise.

Particular thanks are due to Mrs Amber Adams for expert assistance in proof reading, and to the Information Technology Department at Stranmillis College, the staff of the Linen Hall Library, and Paul Campbell of December Publications, all of whom have eased the long path from manuscript to book.

For Amber and Alexandra Adams

CONTENTS

INTRODUCTION

JOHN GRAY

Of those involved in this volume, I was relatively late in recognising Ronnie Adams's unique qualities. True, during the late 70s, I had admired his industry on the Library Association/Public Record Office of Northern Ireland Joint Working Party, and in particular his leading role in ensuring completion and publication of the pioneering *Northern Ireland Newspapers: Checklist with Locations* (1979). I knew that he had very heavy commitments as Deputy Librarian of the Linen Hall Library and wondered why others of us, with larger library organisations behind us, did so much less.

For me the crucial moment in our acquaintance came at some point in 1980. By then Ronnie was Librarian at the Linen Hall which was threatened by imminent closure or take-over by suitors including the Belfast Education and Library Board and Queen's University. At that time, as Irish and Local Studies Librarian in the Belfast Central Library, I was a potential predator, albeit one with increasing misgivings about what was intended. Against that background I visited the Linen Hall and Ronnie Adams.

He reigned in the midst of what, on the surface, appeared to be a scene of irredeemable decay and dilapidation. By many practical standards the Linen Hall was beyond saving. I listened then to a softly spoken but impassioned defence of the cultural role of the library and its collections, its accretion of the small printing of its own community, and its indispensable value for the future. Coming as I did from a library service which, with blinkered determination, still insisted that local studies and Irish studies were 'just part of world civilisation and should be treated accordingly', I was, bit by bit, won over. So, in those critical times for the Linen Hall Library, were many others.

This is, of course, to leap ahead in the chronology of Ronnie's own career. Whence came he on the road to the Linen Hall?

No-one who knew him could have doubted his Ulster provenance, but this was not merely the narrow ground of Belfast and Down in which he subsequently worked and made his home. He was born in Londonderry in 1946, son of a school principal, spent his childhood years in County Donegal, and was educated at Sligo Grammar and High School.

He was to retain a strong affection for that Donegal hinterland later writing on the local poets of the Laggan. There is no doubt that this extra geographical dimension to his experience, an increasingly unusual one in post-partition Ulster, lent a wider dimension to his understanding and appreciation of cultural diversity, and of the importance of local studies.

Moving to Belfast he started work as a library assistant in the public library service in 1965. He was soon seconded to the newly formed Department of Library and Information Studies at Queen's University where he obtained his professional qualification in 1969. It was here also that he met his wife Amber who was also to pursue a career in librarianship.

While this necessary grounding offered no obvious opportunity for Ronnie to exercise what were soon to prove his real strengths, it is significant that, in a private capacity, he was one of the very few who recognised the importance of the tide of ephemeral publications that stemmed from the onset of the troubles in 1968. In this he shared a common interest with Jim Gracey, a friend from library school days, and by now Deputy Librarian at the Linen Hall Library. Gracey was substantially responsible for initiating what is now the Northern Ireland Political Collection at the library. He was assisted in acquiring material by Ronnie who assembled his own considerable collection which was later sold to the University of Ulster.

Ronnie Adams's appointment in 1971 as Assistant Librarian at Down County Library with particular responsibility for local history provided him with a first professional opportunity to play a pioneering role. He launched a bi-monthly listing of new additions to the collection, assembled local history packs for each branch library, and developed a card index to local material of 'every conceivable sort'. As he was later to note by way of characteristic understatement, 'these initiatives had up to then not been practised in the north of Ireland'.

He was an obvious candidate in 1973 for appointment as Deputy Librarian at the Linen Hall Library, again with particular responsibility for local history. He did much to improve organisation and access to the collection. It was also a post which gave him personal access to what he always viewed as 'a matchless collection'. He began to establish another distinction from so many other librarians – he read the books in his collection, and, increasingly, committed the fruits of his research to print.

Work on his thesis, 'A History of Libraries in County Down from the Earliest Period to the Year 1900', for which he received his Fellowship of the Library Association in 1977, did much to establish his reputation as an expert on books, literacy, and their relationship with popular culture. His knowledge of early County Down reading societies no doubt stood him in good stead in securing appointment as Linen Hall Librarian in 1978.

It was an appointment which should have led to long and fruitful tenure. Unfortunately for the library, and perhaps for Ronnie Adams, it was not to be. Again with characteristic diffidence he was subsequently to describe circumstances in which 'increasing uncertainty about the future made forward planning difficult and ensured that managerial duties took up most of my time'. Ronnie would in any case have regretted the pull away from 'continued bibliographical work', but when managerial duty included coping with a demanding and yet badly divided Board of Governors in a library directly faced with closure, the strains were all the greater. In those circumstances his switch in 1981 to the post of Librarian at the Ulster Folk and Transport Museum and to an 'in house' research library, seemed to offer the chance to return to the kind of work he truly relished.

He remained a regular visitor to the Linen Hall. One did perhaps detect a sense of regret that he was no longer in day to day contact with the collections. It remains true that the availability of the collections to anyone owes much to his period as Librarian. When I succeeded him at the end of 1981 most of the hard decisions necessary to secure the survival of the library had been taken, and outlines of future possibilities were in place, many of which have contributed to the subsequent success of the institution.

At the Ulster Folk and Transport Museum, Ronnie succeeded Aiken McClelland whose early death had robbed the province of an enthusiast

3

for, and expert on the small printing of the province. McClelland had enjoyed a relatively free hand in pursuing his own researches, notably on the Orange Order. Matters were never quite so simple in the 1980s. An early constraint for Adams was lack of other staff. Latterly his role expanded when he chaired the Museum's Documentation Committee which initiated planning for and recommended appropriate procedures for use in a co-ordinated computer-based documentation system encompassing all the institution's archival collections as well as its holdings of material objects.

Above all, however, his tenure at the Ulster Folk and Transport Museum did provide a real opportunity to extend his research and writing activities, indeed some 55 of his 70 published articles and books date from this period. Influences at the Museum no doubt encouraged a ready expansion of his interests into the fields of folklife and dialect studies. This, combined with his already far reaching knowledge of more specifically book related aspects of cultural history, gave him a breadth of understanding matched by few.

Part time MA studies at Queen's University's Department of Economic and Social History saw the genesis of his major work, first as a thesis completed in 1986, and then as *The Printed Word and the Common Man: Popular Culture in Ulster 1700-1900* (Belfast: Institute of Irish Studies, 1987). This was widely acclaimed at the time, 'highly commended' in the 1988 Irish Book Awards, and now, almost a decade later, remains an obligatory point of reference for social and cultural historians.

At the Linen Hall we continued to benefit from his breadth of view. In the 1970s he had contributed to *Irish Booklore*, originally a separate journal, but in the 1980s revived as an 'Irish Booklore' section in the *Linen Hall Review*. It was perhaps an indication of the lack of any extensive tradition of research and writing by northern librarians or book collectors that feature material for this section was often hard to secure. Ronnie was a glowing exception to this stricture and appeared to have an unfailing ability to produce extensive articles at short notice with the added merit that they were always authoritative and yet accessible to the lay community.

Typically in November 1993 he took ten days to produce 'From *Green Gravel* to *The Way that I Went:* Folklife, Literature and the Patterson Family of Holywood'. By way of editorial convenience 2,500 words arrived requiring hardly a correction and complete with photographs and captions. By way of more enduring value, here was an article, that as the title alone indicates, brought together strands of family history, local history, bibliography and folk lore.

We were not to know that this was to be his last article. The printer's ink was barely dry when we heard of his sudden and untimely death. Perhaps one should leave him with the final words, both quotations from the introduction to *The Printed Word and the Common Man*. The first reflects his determination to go beyond any narrow or overly mechanistic definition of the proper role of either a librarian or a book-lover:

> A book is not just an object capable of being described bibliographically: it is the medium by which people absorbed ideas and saw reflected their views and hopes.

The second, his verdict that 'the culture was an amazingly shared one – a very broad church indeed', can be applied to the range of Ronnie's own friends and connections many of whom have contributed to this volume. Our scope is we hope creatively multi-disciplinary; we come from many townlands, but we share a common desire to sustain Ronnie Adams's breadth of vision.

CONTINENTAL TRAVEL MEMOIRS: A SOURCE FOR THE PROVINCIAL BOOKTRADE?

BARBARA TRAXLER BROWN

WHEN COMPILING THE HISTORY of the provincial booktrade, certain categories of source material are quite familiar, and keep recurring, regardless of the country in question. Directories of the period, archival records, contemporary newspaper advertisements – all these are featured among the primary sources of most explorations. In the following survey, however, a less frequent primary source is in question, the foreign language travel account: in particular those describing the experiences of Continental visitors to Britain and Ireland during the late eighteenth and early nineteenth centuries.

At the present stage of our survey the language of publication selected for such travel accounts is German. Many publications in this minor genre for that language are extant; indeed they have formed the basis for exploring mainstream Anglo-German cultural relations since the late nineteenth century.[1] Trade and contact between Britain, Ireland and the various German duchies and kingdoms had been favoured by the Hanoverian succession of 1714 – to the extent that by 1769, the British ambassador to the Court of Saxony at Dresden, Robert Murray Keith, was complaining of 'an inundation of English'. Likewise, the number of German visitors to Britain steadily increased. Indeed, according to some estimates based on attendance statistics at Lutheran Churches, the resident German-speaking population of London numbered several thousand by the end of the eighteenth century.[2]

While London and its surroundings attracted the majority of German visitors, others ventured farther afield, including Scotland and Ireland on an itinerary which virtually represented a Northern counterpart of the traditional Grand Tour. Insofar as these visitors, like their British counterparts, represented a social, professional and educational elite, comments on the level of literary culture in various regions, the local booktrade, newspapers and reading facilities do occur, in general apparently eyewitness accounts which often confirm the factual details of other, more widely known standard sources. To gain some insight into the nature of this documentary evidence, and the ways in which it may be mobilised, it is helpful to consider some sample German language publications for the period 1775-1845, noting references to the booktrade and various aspects of reading culture in England and Ireland as they arise.

German language travel memoirs 1775-1845: their nature and accessibility

The most accessible format for this type of source is the formally published travel memoir, whether presented in journals or magazines of the period, or in near contemporary editions a few months or years after the visit. The widest physical availability in most German research libraries for such material, however, would be in the posthumous scholarly and critical editions of the nineteenth and twentieth centuries. For all such published editions – regardless of date – the bibliographical control, the means of locating library copies, has steadily improved since the early 1980s. Quite apart from normal hard copy subject bibliographies, new methods of electronic retrieval and consultation have emerged due to the retrospective catalogue conversion programmes of the major West German research libraries in recent years, for example, at the State and University Library of Lower Saxony in Göttingen, at the Herzog August Library in Wolfenbüttel, near Brunswick, at the Staatsbibliothek-Preussischer Kulturbesitz, Berlin, and at the Bavarian State Library, Munich. (See diagram on following page).

Of all these regional initiatives, the State and University Library at Göttingen in particular has had a very long association with the British Library, in the context of contributing well over 12,000 records from its holdings for the period 1701-1800 to the database of the Eighteenth

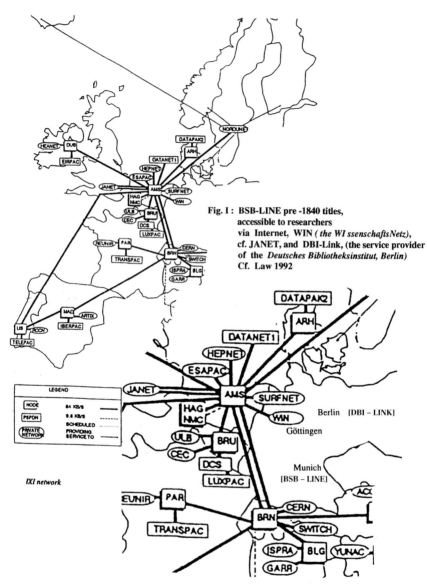

Fig. I : **BSB-LINE pre -1840 titles,
accessible to researchers
via Internet, WIN (** *the WI ssenschaftsNetz),*
**cf. JANET, and DBI-Link, (the service provider
of** the *Deutsches Bibliotheksinstitut, Berlin)*
Cf. Law 1992

Berlin   [DBI – LINK]

Göttingen

Munich
[BSB – LINE]

IXI network

LEGEND

NODE	64 KB/S
PSPDN	9.6 KB/S
PRIVATE NETWORK	SCHEDULED
	PROVIDING SERVICE TO

*Derek Law, European Research Networks In: M. Blake (ed.) The Common Market for
Information. Proceedings of the Institute of Information Scientists, June, 1992,
Bedford. (London, 1992), p.51.*
'Cosine Pilot IXI Topology, 01.04.92'
(prepared by the Joint Network Team)

8

Century Short-Title Catalogue (ESTC).[3] Thereby it is possible to trace and identify contemporary English language translations of German travel accounts concerning various geographic regions during the eighteenth century. In contrast to Göttingen – an eighteenth-century Hanoverian University foundation with close links to England – the catalogue automation programme of the Bavarian State Library at Munich has demonstrated quite an alternative collection profile and emphasis. Comparison of its foundation collections for the period 1501-1840 (*c*.662,000 titles) with those of the British Library, the Bibliothèque Nationale, or the Library of Congress, indicates that approximately 40% of the Munich holdings are *not* to be found duplicated in these other research collections.[4] Since September 1992 electronic retrieval of those holdings has been possible via the Bavarian State Library On-line Public Access Catalogue (BSBOPAC), a networked version of which has been available since November 1994, BSB-LINE on the Internet. Thus a relatively unexploited domain exists for consultation by those interested in exploring references to the booktrade and reading culture of Britain and Ireland, as derived from Continental travel accounts of two hundred years ago. Some of the rewards – and disadvantages – of the historical evidence so revealed may be illustrated as follows.

Similar to the database of the British Library Eighteenth Century Short-Title Catalogue, it is possible to define and search the eighteenth-century records of the BSBOPAC for particular keywords, authors or places of publication. If, for example, a search for the title keywords IRELAND/IRLAND and/or the variant form, IRRLAND, is entered, and the date span restricted to 1700-1800, over one hundred catalogue records are displayed. To illustrate further the retrieval capacity of the BSBOPAC its recorded places of publication are of particular interest. For example, if the search term BELFAST is entered, and the datespan extended to 1700-1840, some twelve entries are retrieved from this research library's foundation collection; among those entries, however, are Samuel MacSkimin's *History and Antiquities ... of the Town of Carrickfergus from the Earliest Records to the Present Time* (Belfast, 1811), the *Collection of Choice Irish Songs... translated by Miss Brooke* (Belfast, 1795) and Tone's pamphlet, *An Argument on Behalf of the Catholics of Ireland* (Belfast, 1791). For NEWRY as a search term, just one publication is retrieved: the

9

Historical Memoirs of the City of Armagh for a period of 1373 Years, by James Stuart (Newry, 1819). For LONDONDERRY, alas, or any of its variants, nothing appears to be extant among this Munich library's antiquarian books. Likewise for the city of ARMAGH.

However, as in the case of some other major German collections, the identification of relevant catalogue entries is by no means a guarantee that the actual book is still available for consultation, i.e. that the Library's holdings survived the vicissitudes of 1939-45. As will be seen later, some potentially very relevant eighteenth-century descriptions of Ireland and England highlighted by the BSBOPAC will have to be obtained elsewhere, since although the catalogue record has survived, the book itself is a war loss, indicated by the shelf-mark note, *(Kriegs)verlust*.

While the above general miscellaneous imprints are of some interest, the *specific* retrieval capacity of BSBOPAC for travel literature may be seen in the following 'hit', the *Neueste Reisen durch Schottland und Ireland* by Johann Jakob Volkmann (1732-1803).[5] Published at Leipzig in 1784, it was intended, as its author mentions, to fill a gap in reference literature about Ireland for the German-speaking visitor. As was quite normal for such travel literature, it adopts the epistolary format, a series of *Briefe* or Letters, covering the various cities and counties of the author's itinerary, starting at Dublin, and continuing to Belfast and even Ballyshannon. Volkmann's other publications were well known as late as the 1930s to historians researching Anglo-German cultural relations, among them John Alexander Kelly. The relative eclipse since then of his travel book on Ireland and Scotland, however, is certainly due in part to the difficulty in identifying such pre-1840 material from traditional, non-automated catalogues.

Once identified, what do these and other titles have to tell us? With reference first of all to the English booktrade, the following episode concerning John Baskerville's enterprise at Birmingham illustrates several aspects concerning the practical availability and value of such foreign language accounts. While London and its surroundings attracted the majority of German visitors as noted above, others towards the end of the century were venturing farther afield, including the English provinces, as well as Scotland and Ireland on their itineraries.

The author Georg Christoph Lichtenberg (1742-1799) visited England in 1770, and again in 1775. As a Professor at Göttingen University, he wrote several 'open' letters to his publisher in Göttingen, Johann Christian Dieterich (1712-1800), as well as to various scientific colleagues. Given Dieterich's profession, it is not surprising that letters to him focused especially on the current news of the English booktrade. From a letter written in St. Paul's Coffee-house, London, on 13th October 1775, it emerges that Lichtenberg had just returned from a visit to Birmingham.[6] Unaware that Baskerville had died earlier that year, he virtually undertook a pilgrimage there to see for himself this centre of excellence in English typographical design. The letter describes in detail his reception by Mrs Baskerville, her surroundings, and how – despite her black silk mourning dress – she took him personally around the foundry, showing the various punches and matrices. Afterwards she treated him not merely to a glass of Madeira and toast, but also to a copy of the *Book of Common Prayer*, and to no fewer than six specimen sheets. There is a reason, though, for the latter: they were not just intended as souvenirs. Ideally everything, all the equipment and materials, was to be sold, along with her husband's secret recipe for printing ink, for about £4,000, transport from Birmingham to London included *gratis*. For ready cash there would be a discount of 5%, otherwise half-yearly credit. Perhaps in the German states, there would be a purchaser?

Such, however, was not to be the case. The material was acquired by Beaumarchais in 1779, and used by him at Kehl, just across the Rhine from Strasbourg, for his celebrated edition of Voltaire's works. Lichtenberg personally assessed the Baskerville legacy as too much of a risk for the German booktrade of the period, literally the wherewithal for a publisher to go bankrupt (as Beaumarchais eventually did). The letter to Dieterich is extant in two versions, and offers a striking insight into the months immediately after Baskerville's demise, when the fate of his life's work was in the balance. In terms of physical availability the late twentieth century editions of Lichtenberg's letters offer by far the most accurate and comprehensive version of his text. Otherwise, even the legibility of such accounts can pose problems. Just as German language publications were normally printed in *Fraktur* up to the mid-twentieth century, so too private individuals normally wrote in a non-roman manuscript convention, *Süterlin*. Accordingly, even where it has survived, the original family correspondence or personal diary underlying many of these travel accounts can be rather difficult to decipher. Yet it is this capacity for personal eyewitness observation of aspects of the booktrade and reading culture which appears to distinguish the best and most rewarding of the travel accounts extant.

This characteristic can also be noted for one of Lichtenberg's direct contemporaries, Sophie von La Roche (1731-1807). In the autumn of 1786 she visited England with her son, the scientist, Carl von La Roche. The family correspondence generated by her visit during those months later comprised most of the travel diary, or *Tagebuch einer Reise durch Holland und England*, published two years later at Offenbach in 1788, and again in 1791.[7] The diary format is worth noting. Just as the title keywords, IRELAND/IRLAND can be used to retrieve relevant database entries in the BSBOPAC, so too can generic terms, like *Briefe*/Letters or *Tagebuch*/Diary, i.e. journal, cf. Boswell's *Journal of a Tour to the Hebrides* ... of the same era. Certainly for German publishing 1700-1801, the *Tagebuch* as a minor literary genre appears to be an indispensable vehicle for the travel memoir, if the sixty-eight entries of the Bavarian State Library may be taken as evidence.

Exceptionally for this class of material, there is a modern English translation of Sophie von La Roche's account. Typical for her circle she is introduced to the well-known Irish scientist and Fellow of the Royal Society, Richard Kirwan (1733-1812). Originally from County Galway, Kirwan's London home attracted some of the best scientific and intellectual talent of the period.[8] His views on one particular author, as recorded by Sophie, help to explain one of the more curious features of contemporary reading culture in Ireland: the popularity, and sustained longevity of interest in the Swiss poet, Salomon Gessner (1730-1788), as described by Adams.[9] Gessner emerges as a common acquaintance of Kirwan and Sophie, as noted by the latter:

> ... giving me messages to Salomon Gessner, for whom he has an exceeding admiration, ... telling me that the entire English nation was likewise agreed upon the works of this noble, gentle spirit, or else Gessner's writings would not have reached their eighteenth edition.

The literary merits of Gessner's rural idylls and Arcadian shepherds, so familiar to the enlightened, Continental milieux of Kirwan and Sophie, are somewhat less obvious today; nonetheless it is clear that Gessner's work had endorsement at the highest social levels, in Kirwan's case, as a future member of the Royal Irish Academy, and Inspector of His Majesty's Mines in Ireland. With this calibre of socio-cultural approval, it is not perhaps so surprising that Gessner's work was published in locations as peripheral – in geographic terms – as Newry, for example, the 'fourteenth edition' of 1783, by Daniel Carpenter; likewise, several decades later, in Belfast by the printer, Joseph Smyth.[10] For more than seventy years, Gessner's *Death of Abel* appears to have been a regular feature of the chapman's pack. This longevity in the canon of popular literature in Ulster is shared by his European contemporaries, Rudolf Erich Raspe (1737-1794), the author of the *Surprising Travels and Adventures of Baron Munchausen* (alias *Gulliver Revived*), Joachim Heinrich Campe (1746-1818), with *The New Robinson Crusoe ...*, and last, but not least, Johann Wolfgang von Goethe (1749-1832) and his *Sorrows of Werter: a German Story*.[11] It is possible that these Continental best sellers from the previous century in the lists of the Belfast printer, Joseph Smyth, during 1826-1850, represent the survivors, the last vestiges, even the relics in a sense, of a Georgian cosmopolitan literary culture, a phenomenon which merits much closer investigation in the context of evolving reading taste in Ireland during the late eighteenth and early nineteenth centuries.

In terms of direct eyewitness narrative, therefore, the travel accounts of the later eighteenth century can yield unexpected avenues of enquiry. At the very least, they have the potential to highlight authors whose reference, or literary value has long since become eclipsed. Specifically in the context of foreign authors on Ireland, the La Roche *Diary* has some further revelations. At Windsor, Sophie is introduced to a 'Mr. Küttner', whom she describes as:

> an estimable German scholar ... who is responsible for some of the best information on the Irish climate, character and customs, for his *Letters*, published in 1785, belong to the finest and most complete sketches of that truly strange land, which is less known even than India.[12]

This author, Karl Gottlob Küttner (1755-1805), is seldom mentioned today in modern German literary history. After studying at Leipzig, a university town second only to Göttingen in cultivating cultural relations with England, Küttner earned a living for over a decade as a private family tutor to distinguished families, first in Switzerland, then England and Ireland. His services resulted in a life-long pension. In 1785, following his return to Leipzig, he edited the *Briefe über Irland* referred to by Sophie von La Roche.[13] Given Küttner's career as a private tutor, some appreciation of local levels of reading culture and book provision may legitimately be expected from his correspondence. The *Briefe über Irland* are recorded in the BSBOPAC; the copy may well have been the one consulted by John Alexander Kelly when he used the Munich Staatsbibliotheck for his researches in the early 1930s.

Surprisingly, in view of Küttner's direct experience of Ireland, and the outspoken praise of Sophie von La Roche, Kelly is quite dismissive of Küttner as a travel writer in general. In particular he mentions how the latter 'borrows freely' from the work of Johann Jakob Volkmann, although he does not make clear if this charge of Kütttner's 'borrowing' applies to Volkmann's earlier publications about *England*, as distinct from the later work of 1784 about Scotland and Ireland.[14] To clarify the validity of Kelly's criticism is today, however, not quite so straightforward as at the time of his original researches. While the catalogue record of Küttner's *Briefe* survives in electronic format in the State Library, the book itself has not been so fortunate: like the Library's copy of Sophie's *Tagebuch*, Offenbach, 1791, it is recorded as a *Verlust*. Pending further database searches of other major collections in the German *Länder*, it would seem that only the British Library in London duplicates today the particular research conditions of Kelly's examination, insofar as it holds all of the relevant Küttner, Volkmann, and La Roche editions.[15]

If it does emerge eventually that Küttner's *Briefe* are plagiarised from Volkmann's account of 1784, this was neither a wise nor commendable procedure. Unfortunately for his successors, Volkmann himself derived much of his text from other authors, in particular from English language originals of the 1770s, and early 1780s. When referring to Belfast, for example, Volkmann describes how '... a certain Magee has a printing-house, which delivers texts with far better type and paper than elsewhere in Ireland'.[16] He is almost certainly thinking of the elder James Magee (1707-1797), the founder of one of the most noted Belfast printing dynasties.[17] However, for anyone familiar with the prolific chapbook trade of this firm, Volkmann's emphasis on the select nature of Magee's productions is rather mystifying. Why should readers in Leipzig and elsewhere have been given this flattering impression of a provincial printing firm in a far distant country? Well, the answer is fairly straightforward. The generous verdict on Magee's expertise is not original to Volkmann at all; instead it is copied, taken from a very well-known source, the *Tour in Ireland* of Richard Twiss, London, 1776, as follows:[18] 'A few books have been printed in Belfast, by one James Magee, in a much neater manner than in any other part of Ireland, both as to the beauty of the types, and the fineness of the paper.' In his footnotes, Twiss even specifies the titles in question - all of them recent, for example, Aikin's *Miscellaneous Pieces in Prose*, Roberts' *Poetical Essays*, Goldsmith's *Poems*. Twiss continues to characterise Magee even further as a former 'taylor, who, by mere dint of genius, made the types, the ink, the paper, and the press.'

Well, in at least one aspect this characterisation is not true: at University College Dublin some of these particular Magee editions are extant, as in the *Miscellaneous Pieces, in Prose*, by John and Anna Laetitia Aikin, alias Mrs Barbauld.[19] The paper for the edition was certainly not made by Magee, or even linked with Belfast at all. Of good quality, a plain Fleur-de-lis countermarked RM, it is probably from the mill of Richard Mansergh, whose paper-making activities are documented from 1768 to 1789, and whose trade office was located in Cook Street, Dublin, near the quays, a very typical location for the trade.[20] Thus this title in Magee's production is far removed from his more commonplace output, of which some 190 examples are recorded in the ESTC. For the purposes of our exploration, however, this particular episode has demonstrated one of the main failings of formally published travel literature in the eighteenth century: the fact that much of it can be derivative, especially through unacknowledged translation. As Black has pointed out for English memoirs about the Grand Tour, a great deal is simply copied from one account to the next.[21] Volkmann clearly had access to the account by Richard Twiss, and in fact he may well have been associated with the Leipzig translation in 1777 of Twiss, *Reise durch Irrland*, recorded in the BSBOPAC, albeit as a lost holding. Certainly, for Arthur Young's *Tour through Ireland*, published at Leipzig in 1780, a few months after the London and Dublin editions, Volkmann is named as one of the two German translators.[22] So the above case does raise a fundamental point: why go to the trouble of locating Continental accounts, consulting them, deciphering them, if the risk is so high for repetition, misinterpretation even, of standard English language sources in any case?

To some extent, this problem of duplication was already well known to contemporary observers; in response perhaps to their criticism a certain maturing of the genre can be noted by the turn of the century. Memoirs become more specific, topical and original. By 1807 the work of Philip Andreas Nemnich (1764-1822) illustrates this trend. As distinct from the spontaneous, anecdotal approach of earlier visitors, Nemnich went to Britain virtually by commission, on behalf of his publisher, J.G. Cotta at Tübingen. His description of manufactures and trading conditions in Britain were originally intended for publication in Cotta's newspaper, the *Allgemeine Zeitung*.[23] In a preparatory journey through the English counties in 1799, Nemnich systematically refers to local newspapers, reading societies, subscription libraries, etc. From his account it emerges that Miles Swinney in Birmingham is virtually the successor to Baskerville there, and that a specimen sheet of the type and ornaments from Swinney's foundry was published in 1799, quite a rare document for the provincial trade outside the Oxford and Cambridge presses.[24] Six years later, in 1805, Nemnich returns, this time including Scotland and Ireland in his survey, as well as England. The book-trade is considered in some detail: for example, the price of a Stanhope press is noted as £100, that of a wooden press in mahogany, £40. This may be contrasted with the common wooden press, retailing at £30. While the above price of £100 for a new Stanhope press does seem exaggerated, nonetheless it is an amount which has been identified for the period September 1804-April 1805, so Nemnich appears to have been correct. He further records printers' ink as selling from 16 pence upwards per pound, depending on quality. Estimates are also provided by him for the titles, circulation and financial worth of the magazine market, plus the number of those employed in the booktrade throughout Britain (about 4,000), the number of new titles per annum (between 700-800) and the value of book exports to the United States (a lamentable £20,000 each year).[25]

On reaching Dublin in 1806, Nemnich resides in Dame Street, in the hotel part of the recently developed Commercial Buildings, the then location of the Dublin Stock Exchange. He describes the spacious Commercial Coffee-House, which is part of this complex, how it is well supplied with various newspapers, and how John Archer's bookshop, 'the most distinguished in Dublin', is located right at the entrance.[26] If these details are checked against local sources, Nemnich proves to be totally accurate. The *Dublin Directory* of Peter Wilson for 1802 describes the Commercial Coffee-House and Hotel, managed by a 'Mrs Gaynor'. The *Directory* also gives John Archer's address at the Commercial Buildings, Dame Street, to which he had very recently moved, for he was still at No. 80, Dame Street, the location of many of his book auctions, in 1800. As for being distinguished, yes, already well before Nemnich's visit, Archer could style himself 'Bookseller to the Lord Lieutenant'. Disappointingly, however, there is no record of any direct conversation between Archer and Nemnich, although from some unnamed source the latter presents the conclusion that scarcely a dozen new titles are produced at present by the Dublin booktrade, following the Act of Union.[27] Nonetheless, the description of the Dublin visit in general is quite vivid and worthwhile.

Conclusion

To summarise, therefore, there has been a dramatic improvement since the early 1990s in the research conditions for identifying and locating editions of historical travel literature concerning Ireland. This improvement is especially true for English and German language publications prior to 1800 and 1840 respectively. The material so retrieved is often capable of yielding new perspectives on existing well-known sources for the booktrade and levels of reading culture; nonetheless, the tendency for plagiarism – and that on a really international scale across European borders – results in a constant need for careful textual collation and bibliographical research when dealing with such authors.

The scale and extent of this new electronic retrieval capacity for antiquarian foreign language imprints emerge all the more clearly when, for post-1840 literature, the traditional typescript, or even manuscript – i.e. in *Süterlin* – card catalogues have once again to be called into service. For the period 1841-1952 in the Bavarian State Library, approximately 2.3 million records are awaiting conversion to electronic format, an undertaking which will last well into the next century.[28] In addition, while the State Library's holdings constitute by far the largest segment of the networked BVB or Union Catalogue for libraries in the *Land* of Bavaria, there do remain very significant collections in other libraries of the region where catalogue conversion is not quite so far advanced.

Simply to illustrate what this situation means in practice, the following case in another Munich research library may be considered. If the subject card indexes of the Deutsches Museum are consulted for the Library's holdings relating to IRLAND, one of the most worthwhile entries is given as the following: Titmarsh, M. A.: *Irländische Zustände. Aus dem Englischen von Carl Emil Lenzor*, Stuttgart, 1845. This edition is part of a travelogue series, namely, *Weltpanorama. Eine Chronik der neuesten Reisen und Abenteuer bei allen Nationen der Welt.*[29] The contribution of Michael Angelo Titmarsh forms volumes 51 to 53 of the series. As a library specialising above all in scientific and technological research, the Deutsches Museum has comparatively few antiquarian editions by English literary authors. This particular holding, however, is certainly quite a rare item, for no other copy of the Stuttgart 1845 German translation appears in the records of the Bavarian State Library, the networked BVB Union Catalogue, or in the 1992 microfiche Central Catalogue for other libraries in the region, (2,625,210 entries).

The text of *Irländische Zustände* is surprisingly rich in details about the facilities of the book-trade in various Irish towns.[30] Despite its apparent rarity, it is one of the most frequent reference sources for the cultural historians of nineteenth-century Ireland, albeit under a much more familiar title, namely *The Irish Sketch-book* by William Makepeace Thackeray, first published at London in 1843. For several of his works during the 1840s, Thackeray used the pseudonym of M.A. Titmarsh. Thus, what initially appeared to be an original contribution by a minor author to the historical complex of German language texts about Ireland, is in reality a duplication, a further extension of an already well-known and well-used source. Once again, it demonstrates the need for careful bibliographical research, when attempting to identify and utilise such literature, above all for the decades after 1840.

Thus on the one hand, the new and planned catalogue databases of European research libraries offer an unprecedented resource for exploration; yet, on the other, the scepticism and cross-checking required for the titles so identified does not always seem to be quite in proportion to the amount of worthwhile evidence which emerges. The experiment continues, however, for although the portrayal given to the distant Continental reader of local booktrade conditions may certainly have been unusual or strange on occasion – witness the Leipzig readers' perception of James Magee – nonetheless the value and interest of this phenomen is too great to ignore, or casually dismiss.

Notes

1   John Alexander Kelly, *England and the Englishman in German Literature of the Eighteenth Century* (New York, 1921). Jeremy Black, *The British Abroad: the Grand Tour in the Eighteenth Century* (New York, 1992), p. 10. Cf. the detailed surveys by C.J. Woods in *Irish Historical Studies*, 25 (1987), 311-321 and 28 (1992), 171-183. Also, Eda Sagarra, *Die 'grüne Insel' in der Deutschen Reiseliteratur. Deutsche Irlandreisende von Karl Gottlob Küttner bis Heinrich Böll.* In: Hans-Wolf Jäger (ed.) *Europäisches Reisen im Zeitalter der Aufklärung* (Heidelberg, 1992), pp. 182-95.

2   Cf. J.G. Burkhard, *Kirchengeschichte der deutschen Gemeinden in London* (Tübingen, 1798).

3   The ESTC Library Location Symbol for Göttingen = GOT.

4   Bavarian State Library, *Alphabetical Catalogue 1501-1840.* (Preliminary edition) (Munich, 1987), vol. I, p. XI. For Internet access to BSB-LINE, enter 129.143.3.1 or 129.143.3.2, then pad 45050080007 starte.

5   Johann Jakob Volkmann, *Neueste Reisen durch Schottland und Ireland: vorzüglich in Absicht auf die Naturgeschichte, Oekonomie, Manufakturen und Landsitze der Grossen. Aus den besten Nachrichten und neuern Schriften* (Leipzig, 1784).

6   *Lichtenberg in England. Dokumente einer Begegnung,* edited by Hans Ludwig Gumbert (Wiesbaden, 1977), vol. I, pp. 310-11. Cf. also *Georg Christoph Lichtenberg. Briefwechsel,* edited by Ulrich Joost and Albrecht

Schöne (Munich, 1983-1992), vol. I, pp. 556-57.

7   Sophie von La Roche, *Tagebuch einer Reise durch Holland und England* (Second edition) (Offenbach am Main, 1791).

8   *Sophie in London, 1786; Being the Diary of Sophie v. la Roche. A Translation of the Portion Referring to England of "Tagebuch einer Reise durch Holland und England"* translated, ... with an introductory essay by Clare Williams, etc. (London, 1933), pp. 281-82.

9   J.R.R. Adams, *The Printed Word and the Common Man : Popular Culture in Ulster 1700-1900* (Belfast, 1987), p. 147, p. 150, and Appendix III, p. 185.

10 Salomon Gessner, *[Der Tod Abels. English] The Death of Abel. In Five Books. Attempted from the German of Mr. Gessner. The fourteenth edition ...*, Newry: printed by D. Carpenter, 1783, ESTC t167968. Cf. Adams, *The Printed Word*, p. 68, p. 179, No. 113, and Appendix VI, p. 196.

11 Cf. Rudolf Erich Raspe, *Gulliver Revived; Containing Singular Travels, Campaigns, and Adventures in Russia, ...* London, 1787. ESTC n017827 and Adams, *The Printed Word*, p. 197 and p. 202. For Goethe's *Sorrows of Werter*, Belfast, 1844, cf. Adams, p. 196, and also Robin C. Alston, *Books with Manuscript. A Short Title Catalogue of Books with Manuscript Notes in the British Library* (London, 1994) p.602. Joachim Heinrich Campe, *[Robinson der Jüngere. English] The new Robinson Crusoe Designed for the Amusement and Instruction of the Youth of Both Sexes. Translated from the original German. Embellished with cuts.* London: printed for E. Newbery, 1790. ESTC n020066, and Adams, p. 195.

12 Clare Williams, *Sophie in London 1786*, pp. 272-73.

13 Karl Gottlob Küttner, *Briefe über Irland an seinen Freund den Herausgeber (M. Schenk)* (Leipzig, 1785). Cf. Woods (note 1) p. 313.

14 John Alexander Kelly, *German Visitors to English Theatres in the Eighteenth Century* (New York, 1978) (first edition: Princeton, 1936) pp. 92-93. Küttner's 16 volume reference work on England was published as *Beyträge zur Kenntniss vorzüglich des Innern von England und seiner Einwohner* (Leipzig, 1791-1796).

15 British Library, 567.c.19 (Küttner 1785); 577.e.41 (Volkmann 1784); 1430.d.16, and 10107.d.29 (La Roche 1791).

16 Volkmann, *Neueste Reisen nach Schottland und Ireland*, p. 404.

17 Adams, *The Printed Word*, pp. 23 ff. and Appendix II-IV, pp. 182-90.

18 Richard Twiss, *A Tour in Ireland in 1775* (London, 1776), p. 78. John Aikin, (1747-1822) *Miscellaneous Pieces, in Prose*, by J. and A.L. Aikin. Belfast: printed by James Magee, 1774, ESTC t085573. William Hayward Roberts (1734-1791) *Poetical Essays, in Three Parts. I. On the Existence of God. II. On the Attributes of God. III. On the Providence of God. By the Rev'd W.H. Roberts, ... to which is added, a Poem on the Immortality of the Soul. Translated from the Latin of Isaac Hawkins Browne, Esq; by Soame Jennyns, Esq; in two books.* Belfast: printed by James Magee, 1774, ESTC t190188. Oliver Goldsmith (1728-1774) *Poems by the Late Dr. Oliver Goldsmith ... To which is prefixed the Life of the Author.* Belfast: printed by James Magee, 1775, ESTC t146126.

19 University College Dublin, Special Collections, ESTC t085573 (UCD 34.U.8/3).

20 James W. Phillips, 'A Trial List of Irish Papermakers', *The Library*, fifth series, (1958) 67-72. Mary Pollard and Charles Benson, : 'The Rags of Ireland are by no Means the Same', in *Long Room* (1970) No. 2, pp.18-35.

21 Black, *The British Abroad*, Preface, p. XIII.

22 Arthur Young, *Reise durch Ireland: nebst allgemeinen Beobachtungen über den gegenwärtigen Zustand dieses Reiches in den Jahren 1776, 1777 und 1778 bis zu Ende des Jahres 1779. Aus dem Englischen von Johann J. Volkmann oder Johann A. Engelbrecht* (Leipzig, 1780).

23 Philipp Andreas Nemnich, *Neueste Reise durch England, Schottland und Ireland, hauptsächlich in Bezug auf Produkte, Fabriken und Handlung* (Tübingen, 1807), p. V.

24 Philipp Andreas Nemnich, *Beschreibung einer im Sommer 1799 von Hamburg nach und durch England geschehenen Reise* (Tübingen, 1800), p. 131. Cf. John Feather, *The Provincial Book Trade in Eighteenth-century England* (Cambridge, 1985), p. 101.

25 Nemnich, *Neueste Reise durch England, Schottland und Ireland*, pp. 158-66. Cf. Horace Hart, *Charles Earl Stanhope and the Oxford University Press* (London, 1966), p. xviii.

26 Ibid., p. 651.

27 Ibid., p. 160. It is noteworthy that Archer had quite a sustained interest

during the 1790s in publishing German authors, in particular, Friedrich Schiller (1759-1805). Cf. *[Die Räuber. English]* The Robbers : a *Tragedy ... The third edition corrected and improved.* Dublin : printed for J. Archer, 1799, ESTC t169259. Also *[Don Carlos. English]* Don *Carlos: A Tragedy. Translated from the German of Frederick Schiller,* ... Dublin, printed for John Archer, 1799, ESTC t125181.

28   Bavarian State Library, *Alphabetical Catalogue 1501-1840*, vol. I. p. XII ff.

29   *Weltpanorama. Eine Chronik der neuesten Reisen und Abenteuer bei allen Nationen der Welt, mit besonderer Rücksicht auf die politischen Ereignisse der Gegenwart. Nach den besten Quellen des Auslandes. 51ster bis 53ter Band. Irländische Zustände von M.A. Titmarsh* (Stuttgart, 1845). Cf. Titmarsh (Michael Angelo) pseud. [i.e. William Makepeace Thackeray], *Irländische Zustände geschildert von M.A. Titmarsh. Aus dem Englischen ["The Irish Sketch Book"] von C.E. Lenzor.* 2pt. Stuttgart, 1845. [British Library 10390. aaa.16].

30   Adams, *The Printed Word and the Common Man*, p.146.

A BALLYMENA BUSINESS
IN THE LATE EIGHTEENTH CENTURY

W. H. CRAWFORD

LIKE THE LATE AIKEN McCLELLAND, his predecessor as librarian of the Ulster Folk and Transport Museum, Ronnie Adams took great pleasure in perusing the eighteenth-century volumes of the *Belfast News-letter*. In 1985 he published an article in *Ulster Folklife* quoting from some of the earliest surviving issues to show the use that can be made of the newspaper press in researching social history. One of the pleasures of working with him in the Museum was his evident enjoyment of social history and he loved to be kept informed about interesting material turned up in research elsewhere. I did show him a handbill published by a Ballymena merchant, Alex Mitchell, in 1776 and found in a collection of material from Ballymena now in the Public Record Office of Northern Ireland.[1]

Recently I took the opportunity to examine this collection more thoroughly and discovered a valuable cache. Among papers deposited by the Young family of Galgorm are two volumes of business records created by the said Alex Mitchell: a day-book kept between 1783 and 1787 with some subsequent entries up to 1797, and a journal from 1776 to 1817. Although they are not in themselves sufficient to provide us with an accurate account of his business affairs, they do throw much light on elements of his business, the mechanics of transactions, and the identity of his customers. They are supplemented by some other documents, notably an inventory of his goods and chattels taken after his death in 1823 and details about his purchase in 1787 of the townland of Farranacushog, not far from the village of Clogh in County Antrim. This essay reflects an initial attempt to come to terms with this material which deserves much fuller treatment because of the paucity of information about everyday life in Ulster in the late eighteenth century.

To place Alex Mitchell in his contemporary setting, however, it is necessary to return to the *Belfast News-letter*. The earliest reference to him in advertisements is in 1769 and the information there, accords with the earliest entries in Mitchell's journal. Between 1769 and 1800 the name Alex or Alexander Mitchell appears in the Personal Names Index seventy-nine times.[2] Although all these references are not to Alex Mitchell of Ballymena (that of January 1787, for instance, was to a Lisburn linen draper) the great majority are. We still have to find out about his family background and his early training and we would like to resurrect him as a member of his local community.

Alex Mitchell would have considered himself a hardware merchant but in that guise he provided a much wider range of services than we might at first imagine. Certainly he was a house-furnisher although he did not sell furniture. He provided all kinds of kitchen gadgets from bellows and fire-irons to coffee-mills and box-irons, bottle-coasters and bread-racks to 'tea kitchens' and nut-crackers. For urban living bells and bell-hooks, sash-pulleys and weights, candle-sticks and snuffer-trays were readily available, as well as sugar-cutters, brass-cocks, and barrel-ouncels. As an ironmonger he sold razors, lancets, phlemes (for bleeding cattle), and all kinds of cutlery, knives, scissors, and shears; as a jeweller, ear- and finger-rings, lockets, necklaces, watch-keys and chains, seals and trinkets, snuff- and tobacco-boxes (without their contents) whether enamelled, paper [papier mâché], or gilt. These took him into the realms of 'silver and set [with glass] knee, shoe, stock [cravat] and breast buckles' which could be purchased more cheaply in 'plated, pinchbeck, sanguine, copper, steel, brass, or Bath metal'. Buttons were 'plated, silvered, gilt, lacquered, livery, woven, or horn'. There were hair-pins and cloak-pins. 'Temple and common spectacles' are also listed on his handbill, dated 6 September 1776.

On consideration, all these products appear obvious, just the things a shopkeeper would stock in the late eighteenth century. And yet we don't associate them with Ulster life at that time. We have been blinded by the commonly held notion that Irish society was too poor to purchase them. We forget that every society has at least two cultures, one for the 'haves' and one for the 'have nots'. This paper will suggest that the prosperous element of the community in and around Ballymena was more considerable than we might suspect. Just as significant is the evidence from Irish import statistics that the total value of hardware imported into Belfast increased from £2,971 in the 1770s to £20,062 in the 1780s. This great increase coincided with similar large rises for Newry (from £3,336 to £16,341) and Londonderry (from £1,872 to £18,438).[3] Alex Mitchell's business records help us to understand the nature of this important change. Without them we might overlook, for example, the numerous craftsmen who catered for and depended on the wealth of the local community for their living. They depended also on hardware merchants like Mitchell to import tools and parts essential for their products. In 1762, for example, another Ballymena shopkeeper had advertised material for saddlers, staymakers, wig-makers, whipmakers, and reed-makers.[4] We could add shoemakers, clockmakers, masons, weavers, and others such as chandlers, brewers, and distillers. Their industry created the distinctive character of the provincial town in the Ulster of the late eighteenth century.

When everyone and everything relied for transport on the horse, the saddler, the blacksmith, and the wheelwright played key roles in the community.[5] For the saddler Mitchell imported 'iron, steel, washed and plated spurs; plated and "tooth and egg" stirrup irons; bridle bits, and variety of buckles and drops for them'. The leather, of course, would have been obtained from a leather-merchant. Although the commonest form of transport was still the wheel-car with its solid wooden wheels, the local gentry, the better-off clergy and merchants as well as some professionals such as attorneys, and hearthmoney collectors, liked to drive about in well-sprung chaises: even John Wesley enjoyed such a conveyance on his later visits to Ireland.[6] It was only the wheelwright who had the skill to make and repair the large dished and spoked wheels of those vehicles.

Mitchell's most regular customers among the craftsmen were carpenters and he provided them with a great variety of tools made in Birmingham and Sheffield.

Hand, Tenon, Sash, Dove-tail, and Lock Saws
Gouges, Chisels, Plane-Irons, Foot Adzes, Drivers, Lathing

Axes, and Hammers; Augers, Gimblets, Tap-borers; Dowel,
Centre, and Spool Bits
Sundry kinds of Rasps and Files
Compasses, Rules, and Yards
Best and Common Black Lead Pencils.

If he concentrated on fitting out houses and shops, the carpenter would need such fittings as 'japanned knockers for doors, door handles and catches, spring latches; brass, mortice, gilt, and iron-rimmed locks'. If his inclination was to cabinet-making he could obtain iron and brass hinges and locks as well as 'a large assortment of brasses for drawers, desks, tea-chests, and clock-cases'. On 2 July 1783, for instance, Peter Wallace of Shanescastle purchased:

8 plain rose escutcheons and handles	@ 6/6 dozen	£0. 4. 4
6 key escutcheons	@ 2/= dozen	0. 1. 0
1 pair folding desk brass hinges	@ 10/= dozen	0. 0.10
1 pair Prospect brass hinges	@ 4/= dozen	0. 0. 4
3 dozen wood screws	@ 4d dozen	0. 1. 0
14 brass knob screws		0. 0.11½
2 large brass knob screws	@ 18d dozen	0. 0. 3
3-bolt brass desk lock		0. 1. 8
1 Prospect brass desk lock		0. 0. 8
5 till locks	@ 8/= dozen	0. 3. 4
	Bill furnished	0.14. 4½

Cabinet-makers such as Peter Wallace had the skill and the tools to construct good serviceable furniture in local hardwoods and some of their pieces may have survived into our own times. We are likely to overlook them in our search for vernacular furniture, especially the ubiquitous but often crudely-finished dresser. A regular never-ending employment for carpenters was making coffins for which Mitchell offered 'silvered, fine metal, iron and tin coffin furniture of all sorts and prices with letters, figures, (decorations such as angels and cherubims, flowers and squares), lace, nails and pins'. Their survival is very unlikely, but they would probably differ little from the carvings on many eighteenth-century tombstones. At this point, however, it is worth considering how the ready availability of such cheap decorations for everyday objects might have stifled an earlier local tradition of design.

Scrutiny of Mitchell's handbill indicates that he sold guns and pistols as well as money-weights and scales but, strangely, it makes no reference to his service to the farming community. Yet his cashbook shows that in 1783 he imported from Sheffield 109 dozen of No.1 Rib and 40 dozen No.2 Common Sickles as well as 25 dozen scythes. In 1784 he imported 200 dozen sickles and sold them to retailers throughout the district. On 7 September alone he sold more than 50 dozen sickles and another 85 dozen by 14 September. He charged 5s 6d a dozen for the No.1 Ribs and 4s 6d a dozen for the No.2 Commons. A 1786 account mentions Robert Turner, 'sickle smith' of Ridgway near Sheffield. In the context of these sales it is all the more surprising that there are no other references to sales of farm implements, except the occasional spade. There is, however, a valuable section on selling flour from the Crumlin mill of Thomas Ashe & Co. on commission: Crumlin was the first flour mill to operate in Ulster and flour was considered more acceptable than oatmeal to the refined palates of the well-to-do.

Although the handbill does not refer to Mitchell's role in furnishing chapmen and pedlars with merchandise to carry through the countryside, his account book does contain accounts with six pedlars and with another six individuals whom he described variously as chapmen or pedlars. The 1780s account book suggests that most of this business took place in the previous decade but a few details are noted in it. On 4 October 1783 John McCully purchased '5 pieces of garters @ 10/= a dozen,= 4/2; 2 pieces of frieze fringed @ 12d = 2/=; 1 dozen pen-knives @ 4/=; 1 dozen shears @ 2/6'; and on the 27 December a pedlar named Bonner bought '1 dozen combs @ 1/7½; 1 bolt of scarlet tape @ 1/1; 6 knives @ 2/9 per dozen; a card of buttons and 2 sheets of pins'. Earlier that year, in February, James and Mary Calderwood, rag-gatherers, had purchased '2 lb. field pins 7/=; 2½ dozen No.12 pins @ 3/6 per dozen = 8/9; 13 hundred common needles = 4/4; 2½ hundred darning needles = 1/10½; 1 sheet Crown pins = 1/3'; they paid in full on 8 July. On 3 April Mitchell recorded that:

I got from David Boulton, Pedlar, one watch No. 608 Maker's name D. Edmonds, Liverpool, and one watch No. 11039 Bawcutt, London and gave up his note that I had from him in 1779 for £5/8/3½ in full 3 Nov. Sold those two watches to two men who called themselves Michael McLoskey and Hugh Maguiken and got for them both same time five and a half guineas in full.

The handbill makes no reference either to Mitchell's involvement in the emigrant trade. It is not possible to determine when Mitchell became interested in this trade: his name does not appear in the list of ships engaged from Ulster ports in the years 1771-5.[7] By 1784 he was experienced for in that year he recorded how he had disbursed forty dollars that he had received from William McHendry of Baltimore in favour of his uncle, Alex Craig. Advertisements in the *Belfast News-letter* note that he was taking freight for a voyage to South Carolina in 1787. His cash-book noted in April 1788 that he had taken two bookings for another voyage from Larne to South Carolina, and another in June 1789 to Philadelphia for two passengers; each intending passenger paid a deposit of one guinea (£1. 2s. 9d.) for a passage agreed at four guineas. Mitchell's journal refers to individuals who had emigrated. About George Allen, a carpenter from Randalstown, he wrote 'Lost all this as he's gone to America and is since dead'. About another carpenter, William Scott of Ballygarvey, he was able to note: 'By cash received per self in full when he was going to America'. And he must have been pleased to record: 'I received from William Auld who is now in Philadelphia in March last [1784], one watch No.0 Maker's name Humphrey White, Fairford, for the account he owed me of a book account'.

From an examination of the goods and services Mitchell offered we pass to consideration of the mechanics of transactions. Small purchases were paid in cash and surprisingly large amounts of cash must have been kept in the shop till: in the day-book Mitchell recorded on 12 May 1787: 'About a quarter after 12 o'clock in the day one hundred guineas was stolen out of the drawer of the counter by a person unknown', and there is no subsequent reference to this serious loss. The day-book was used to enter all credit transactions, usually with a note to identify the individual who made the purchase, often a friend or servant of the buyer: in one case, 'a red-haired boy'. The margins contain comments such as 'paid' or 'settled'. These debts were then transferred to the journal which recorded the state of each customer's accounts: these 219 customers are usually identified by their profession or trade and their place of abode.

Throughout Ulster, until the early years of the nineteenth century, almost all transactions were in cash. It has been suggested that it was the demand for gold by the landlords (for rents) and consequently by the peasant weavers, that made the successful operation of a local banking or large discounting business impossible.[8] The emphasis of this explanation should be shifted from the landlords to the weavers, however, because all linens had to be sold in public markets and in the hurry of transactions between linendrapers and thousands of weavers, cash created fewer problems.[9] It was not only in Ulster that weavers and traders continued to be suspicious of banknotes. In contemporary Lancashire 'traders of this period looked with distaste on notes of any kind, not only because, since these were payable to bearer, there was danger of theft, but also because of a long experience of over-issues and failures of note-issuing banks in all parts of England'.[10]

In Ulster it was the linendrapers who needed cash to purchase the cloth and they paid for it in the bills of exchange that they had received in payment from dealers or factors in Dublin or Britain. The bill of exchange had developed as the means of settling debts between people at a distance from each other. If A and B were two Belfast merchants and C a merchant in London: A owed C £1,000 and C owed B £1,000. C therefore drew a bill on A and sent it to B who presented it for payment to A; the transaction was settled without sending any cash. It was a point of courtesy for C to notify A immediately that he had drawn on him so that A could make arrangements to pay. Alternatively, one person owed another £100 for goods on which he was to have credit for three months. So that the creditor did not lie out of his money for that time the debtor sent him a bill promising to pay the money in three months. If the creditor needed his money before that date he could sell the bill at a discount. The bill of exchange was, therefore, a negotiable instrument and could pass through the hands of several people before being presented for payment when it became due. Each endorser had to write his name on the back of the bill and was held responsible jointly with the other endorsers if the bill was not accepted on the day of payment. A bill could be refused on a technicality such as the failure to have it stamped (for stamp duty) or endorsed, but it would be enforced in law if it was proved to be good.

To evade the trouble of drawing a bill and the expense of paying stamp duty, it was common practice for merchants to retain a supply of bills from which they would select a bill or bills of the right maturity to make up the sum due. This was Alex Mitchell's practice. In May 1783, for example, when he went to England for a month, he took with him seven bills totalling £384.10s.6d., three of them drawn on Pooley & Fletcher of London, one on John Wilson of London, and two on Reed Darby & Co. He managed to obtain these London bills within a month about Ballymena itself, probably from bleachers and linendrapers. In 1775 a County Down agent had complained that to obtain a London bill for as much as £450 he had been 'obliged to travel above forty miles after having taken many shorter rides through the country in vain to procure a safe one'.[11] Only major linen firms would have had such considerable credit resources in London.

Mitchell's dealing in bills, however, was not confined to purchasing bills to pay his debts and provide services for his customers. It was part of his much greater role in providing liquidity for the local economy. The transactions recorded in his day-book show that he lent money very extensively, in large or small amounts. This must have been vital for many businesses. In November 1785, for instance, Mitchell lent Alexander Brown, a Ballymena chandler, 120 guineas in several sums over a period of eighteen days. He was repaid 50 guineas on 18 January, and 40 on 6 February and the balance by a Dublin bill and cash on 22 February; for this he charged 2 guineas in interest. At the same time, Mitchell was linked into a very much larger credit network. He had enough capital to purchase bills of exchange at a discount and sell them on to other contacts in the network. On 8 January 1783, for instance, he bought off Robert Holden his draft dated 10th, on Nathaniel Wilson of Belfast for £50 at 31 days sight. He gave the boy that brought the bill 43½ guineas (@ £1. 2s. 9d. per guinea). The bill he sent to David Henderson of Belfast on the 15th and received from him by Hugh Holden on 22 February 44 guineas. From the day-book we can analyse his bill purchases and outlets for disposal throughout 1783, for instance. His main contact was James Cathcart in

Dublin and it was he who supplied Mitchell with cash on at least one occasion through the 'carrier' or 'carriman', Gavin Saunderson, to the tune of over £300: 'Cash received from James Cathcart per Saunderson's pack'. Mitchell had sent a similar amount of cash to Cathcart earlier in the year. Mitchell had probably been recommended to Cathcart by Hugh Crawford of Belfast who was the main broker for his Belfast bills. More than sixty per cent of the bills in 1783 were drawn on Dublin with Belfast and Lisburn accounting for just over twenty per cent and London less than ten per cent. It will be interesting to find out if the London and Belfast percentages rose over succeeding years in accordance with increasing imports from Britain into Belfast. Mitchell used two other Dublin contacts: James Morgan of Pill Lane and Robert Blackley, but James Cathcart seems to have handled the major bills. Often they were sent to Dublin by post, not a hazardous operation because the bills would be cashed only by the individual against whom they were drawn. These dealers or brokers seem to have credited Mitchell with the bills he sent and to have forwarded for payment bills drawn against Ballymena men to pay merchants elsewhere. Mitchell had three other Ballymena colleagues, David Kerr, John Alexander and Samuel Mitchell (his brother?) all prepared to co-operate with him to raise cash to purchase bills of exchange. This co-operation was very valuable in saving him at any time when his resources were stretched to the limit. The day-book shows that Kerr brought Mitchell cash from Hugh Crawford in Belfast: an indication that this was a tightly knit network.

Among the bills that were transmitted to Dublin were pensioners' bills. These were sent out twice a year by the government to retired soldiers and they cashed them with merchants such as Alex Mitchell. Mitchell sent these to James Cathcart in Dublin by the carrier, Peter Raney. In September 1783 he sent nine pensioner's bills but this rose to seventeen by February 1784 and thirty by August 1786, probably the consequence of disbandment of soldiers and sailors after the American War of Independence. Among them was a 'King's Letter Man', responsible for carrying secret government correspondence, and his pension was twice as large as the others. The *Annals of Saintfield* records for 5 January 1824 the death of Anthony Stoddard, aged 98, who had served in the army for eight years and received a pension of 6d a day for sixty years – this suggests that he had served in the Seven Years War (1756-63). More information about these pensioner's bills is provided by an advertisement in the *Belfast News-letter* of 28-31 August 1787:

> LOST – on Tuesday the 21st instant, on the Road between Belfast and Doagh, (supposed near to Doagh) a POCKET BOOK containing four pensioner's bills for £3. 17s. 6d each, viz John Flack, John Willson's, Anthony Grogan's and James Bouley's: There was some other papers in said Pocket-Book, none of which can be of any use to any Person except the Proprietor, as the payment of the notes is stopp'd at the Pay Office, Dublin. Whoever returns the same to Mr. Hugh Crawford, Belfast; Mr. James Jameson, Doagh; or Mr. Alexander Mitchell of Ballymena will receive a reasonable reward.

In the opposite direction, from Dublin, came lottery tickets in profusion. Several pages in the day-book contain lists of lottery numbers and their purchasers.[12]

All of these transactions move us to reflect on the structure of this society. How did it fit into the wider national and even international picture? Even a cursory analysis of the 219 names noted in Alex Mitchell's journal indicates a society that was increasing in wealth and complexity. We expect the major and minor gentry, the ex-army officers, and the strong farmers but we have not made sufficient allowance for the impact on the community of the 12 linendrapers, the 6 innkeepers, or the 29 merchants. Nor should we overlook the 4 attorneys (including Roger Casement of Ballymena), 2 gaugers, 2 surveyors, 2 hearth-money collectors, and the Inspector of Linen. Many of these people can be identified in contemporary advertisements of the *Belfast News-letter* and we should be able with the help of genealogists to build up a more detailed picture of the society that these people inhabited. Registry of Deeds memorials are invaluable for fleshing out the bones of eighteenth-century society. For the early nineteenth century it should be possible to reconstruct the map of Ballymena using surviving estate maps, ordnance survey maps, and the records of the first valuation. The prospects are good for research into the history of Ulster provincial towns in the late eighteenth century.

Notes

1   Public Record Office of Northern Ireland, Young of Galgorm MSS D.1364.
    I wish to thank the Director for permission to draw on this material.

2   See the *Belfast News-letter Index 1738-1800* [on microfiche], ed. by John
    C Greene (Ann Arbor: UM1, n.d.)

3   See W.H. Crawford, Change in Ulster in the Late Eighteenth Century in
    T. Bartlett and D.W. Hayton, eds, *Penal Era and Golden Age* (Belfast,
    1979), pp. 193-9.

4   *Belfast News-letter*, 27 July 1762: Moses McKee.

5   See M. McManus and S. O'Kane, *Hot Shoes and Heavy Metal* (Ulster Folk
    & Transport Museum, 1992) on the importance of blacksmiths in the
    community.

6   John Wesley, *The Journal*, ed. Nehemiah Curnock (London, 8 vols, 1909-
    16), *passim*.

7   R.J. Dickson, *Ulster Emigration to Colonial America 1718-1775* (London,
    1966), Appendix D, Synopsis of Emigrant Shipping Advertisements,
    1771-1775, pp. 238-81.

8   L.M. Cullen, *Anglo-Irish Trade 1660-1800* (Manchester, 1968), p. 174.

9   W.H. Crawford, The Evolution of the Linen Trade in Ulster before
    Industrialisation, *Irish Economic & Social History*, XV, (1988), 39.

10 T.S. Ashton, *An Eighteenth-Century Industrialist: Peter Stubs of
    Warrington 1756-1806* (Manchester, 1939), p. 102.

11 W.H. Crawford, *Letters from an Ulster Land Agent 1774-85* (Belfast,
    1976), p. 9.

12 For the importance of lotteries see Cullen, *Anglo-Irish Trade*, p. 186.

'BY APPOINTMENT TO EMPERORS': MARCUS WARD AND COMPANY OF BELFAST

ROGER DIXON

PRINTING AND PUBLISHING IN BELFAST was one of Ronnie Adams's abiding interests. Some years ago there was talk of mounting a major exhibition in Belfast on Marcus Ward, and Ronnie and I discussed writing articles to accompany it. Ronnie's article was going to deal with the publishing side of the business and I was to cover the illuminated addresses, calendars, cards and other illustrative material. Unfortunately the exhibition project was shelved and the articles were never written, but Sally Skilling, who was Ronnie's deputy for many years, has informed me that Ronnie had resurrected the idea of an article about the firm some months before his death. Unfortunately this never came to fruition, but I am honoured to offer this contribution on a subject in which Ronnie had shown much interest.

The firm of Marcus Ward and Company which dominated the printing business in Belfast for almost a century and eventually gained a world-wide reputation for its products, began life at the very beginning of the nineteenth century with John Ward. Ward, like a number of other prominent business men of the time, was involved in paper manufacture and in 1802 he formed a partnership with two other of the main players in this business, Robert Greenfield and James Blow.

The new partnership was announced in the *Belfast News-letter* and stated that:

> Robert Green, James Blow and John Ward announce their
> cooperation in the new firm of Blow, Ward and Co., at 97 Ann
> Street next door to Joy's Entry. They have taken the concerns
> of Mr. Daniel Blow.[1]

Although the chief concern of the partnership was paper manufacture, it was at this time that enterprising paper makers were looking for new uses for the paper and often branching out into associated businesses. John Blow of Dunadry, for instance, was not only one of the founders and proprietors of the *Belfast Commercial Chronicles* he was also the manufacturer of the paper on which it was printed. For the enterprising John Ward printing and the manufacture of stationery was an obvious avenue for him to pursue although this appears to have remained a minority interest with the firm until after his retirement.

The initial partnership with Blow and Greenfield ended in the 1820s and Ward formed a new company of John Ward and Sons. The core business remained paper manufacture which the company undertook on quite a large scale with mills in Coleraine and Comber as well as Belfast. The printing and wholesale stationery business was run from the Belfast site which John Ward managed himself, his sons F.D. Ward and Marcus looking after the Coleraine and Comber mills respectively. This arrangement carried on until the early 1830s when John Ward retired and Marcus moved to take over the Belfast side of the business.

By the time of John Ward's death in 1836 the Wards were already a wealthy and respected family in Belfast. The local papers all carried substantial obituaries containing glowing tributes to this obviously popular man. They are, however, short on detail on his business affairs. The *Northern Whig* states that 'For a great length of time Mr Ward was extensively engaged in trade and his integrity and urbane manners secured him the respect of all with whom he either transacted business or who formed the circle of his private acquaintance.'[2] The *Belfast Commercial Chronicle* gives a detailed account of his funeral from his house in Ballymacarrett (Jackson Hall) to his final resting place 'the family burying-ground behind the Poorhouse'[3] (Clifton Street Graveyard). The portrait of this 'gentle and kindly man' printed by N.J. Crowley RHA (1819-57) is in the Ulster Museum's Collection.

With John Ward's death Marcus began increasingly to develop the printing and stationery manufacturing side of the business and moved away from paper manufacturing. To do this he formed the new firm of Marcus Ward and Sons. Martin's *Directory* of 1840 includes a two-page advertisement for the new company offering a wide range of stationery along with ornamental bookbinding, letterpress and lithographic printing. The business obviously prospered for by 1842 more substantial premises were required and the firm moved to 6 Cornmarket.

The firm was not only growing, it was acquiring skills, particularly in lithographic printing. It is a measure of Marcus Ward's ambition for the firm that he began to examine the potential of colour lithography as early as the 1840s. Although the process of lithography had been invented at the beginning of the nineteenth century, it was not until the 1840s that it began to be seriously exploited for full colour reproduction. Marcus Ward ensured that his firm was among the pioneers of the process.

Sadly Marcus Ward died at his home in King Street in 1847 at the comparatively young age of 41, so he was unable to see the success of his company at the Great Exhibition of 1851 where its colour lithography work won a prize medal in the fine arts section. Luckily he had a capable widow and sons ready and able to take on a thriving and growing business. First his eldest son Francis David Ward became a partner, soon followed by the eldest son of his second marriage, John Ward. John, who was to play such an important role in the firm's future, had not been originally interested in entering the family business at all as he wanted to become an architect. From his earliest days he had exhibited a keen interest in art and had been one of the first students at the government school of Art and Design in Belfast, where according to his obituary he distinguished himself in the drawing classes.[4]

From his entry into the firm he had ambitions to raise its artistic standing and organised art exhibitions on the premises. These were the first of their kind to be held in Belfast and excited a good deal of interest. He was greatly aided in his artistic endeavours by John Vinycomb from Newcastle upon Tyne who was taken on as artistic director the year after John became a partner. Vinycomb was not only a superb illuminator; he was also to become a world-renowned authority on heraldry. He took John Ward's idea of art exhibitions a step further by starting art classes in the works after closing hours. The cost was only a penny a class and it was open to all. It was under Vinycomb that the Art Department gained its enviable reputation not just for colour lithography but for the creations of illuminated addresses. Most of the crowned heads of Europe at one time either had Marcus Ward illuminated addresses presented to them or had commissioned one themselves. Among the firm's customers were the British Royal Family and Napoleon III.

The firm's growing success necessitated a further move in 1855, this time to Donegall Place where it occupied a large block stretching through to Fountain Street at the rear. The extra space was needed to hold not only an increasingly important Art Department but also the latest in steam-powered printing machinery. It was this combination of high artistic standards, matched to the latest in Victorian technology, which initially gave Marcus Ward the edge over existing competition. Again in chromo-lithography they were to lead the way. The *Dublin Builder*, in an article entitled 'Chromo Lithography in Belfast' reported that 'Messrs Ward and Co., have just issued specimens of chromo-lithography which we cannot praise too highly... we have rarely seen better examples of this truly difficult art.'[5]

The Donegall Place works were opened with great ceremony and festivities. John Ward, although the younger partner, took the leading role in the proceedings, even composing and singing his own song written specially for the occasion. He sang it at a special ball to which all the workers were invited and in it describes and praises all the departments in turn.

> I'll give you a toast to honour it,
> Strive with all sinceritie;
> The health of every bee in this hive
> Of busy industrie.
>
> The litho department and Thomas Shields
> No man could better be;
> For with kindness and firmness his power he wields
> With im-partial-itie.

The health of the coves with artistic feeling,
Designing suaves they be;
Vinycomb, Perry, Goodman and Keeling,
And all their fraternitie.

To their genius we owe the best of this show
The shields and texts around:
Their designs, historical, quaint, allegorical
With talent and wit abound.[6]

There were many more verses and on this happy occasion it could indeed be said that talent and wit did abound not just in the work force but also in the person of John Ward.

The period at the Donegall Place premises was to prove, in commercial terms, the most successful in the company's history and with increasing success at international exhibitions and a growing market for their wares the company began to establish branches outside Belfast. The first of these was established in Dublin in 1865. This was the year of the Dublin International Exhibitions at which fortuitously the company won an award. The manager of this new branch was William Yeates who was later to replace John Ward as a partner in the firm. It was Yeates who first introduced Vere Foster to the firm. Vere Foster was a wealthy Anglo-Irish philanthropist whose particular interest was in public education.[7] The introduction of Foster to the firm proved timely for he was working on a series of what were known as copy books. The concept of the copy book was that it would contain lines of neatly written letters, words and phrases with blank spaces below to allow children to reproduce the characters. Foster's copy books had the virtue of being a cheap and effective way of teaching children and even adults to write legibly.

At the time of Foster's meeting with Yeates the first of these books was being printed in Dublin but the printer appeared unable to cope with growing demand and Foster was dissatisfied with the work. Satisfactory terms were agreed with Marcus Ward and Co., and the work was transferred to the Belfast works. It is important in the light of what was to follow to understand that Marcus Ward was never the publisher of these books, merely the printer. Foster paid for the design work and carried out his own marketing, and he was in a position to terminate the contract for the printing when he wished. This put the company in a very weak position to protect what was to become the most profitable part of their business.

On making the acquaintance of the partners Foster quickly formed a close friendship with John Ward. With John's involvement Foster's relationship with the firm changed considerably, but the contracts did not. Not only did John have ideas and enthusiasm for the copy book project, he understood to a much greater extent than Foster what was possible with the use of modern printing techniques. In 1867 at John's suggestion Foster embarked on a series of drawing copy books. John had long been interested in the teaching of art and argued that if writing could be taught in this way so could drawing. Eventually these books covered not only landscape and figures but also mechanical drawing and even geometry. Like the writing copy books these proved an astounding success and made John eager to see the concept taken even further. By the end of the 1860s he had persuaded Foster of the feasibility of producing a full colour guide to water colour painting. The first of these beautiful books appeared in 1872 printed by the latest in colour lithography technology. They were a departure for Foster whose real interest lay in public elementary education and because of the high costs of colour reproduction they proved outside the price range of many of his original customers. In fact they were a financial failure and never justified the expenditure in purely commercial terms. However they were a great artistic success and provided a useful vehicle for advertising the company's progress in colour printing.

Although the idea for the colour series was John's, as with the other books, Foster paid for the designs which were carried out by the best artists available including John Vinycomb and William Thornton. Foster it seems was also lending money to the firm to help pay for the state-of-the-art lithographic equipment that John deemed necessary for the work. In fact it appears that John was borrowing from a number of sources to fund the firm's expansion and had on his own admission overvalued the stock to raise bank loans. This practice was to rebound on him when he was paid partly in stock on his departure from the firm. However at this stage the loans seemed justified with markets expanding and copy book orders amounting to £150,000. In fact in terms of volume alone copy books were among the most successful publishing ventures of all, with the final production figure approaching four million copies.

Aside from the production of copy books the company's other interests were blossoming and a new London office and showroom were established in Chandos Street, Covent Garden, in 1867. William Ward, John's younger brother had been accepted as a partner in 1864 and he was sent to manage it. William appears to have been an enterprising young man who shared some of his brother John's characteristics, particularly his ambition. The firm continued to exploit the burgeoning international exhibition movement to parade its works before a wider range of possible clients. The exhibitions in Paris in 1867, Dublin in 1872 and Philadelphia in 1876 saw it again winning medals, not just for colour printing but also for bookbinding and illuminating. Advertisements of the time give an indication of the full range of products, listing the firm as publishers, wholesale stationers and manufacturers, lithographers, artistic designers, illuminators, engravers, dye sinkers, embossers, bookbinders and much more. It is little wonder that the premises in Belfast were proving too small to contain all these activities along side the printing of the copy books. A temporary solution was found by further developing the Donegall Place site with the addition of two large new buildings.

Throughout the 1860s and early 1870s the company continued to be dynamic and successful, easily assimilating new ideas and constantly searching out fresh markets for their products. One of the most successful outlets they found for their expertise in design and colour printing was in the production of calendars and greeting cards. It seems that Marcus Ward and Co. invented the tear-off calendar[8] and they were certainly among the earliest mass producers of greeting cards. These cards were little known before 1860 and owed their popularity to the arrival of a uniform postal delivery service in 1839 and the invention of colour lithography which made the products comparatively cheap to mass produce. Christmas cards under the Marcus Ward name first appeared in 1867, soon to be followed by a full range of greeting cards from valentines to mourning. A lot of the designs for these originated with the London branch which under William Ward's direction had gradually been transformed from being a showroom and distribution centre to a very productive artistic unit, employing twenty-four artists and designers. William, as manager, appears to have had an ability to spot rising talent among the new generation of artists. It was he who recruited Kate Greenaway to the firm. As early as 1868 she was commissioned to execute drawings for the firm and the first valentine card designed by her had the 'unprecedented sale of 25,000 copies inside a couple of months.'[9] She remained with the firm for a decade and was engaged principally in illustrating children's books and designing cards. Long after her departure the firm was able to make good commercial use of their old designs which remained immensely popular with the public. By the 1870s material including books were being published under the imprint of Marcus Ward and Co., of London, and significantly the company's exhibits at the Philadelphia exhibition of 1876 also gave the company's address as London.[10] It seems likely that William Ward was interested in increasing the independence and status of his London branch.

The firm, indeed, considered moving their entire manufacturing base to London; however they were swayed to remain in Belfast by Vere Foster and John Ward. Foster was insistent that he wanted the printing of his books to be carried out in Ireland. This had far reaching effects as the Donegall Place site was proving too small even with the additional buildings, and a new works building was urgently required. The firm was later to claim that the new works were built on the strength of and on the continuing expectation of copy book printing. This seems foolhardy given the weak contractual arrangements that underlay the venture.

The new building was erected on a greenfield site just off the Dublin Road and covered four and a half acres. It was double the size of the previous works and eventually was to employ fourteen hundred men.[11] However, by the time of the opening in 1874, serious trouble was already brewing between the partners. The principal antagonists in the dispute appear to have been William Yeates and William Ward on one side with John Ward opposing them. Vere Foster attempted to intervene between the factions but to no avail. When the split finally came in 1876 it was far from amicable. John Ward agreed to leave the partnership and relinquish all his interest in the firm including the goodwill, and in return he was to receive a cash settlement and £16,000 in goods. These terms caused greater difficulties, mainly due to John Ward's previous practice of over valuing the stock in raising loans. This particular matter was settled after a good deal of acrimony and at the end of a two year period the firm paid

John the considerable sum of £35,578.19s.5d. This sum was to include goods, goodwill and 'his share interest claim and demand in the several premises constituting the Royal Ulster Works'. This settlement however was far from the end of the matter because a further and more serious dispute arose over the Vere Foster contract.

Throughout his association with the Wards, Foster had worked closely with John and formed a close friendship with him. As a result when the split became inevitable he offered to withdraw his business from Marcus Ward and Co. and give it to John. This cannot have made commercial sense for Foster, as once the partnership ended John would no longer own a printing works to carry out the work. Nevertheless John accepted the offer. After the dissolution of the partnership Foster agreed to let Marcus Ward and Co. continue with the old arrangement for printing the copy books for a period of two years. At the end of this he decided to withdraw entirely from the copy book enterprise and offered to sell it all to John for £3,000. This was a very generous offer which John accepted with alacrity. Foster then wrote to the company terminating the printing agreement and requesting the return of all the property associated with the venture including text, plates and lithographic stones. The company refused to return the stones on the rather shaky ground that although Foster had paid for the work carried out on the stones, the stones themselves were company property.

As the value of the work far exceeded the value of the stones the company appears to have had a weak case from the beginning. The real issue however was the loss of the business and by retaining the stones they presumably wished to stake a claim to the copy book venture. The result was a series of expensive and highly damaging law suits in which Foster and John Ward sued the company for the return of the stones and the company sued John Ward for breach of contract. The argument presented by the company barristers was that John Ward 'had released and assigned all his share in the goodwill' but 'by an arrangement with Vere Foster had violated that deed'; as a result 'loss and damage had accrued to the firm'. Throughout the court hearing the company stressed that the Vere Foster business constituted 'the most valuable portion of their trade and business'.[12] The legal proceedings dragged on for four years with a considerable amount of vindictiveness being displayed by both sides.

C.J. Brett, who had been Marcus Ward and Company's solicitor, represented John Ward against his old client and pursued the case with vigour. It is interesting that Brett and Foster tended to blame William Yeates who was now a full partner in the company for the whole sorry affair. Writing in 1881 Brett says of Yeates 'He made this quarrel between the brothers for his own ends ... ousted the man who was his master and got two feeble men under his power instead. The brothers worked amicably together for thirty years until he appeared on the scene'.[13] This was perhaps a biased view as it is hard to see William Ward in particular as a feeble man. However, there is no doubt but that Yeates felt John Ward had done the company a serious injustice perhaps with some cause as it was he who had attracted Foster's business to the Company in the first place and not John. In a letter to Brett written in March 1880 John reports that 'Yeates says if no justice is to be found in the world he will leave it'.

However Yeates did not get the justice he sought from the courts nor did he leave the world. Marcus Ward and Company lost the case and the subsequent appeals. John Ward emerged as the undoubted victor: not only had he the money paid to him by the company but he had also acquired Foster's copy book business for a small sum. Once the case was over he sold the copy book business to Blackie and Son of Edinburgh at a considerable profit and set off up the Nile to follow his real interests of art, archaeology and travel, particularly in Egypt and the Sudan. He was later to emerge as one of that select band of British Empire Egyptologists which included Viscount Kitchener, Sir William Wilcox and Sir John Gaston. Spending the summers in Ireland and the winters in Egypt, he continued to paint and write happily into his old age. His books such as *Pyramids and Progress: Sketches from Egypt* (London, 1900), *Greek Coins and their Parent Cities* (London, 1902) and *Our Sudan: its Pyramids and Progress* (London, 1905) received respectful reviews in learned journals and enjoyed moderate sales. John Ward died a wealthy and respected man in 1912, and, despite the fact that he had not lived in Ireland for some time, the local papers all found space for long and laudatory obituaries of this fascinating man.

The company he left did not fare so well. It had to find the money to pay off John, it had to pay considerable legal costs and compensation and it had lost its most profitable business, namely the copy books. However it was not, as is frequently assumed, ruined by this unfortunate series of events. The company still had an enviable reputation and a highly trained workforce; what it lacked was adequate capital and new business to make up for the loss of the copy books.

In an attempt to raise capital the firm at first took on a new partner, Mr John Stone, then in 1883 it became a limited company. The quality of its products remained as high as ever and medals continued to be won at international exhibitions all over the world. As late as 1897 it could still win a gold medal for its lithography and stationery at the Victorian Era Exhibition in London. As a publisher too it could still set the standard. R.M. Young's *The Town Book of the Corporation of Belfast* (Belfast, 1892) was hailed by *The Athenaeum* 'as the most beautiful of recent books' and *The Times* praised 'the taste of these well known publishers.' Its Royal Irish Linen writing paper made from cuttings left by the Belfast linen industry continued to be in demand from anyone with pretensions to be part of society.

Throughout the 1880s expansion continued with new branches established in Cape Town, New York and Melbourne and a grand new London headquarters was opened in 1884. Designed in the latest arts and crafts style, Oriel House, as it was called, was unfortunately to be the last building ever built for Marcus Ward and Company. Although artistic accolades continued throughout the 1890s competition was increasing and raising adequate capital remained a serious problem. The company which has been at the forefront of technological advance in the 1850s and 1860s was beginning to look distinctly old fashioned as the century drew to a close. Photographic processes were reaching a stage of sophistication where they could now handle most reproduction work. The Company appears to have made some half-hearted moves into this area of technology but to no avail. The money and perhaps even the will for a major reconstruction of the business were absent. Expansion in the 1880s had been replaced by retrenchment in the 1890s. Francis Davis Ward, the senior partner, was over seventy and William Ward, perhaps anticipating the end, had started his own company in 1896 so the will to fight on was absent.

In 1899 the Company admitted defeat and wound up the business, paying off all creditors and share holders in full. One thousand four hundred men, the majority of them skilled craftsmen, lost their jobs and a name that had made Belfast world famous was no more.

It is tempting to speculate as to what the fate of the firm might have been if John Ward had not left the partnership and taken Vere Foster's business with him. The received view has been that these events undermined the Company to such an extent that it was unable to recover, and certainly the capital paid out to end the partnership and settle the legal fees was sorely missed. The loss too of Foster's business was a blow, but it must be said that the market for the copy books had already passed its peak by 1876 and in fact production of them ceased altogether in the 1890s, some years before the Company closed.

So although the abrupt loss was serious the eventual diminution of the work and the profit were inevitable and the Company was unwise to rely on it so heavily. Certainly if, as was claimed in court, the Royal Ulster Works was built on the strength of Foster's business, this was the height of folly given the weak contractual arrangement underpinning it and its inevitable decline. It is interesting to observe that when F.D. Ward died in 1905 his obituaries were unanimous in apportioning blame for his Company's failure on foreign, specifically German competition. A year later the *Journal of the Royal Society of Antiquaries of Ireland* took up the same theme stating in reference to the Company that 'this Irish firm, which for thirty years held its supremacy against all competition, could not withstand the long-hour labour systems and technical training of the German workshops.'[14] Typically John Ward was in no doubt as to the real reason for the Company's failure. Writing to Brett about the Company in 1876 he states with what appears to be unholy glee that 'they [the partners] have begun to fight among themselves already... From all I learn they have much need of me in the place – all work is sticking and no new ideas launched whatever. It may well be worth their while to pay me a £1,000 a year to manage their business.'[15]

Whatever the real reason, (and it was certainly a combination of factors including, as John Ward suggests, a lack of entrepreneurial skills), the closure was a serious blow to the city of Belfast. Skills, capital, employment and training opportunities were all lost. Thankfully for future generations the products of the Company have always been recognised for their quality, and large numbers have survived particularly in the collections of the principal libraries and museums in Ulster. If you look at the quality of the design work, the colour reproduction and the hand illumination you will realise that these were indeed the products of a very civilised and artistic city.

Notes

1   Quoted by A. Deane 'Belfast in the Past. Ward Family Photographs', *Belfast Museum and Art Gallery Quarterly Notes* (December 1938), p. 3.

2   'Obituary of John Ward', *Northern Whig*, 8 December 1836.

3   'Obituary of John Ward', *Belfast Commercial Chronicle*, 8 December 1836.

4   'Death of Mr John Ward, J.P., F.S.A.' *Belfast Telegraph*, 19 February 1912.

5   'Chromo-lithography in Belfast. Marcus Ward and Company', *The Dublin Builder*, vol V, no 73 (1863), p. 10.

6   The song 'Vive la compagnie', quoted in full by S. Leighton in 'A Famous Ulster Art House. More about Marcus Ward and Company', *Belfast Telegraph*, 2 May 1924.

7   For a full account of the life of this fascinating man see Mary McNeill, *Vere Foster, 1819-1900, an Irish Benefactor* (Newton Abbot, 1971).

8   'Death of Mr John Ward', *Northern Whig*, 19 February 1912.

9   *Northern Whig*, 19 February 1912.

10   Betty Elzea, The Wards and the Sloans', *Delaware Art Museum Occasional Paper*, 3 (1990), p. 20.

11   'The Royal Ulster Works Belfast', reprinted from *Pictorial World 1888-91*, pp. 10-14 in *Industries of the North One Hundred Years Ago* (Belfast, 1986).

12   'Important Belfast Partnership Case', *Belfast Morning News*, 25 February 1881.

13   PRONI. L'Estrange and Brett Papers. For a full account of the case based on these papers see Diane Gracey, 'The Decline and Fall of Marcus Ward', *Irish Booklore*, 1(1971), 186-202.

14   'Obituary of F.D. Ward', *Royal Society of Antiquaries of Ireland Journal*, series v, 16(1906), pp. 100-101.

15   PRONI. L'Estrange and Brett Papers, quoted in Gracey, 'Decline and Fall', p. 199.

AN INTRODUCTION TO THE LITERATURE OF TRAVEL IN IRELAND 1600-1900

JOHN E. GAMBLE

THE LITERATURE OF TRAVEL AND TOURISM in Ireland can be a rewarding source of information for the historian, folklorist, educationalist and general reader. Travellers' accounts of their tours in Ireland, while personal and often idiosyncratic are nonetheless contemporary accounts of people, places, events, manners and customs.

However the search for specific information can be time consuming as there are known to be over seven hundred Irish tour books, covering the past three centuries, together with a great number of guide books. Other Irish tours appear in periodicals, and as contributions to books, such as the interesting tour by Dr Thomas Molyneux in 'Ye North of Ireland in 1708', included in R. M. Young's *Historical Notices of Old Belfast* (Belfast, 1896). Many tours exist only in manuscript, never having been published, while other material relating to travel is found in non-apparent titles, like Dr Alexander Knox, *Irish Watering Places... with an Analysis of the Mineral Springs by Dr. R. Kane* (Dublin, 1845), which provides information on almost forgotten purposes of travel, such as taking the spa waters. Many visitors to Ireland did not recount their travels in travelogue form, one of whom was John Howard, the prison reformer, who used the fruits of his findings to encourage others to visit prisons in Ireland.

Professor Constantia Maxwell provides a fine introduction to travellers' accounts of Ireland in her book entitled *The Stranger in Ireland* (London, 1954), in which she describes some of the major works, with a synopsis and poignant comments which assist the reader and researcher to categorize according to his or her requirements. This book and other helpful works of reference are listed in a short bibliography at the end of this article.

Seventeenth-Century Travellers

In the seventeenth century there was very little printed material in the form of actual guide books available for the traveller. John Woodhouse's book *A Guide for Strangers in the Kingdom of Ireland* (London, 1647), provided details of fifteen principal and twenty four minor roads in Ireland. Thomas Dinely, an English antiquarian, made a tour through Ireland during the reign of Charles II. He illustrated it himself, and provides us with a major source for the history of the Irish fortified house. His journal was published in the *Journal of the Royal Society of Antiquaries of Ireland*, vols. 4, 5, 7, 8, 9, 34 & 43 between 1856 and 1913. This work was also printed in a limited edition at Dublin in 1870, only fifty copies being printed, edited by J. Graves, and with an introduction by E. P. Shirley.

Fynes Moryson, born 1566, was an inveterate traveller. He was Mountjoy's secretary in Ireland, and a highly educated man. In his travels, he described Ireland province by province. He speaks of the climate and the fertility of the soil, the great number of livestock, birds and fish to be had, but condemns the Irish as slothful, and living on a poor diet. In this approach, he reiterated the opinions of Barnabie Rich and Edmund Campion who had also spoken unfavourably of the Irish people. His work was first published in 1617, again at Dublin in two volumes octavo in 1735, but the most readable edition is the edition published in Glasgow, 1907/8, in four volumes.

One of the most exciting travellers in Ireland in the late sixteenth, early seventeenth century was Captain Don Francisco De Cuellar, a Spanish captain of the Armada. The best edition of his travels is that edited by Hugh Allingham, (an uncle of William Allingham), *Captain Cuellar's Adventures in Connaught & Ulster, A.D. 1588* (London. 1897). Captain Cuellar tells how, after the loss of his ship off the Irish coast, he travelled through Ireland. Here we find interesting accounts of his conversation using sign language, and the Latin tongue emerging. His graphic description of the people is found in the following narrative at page 61:

The custom of these savages is to live as brute beasts among the mountains. Thy live in huts made of straw; the men are large bodied and active as the roe deer. They eat once a day, usually butter with oaten bread; they drink sour milk, they do not drink water. They clothe themselves with tight trousers and short loose coats of very coarse goats hair, and blankets, and wear their hair down to their eyes. They are great walkers, and carry on perpetual war with the English. Their chief inclination is to be robbers and plunder each other. The most of the women are very beautiful, but badly dressed, they wear a chemise and a blanket. They are great housekeepers, and call themselves Christians. In this kingdom there is neither justice or right, and everyone does as he pleases.

Cuellar hid at Dunluce for six weeks being kept by a very good woman, and later by a Bishop who went around in the 'garb of a savage'. He had in all spent seven months in Ireland, and in his own words was 'naked and shoeless, and among mountains and woods, with savages' (p. 46) before escaping to Scotland and Spain.

Eighteenth-century travellers

The best known travel book about eighteenth-century Ireland is undoubtedly that of Arthur Young, who wrote his *Tour in Ireland* from the findings he made during 1776 and 1777. The work was first published by subscription in quarto format in 1780. It had two plates, executed by Mr I. Taylor - a fontispiece of Powerscourt Waterfall, and a plate of an Irish cabin; 2 parts in one volume, 384 pp. plus 72 pp. Young had hoped for 500 subscribers in England and 400 in Ireland. However, he had to scrap many of the plates which he had prepared through lack of support from his subscribers.

He had spent nine weeks in Dublin checking records and accounts, and later spent a year as a land agent in Co Cork. However his tour was in actual fact written from what he called 'his minutes'. This was because of an unfortunate incident on the author's return to England. On his journey between Bath and London his trunk which contained the private journal kept by him on the tour, together with specimens of soils and minerals, was stolen. Young was left with only 'his minutes', and perhaps this is the reason that there is a lack of humour and anecdote in the Irish Tour. (Some Irish anecdote can be found in his autobiography, edited and published in 1898.)

When he visited the country, Irish agriculture was at least fifty years behind that of England. This motivated him to publish an account of his travels and findings in order to advise about the newer methods of farming in England, and to increase the knowledge of agricultural conditions in Ireland. He was deeply interested in the Irish peasants and their penury, and gives detailed accounts of their lifestyle and homes or cabins. He deplored the lack of lodgings and good inns in the towns, and examined in detail the emigration of the Ulster Presbyterians, whose position as dissenters led to widespread discontent. Young applied statistical methods to the study of agriculture, and his tours resulted in the publication of about 250 books and pamphlets. He argued for the abolition of state control in agriculture, attacked government measures which crippled the wool industry, and argued that the Irish bounty on linen was an impertinence. He disapproved of the Penal Laws, and did not hurry like other travellers. He had a great regard for potatoes and turnips, but largely ignored antiquities, though he did note fine houses in a brief but accurate manner. He made his first journey by post chaise and horse in 1776, and his second in 1777.

The first edition of his *Tour in Ireland* published at London in 1780, quarto, was immediately reprinted in Dublin in two volumes, octavo. This was followed by a second English edition, in two volumes, octavo, 1780, at London, with five plates. This is perhaps the most desirable edition. In 1800, a French edition by C. Millon omitted part one altogether, printing part two and adding nearly 300pp, from other sources, in two volumes. In 1798, Mavors, British Tourist's Pocket Companion, published only 54 pages of Young, and this was regarded as enough at the time, yet this same publication gave some 62 pages to printing extracts from Holmes's *Tour in Ireland* in 1797. Young was also printed in extract in John Pinkerton, *A General Collection of... Voyages and Travels* (London 1808/14), and in 1887 an abridgment of Young's *Tour* appeared in Cassell's National Library edition in cloth and paper back. This was edited by Professor Henry Morley, and the edition was based on the extracted and edited edition of Pinkerton. The price for the paper edition was 3d., and cloth 6d., for the 192 pages. The best nineteenth-century edition was edited by A. W. Hutton in 1892. This edition was properly divided into suitable chapters, the print type size in part two was made similar to part one, and an index and a bibliography were added. Constantia Maxwell selected and edited an edition in 1925, published by Cambridge University Press, in 244 pages (and later reprinted by the Blackstaff Press Belfast, 1983), with a frontispiece from the *Post Chaise Companion*, and a useful map of Young's itinerary. Maria Edgeworth described his book as 'The first faithful portrait of the inhabitants of Ireland.'

An almost forgotten eighteenth-century traveller in Ireland was Dr Richard Pococke, who travelled to Connaught in 1749. Unfortunately the manuscript of this tour was lost, however he made a more extensive tour to other parts of the country in 1752, and Dr G. T. Stokes published an account of this tour in 1891, entitled *A Tour in Ireland*, from the original mss. in Trinity College Dublin, which had long been supposed to have been lost. Bishop Pococke was one of the first major travellers to explore the *terra incognita* of Ireland, mainly in the North and North-West of the country. It is a most important tour, and covers the effects of the Penal Laws, and contains important references to Charter Schools, the clergy, manufacturers, the peasantry and natural history, causing widespread interest in the Giant's Causeway.

This tour of Pococke's in Ireland in 1752, though remaining unpublished for one hundred and thirty nine years, preceded Arthur Young's tour by a quarter of a century, and is of significance because he visited parts of Ireland which Young did not venture into. An example of the type of narrative we can find in his tour is best illustrated by his notes on the great festivals and coming together of the clergy and people and the landlords and tenants for great feasts. He even comments on the short waistcoats, round hats with narrow brims and breeches of the men, and the short jackets, petticoats with coloured ribbons and the handkerchiefs on the heads of the women. He describes the condition of the people, and there are detailed references to the use of rushes, scallops and tallow for lighting.

Our next traveller is the distinguished Le Chevalier de La Tocnaye (Jacques Louis de Bougernet), a Breton by birth. The first edition of his

51

Irish tour, in French, was published at Dublin in 1797 under the title *Promenade d'un Francais dans L'Irlande*. There was a Cork edition of 1798, mentioned by Constantia Maxwell, not in the British Library catalogue, which lists an English edition of London 1799, in two volumes, duodecimo. A French edition was published at Brunswick in 1801, and a German edition at Erfurt, translated from this Brunswick edition, also in 1801, in two volumes. The Belfast edition of 1917 was edited by John Stevenson, who made a good text available, leaving out the swear words! (This edition was reprinted by the Blackstaff Press Belfast in 1984 with new introduction by J. A. Gamble.) Stevenson thought that La Tocnaye had no style, and he objected to La Tocnaye's plagiarisms from other writers, and the portions entered out of courtesy to La Tocnaye's friend General Vallancey. Stevenson adds the rejoinder that the text printed in French in Dublin was full of errors to start with. With regard to the four plates used in the French language edition of 1797, it is interesting to record that they are numbered 10, 5, 4 & 3. It appears that the plates for these engravings were donated by General Vallancey after they had been used in some of the General's own books, and they were given to La Tocnaye by Vallancey because La Tocnaye encountered some financial difficulties in publishing the Dublin edition at his own expense, hence the answer to the numbering enigma and their absence in English editions.

The last of our eighteenth-century travellers, the Reverend John Wesley, may seem an unusual choice, but his many visits to Ireland tell us much about the people and places he visited. The reason for his visits to Ireland was to promote and extend the cause of Methodism. The accounts of his visits are to be found in his Journals. These Journals were made up from his diaries, begun in 1725, and continuing until his death in 1791. They have been published many times, but the best edition to date is that edited by N. Curnock in eight volumes, between 1909 and 1916. Wesley first came to Ireland in 1747, and altogether he visited Ireland twenty one times, crossing Ireland in a most bewildering fashion, north, south, east and west, establishing Methodist societies wherever he went, and staying in the homes of the gentry and poor alike.

Although very wrapped up in his mission, he shows remarkable curiosity about the places he stopped at, and many of his descriptions show keen observation. He covered three thousand miles each year, mainly on horseback, and while the romantic did not appeal very much to him, he does comment upon trim gardens, cultivated lands and landscape.

His accounts of people like the La Trobe family, and other prominent titled and business people, are of value because of his disregard for a person's rank. His interest in the working classes predominates, as it was from this class, though not exclusively, that he gained most of his followers. His account of the meeting of the butchers of Ormonde Market and the weavers of the Liberty, resulting in ferocious bloody battles, and indeed the burning of the Swaddlers' or Methodists' chapel after one such riot, provide vivid and authentic comment on the manners and customs of the times. In his journal entry for 31 May 1750 he describes the practice of keening at wakes as 'not a song but a dismal inarticulate yell, set up at the grave by four shrill voiced women who were hired for the purpose; none shed a tear for that was part of their bargain'.

His journal entry for 1777 regarding Ulster stated that the ground was cultivated as in England, and that the cottages were neat and clean. He described Kilkenny as one of the pleasantest cities in the Kingdom, even though they did throw stones at him there. He didn't particularly like Sligo, as his post chaise got stuck in the muck, and he had to be rescued on the shoulders of some locals. An amusing journal entry relates to the sermon he preached to a captive audience on the Grand Canal barge from Dublin to Prosperous when, he says, 'they were all attention'! In 1785 he wrote that 'the poor in Ireland are in general very well behaved. All the ill-breeding is among the well-dressed people'. He observed the fine singing of the people at his services, and undoubtedly the Irish love for music found a lively and passionate outworking in the songs and hymns of the Wesley brothers. His journals and travels show his concern for the oppressed. He tells of a poor man blowing a horn, struck suddenly by a gentleman, who knocked him to the ground. He tells also of his own preachers who were often struck and whipped by the gentry in the markets, especially at Ballymena.

His journals record the advent and growth of the Irish Sunday School Movement as being well organised. John Wesley also visited hedge schools, where he notes how ill-fed, ill-clad and ill-taught the children were. He recognized that the schools run by the Incorporated Society through his lifetime and indeed until 1832, were disliked by the Catholic people, but on this point one wishes he could have been more explicit. A detailed study of John Wesley's visits to Ireland has not been published, and such a work would well serve as a commentary on the religious and social life of the people in eighteenth-century Ireland but his journals may be easily perused by the use of the extensive index.

Nineteenth-century Travellers

The greatest Irish tour book published in the nineteenth century was the well known work by Mr and Mrs S. C. Hall, *Ireland, its Scenery and Character*. The first edition in three volumes took three years to publish, between 1841 and 1843. It was issued originally in monthly parts, as well as divisions, and was advertised that it would contain forty eight engravings on steel, with eighteen maps of the counties of Ireland, and about five hundred engravings on wood. The aim of Mr and Mrs Hall was to promote the welfare of Ireland and to give a faithful picture of the condition and character of the country, which they had collected during five tours in Ireland subsequent to the year 1825. It was illustrated from drawings by Creswick and others, engraved on steel, and by woodcuts. Over eighteen artists were commissioned, including such famous names as Croker, Maclise, Nichol, O'Neill, Prout and others. The Hall Virtue undated edition circa. 1845 includes a great number of Bartlett plates, as well as vignette views and the maps, which are usually coloured. It generally contains approximately 100 plates, 16 maps and engraved titles. There is another edition of Hall's *Ireland*, published in New York, circa 1880, and published by the firm of Lovering. The plates are similar to those in the earlier British editions, except that it has the addition of some coloured plates of Irish mansions similar to those found in Morris's *Seats of the Noblemen of Great Britain* (London, 1870). These extra plates are overprinted in the bottom left-hand margin.

Hall's work contains fascinating and unusual information relating to pre-famine Ireland, with significant descriptions of the linen and other industries. Folklore and folklife abound in the pages of this monumental work, with descriptions of funerary practises, education, hedge schools, marriage and related customs, such as the use of the claddagh ring in Galway, all of these described with the same assiduous attention to detail.

A less well-known but fascinating tour in Ireland was published in

1844 by a Dr James Johnson from Ballinderry, Co Antrim, *A Tour in Ireland, with Meditations and Reflections* (London, 1844). Dr Johnson informs us that he spent the first eighteen years of his life in Ireland and made subsequent tours there. He was born in 1777, and died in 1845. He was apprenticed to a surgeon apothecary in Portglenone, and spent two further years in Belfast before graduating as a surgeon in London in 1798. He became a naval surgeon and sailed to Newfoundland, Egypt, India and China, publishing many books about his travels, and a number of books on the popular topic of pilgrimages to spas, and excursions to the principal mineral waters. He resided in Portsmouth and it was from there that he made this tour to Ireland. He said that 'Ireland is that which calls forth the most frequent and the most conflicting emotions in the mind of a traveller; ...laughter and grief, indignation and pity'. (p. iii)

The year 1844 was one of fierce political passion surrounding the Repeal of the Union and the state trials of Daniel O'Connell and others. Dr Johnson was obviously very excited to be in Ireland in such a significant year during the Repeal Crisis. He said 'It has seldom been the lot of a traveller to stand as I did on the sacred hill of Tara surrounded by three hundred and fifty thousand wild Irishmen ...without seeing a broken head or hearing an angry expression'. (p. iv) He goes on to say 'I am slave to no sect, and wedded to no party, ...(yet) the atmosphere of Ireland besides hydrogen and other inflammable ...materials contains a large excess of laughing gas'. (p. v) His sense of humour comes out through this valuable record of turbulent Ireland in the years immediately preceding the great famine of 1847. His text gives us a clue to the impending catastrophe. He says, 'In no country in Europe is there a better supply of physic and a worse supply of food than in 'oule' Ireland. In almost every village we see a dispensary for the gratuitous relief of the sick, but alas for two-thirds of the people only half-boiled potatoes as food'. (p. 14)

He expresses some cynicism about his visit to Trinity College Dublin which he says 'is called Trinity because it opens to Protestants, Papists and Dissenters'. (p. 23) He constantly pokes fun at religion in Ireland, which he calls 'the odium theologicum', (p. 15) and says that 'the superabundant supply of fresh water during nine months of the year ...gave the Irish a keen relish for Father Mathew's champagne'. (p. 27) Dr Johnson was astute enough to point out the significant effects of Father Mathew's astonishing teetotal mission in Ireland, as up to 1842 three million people had signed the pledge, and this created a great diminution in crime. He noted that in 1839 over 26,392 were brought to trial, while two years later in 1841 the number of persons tried dropped to 20,790. Dr Johnson's tour in Ireland is especially scintillating for his description of Irish customs, people and transport. The jaunting car he found amusing, and said that:

> some complain that half the passengers turn their back on the other half, and only see one side of the road. However, one side of the landscape is as good as the other, and anyway it's like one side of a question, it is far more easily grasped than both sides. At any rate, the conversation of half the travellers we met is worse than useless. (p. 121)

He was less tolerant and amusing about the mendicants or beggars who, he said, 'were the greatest of all pests to the traveller' (p. 167) and their general cry was 'och and will Dr Johnson pass through Tuam without throwing a half-crown to the poor crathurs that are starving here'. (p. 16)

Despite the poverty of the people, he praised their generosity in penury, stating 'the poor Troglodyte of the bog or the mountain in Ireland will share his last potatoe [sic] and bed of straw with the wandering mendicant or passing stranger' (p. 13) and he explains the oft used term of 'potatoes with bones in', which meant that the potatoes were par-boiled so that the centre was raw and hard like a bone, rendering it indigestible and thereby alleviating hunger pangs.

He provides us with two excellent descriptions of pre-famine Irish customs, one a wedding and the other a wake. For the wedding a match was made and a certificate obtained from the Parish Priest for a fee of five shillings, and a further Bishop's fee of seven shillings and six pence. The bride's father would pay for a good dinner and the bridegroom's friends would come along to the dinner and donate up to fifty pounds. The ceremony was in Latin, and generally before Lent. The bride cake or wedding cake was blessed by the Priest's stole. It was then cut by the Priest into small slices, and each guest took a slice and left a donation for the Priest. Wine and punch followed, usually with high spirited festivities. At the wake, he was overwhelmed by the howling of the keeners (the old women who wailed), and he continues, 'Thanks to Father Mathew the poteen has now almost disappeared from the homes of mourning though tobacco and snuff have happily usurped its place.' (p. 190) He felt that amid the 'fictitious wailing' and 'indecent mirth' there was very real grief and sadness among the poor. In the funerals of the upper classes he condemns 'the display of carriages... filled with well-dressed and merry-looking people'. (p. 190) Near Loch Corrib, Dr Johnson's carriage met a funeral train of all sexes, an Irish mile long. His driver pulled off the road and it took forty-five minutes for the procession to pass. He curiously adds 'I am much surprised that the Priest rarely officiates in the Churchyard.' (p. 196)

Many and varied are the aspects of Irish life and character found the among the pages of Irish travel literature and, as Sir Thomas Browne said in his *Religio Medici*, 'large are the treasures of oblivion; more is buried than recorded'.

Select Bibliography

ALLINGHAM, Hugh. *Captain Cuellar's Adventures in Connacht and Ulster AD1588*. London, 1897.

ANCIENT *Irish Histories. The Works of Spencer, Campion, Hanmer and Marleburrough*. In two volumes. Dublin, Hibernia Press, 1809. [Volume 1 contains Spencer's 'View of The State of Ireland' and Campion's 'Historie of Ireland', 1-266, 1-204 pp.]

ANDERSON, John P. *The Book of British Topography*. London, 1881.

[BRADSHAW COLLECTION]. *A Catalogue of the Bradshaw Collection of Irish Books in the University Library, Cambridge*. [Cambridge], 1916. 3 vols.

CARR, Sir John. *The Stranger in Ireland, 1805*. London, 1805. Anr. edition: New York, 1807.

CARTER HALL, Samuel and HALL, Anna Maria. Mr and Mrs S.C. Hall. *Ireland it's Scenery and Character etc*. London, 1841/3. 3 vols.

CHETWOOD, William R. *A Tour through Ireland*, part 1. London, 1748.

DE LATOCNAYE. *Promenade d'un Francais dans l'Irlande*. Dublin, 1797.

DINELY, Thomas. 'Journal of his Irish Tour in 1680.' in *Royal Society of Antiquaries Journal*, vols., 4,5,7,8,9,34 and 43. Also issued in a limited edition (50 copies). Dublin, 1870. Edited by J. Graves and with an introduction by E.P. Shirley.

FORDHAM, Herbert George. *The Road Books and Itineraries of Ireland 1647-*

1850. Dublin, Bibliographical Society of Ireland, 1923.

GAMBLE, Jack. *'Old Irish Travel Books Relating to Co. Antrim.'* The Glynns, 8 (1980), 57-62.

HALL, Rev James. *A Tour through Ireland Particularly the Interior and Least Known Parts*. London, 1813. 2 vols.

HEANEY, Henry J. 'Tourists in Ireland 1800-1850' [an annotated bibliography]. Londonderry, c.1967. [Unpublished thesis].

HENCHY, Patrick. *A Bibliography of Irish Spas*. Dublin, Bibliographical Society of Ireland, 1958.

HYDE, Douglas and O'DONAHUE, D.J. *Catalogue of the Books and Manuscripts Comprising the Library of the late Sir John T. Gilbert*. Dublin, 1918.

JOHNSON, Dr James. *A Town in Ireland: with Meditations and Reflections*. London, 1884.

KNOX, Dr Alexander. *Irish Watering Places: with an Analysis of the Mineral Springs*. Dublin, 1845.

MAXWELL, Constantia. *Country and Town in Ireland under the Georges*. London, 1940.

MAXWELL, Constantia. *The Stranger in Ireland from the Reign of Elizabeth to the Great Famine*. London, 1954.

MORYSON, Fynes. *An Itinerary Written ... first in the Latin Tongue and then translated by him into English*. London, 1617. [Part two contains the *Rebellion of the Earl of Tyrone*] also 2 vols. Dublin, 1735 and 4 vols. Glasgow, 1907/8.

O MUIRTHE, Diarmuid. *A Seat behind the Coachman, Travellers in Ireland 1800-1900*. Dublin, 1972.

POCOCKE, Dr Richard. *Pococke's Tour in Ireland*. Edited with an introduction and notes by G.T. Stokes. Dublin, 1891.

WESLEY, Rev John. *The Journal of the Rev John Wesley AM ... enlarged from original MSS, with notes from unpublished Diaries*. Maps and illus. Edited by N. Curnock. London, 1938. 8 vols.

WOODHOUSE, John. *A Guide for Strangers in the Kingdom of Ireland ...* London, 1647.

YOUNG, Arthur. *A Tour in Ireland, with Observations on the Present State of that Kingdom*. London, 1780 4to. London and Dublin, 1780, 2 vols 8vo. Anr. edition edited by A.W. Hutton. London, 1892.

YOUNG, R.M. 'Dr Thomas Molyneux, Journey to ye North, August 7, 1708'. In *Historical Notices of Old Belfast ...* Belfast, 1896, pp. 152-160.

BETWEEN REVOLUTION AND FAMINE: PATTERNS OF EMIGRATION FROM ULSTER 1776-1845

TREVOR PARKHILL

ACADEMIC STUDIES OF, and popular interest in, the movement of people from Ireland to America have tended to concentrate on the colonial period of Scots-Irish migration or on the great exodus from the south and west of Ireland which was such a feature of the Famine and its aftermath.[1] Each of these two periods has, moreover, been studied without sufficient regard for the other. The evidence that is available on emigration in the period which straddles the War of American Independence and the Great Famine suggests that, rather than being simply a chronological link in the continuum of Irish emigration, it retains aspects of the eighteenth-century experience, while shaping the pattern of the radically different nineteenth-century migration. It is also a period significant in its own right: it sees the establishment of a regular pulse of emigration which quickens by the 1840s, the development of assisted and chain migratory patterns within families and communities, and the opening up of Canada for emigrants. In all of these, and in an estimation of the numbers of emigrants from Ireland pre-1845, the nine counties of Ulster can be seen to have had an influential and prominent role.

The question of how many people emigrated from Ireland and from Ulster in the pre-famine period has attracted a number of tentative totals but rounded estimates are the best that the available evidence permits. Not until 1851 did the Census Commissioners record data precise enough to allow accurate annual totals of emigrants from each county and province to be calculated. It is significant that in the period 1851-1901, usually associated more closely with emigration from the south and west,

Ulster emigrants made up 29% of the 3.75 million recorded emigrants, a percentage more or less proportionate with its share of the population.[2] The Ulster contribution to pre-famine emigration can be better estimated in terms of percentage than in precise numbers and, when the evidence that is available is considered, it is a reasonably safe extrapolation that the numbers of emigrants in the pre-famine period who were of Ulster origin were considerably in excess of 30% of the total, whatever it is.

In lieu of official statistics, passenger lists offer the best numerical study of emigrants. There are four main series of passenger lists recorded on both sides of the Atlantic between 1803-46 and, while these cannot be any indication of absolute numbers, they are at least useful for outlining a pattern of the county of origin of emigrants.[3] In this respect, the Boston immigration lists 1803-06 are the most reliable: almost 80% of the 3,215 passengers whose location in Ireland can be established with some certainty came from the nine counties of Ulster.[4] The other set of passenger lists, for New York for the period 1820-46, are less helpful than the Boston series with information on the county of origin. Cormac O Grada has separated the New York lists into two distinct periods: between 1820-34, 39% of the Irish immigrating into the United States through the port of New York were of Ulster origin; for the period 1835-46 this had fallen only slightly to 36.7%.[5] It has been shown elsewhere, by Adams, MacDonagh *et al*, that the decade immediately before the Famine witnessed an acceleration in emigration from the three other provinces and it is this which accounts for the declining share of Ulster. For the period before 1840, however, emigration from Ulster appears not to have fallen below 40% of the national total; and for much of the period before 1840 was, in all probability, considerably higher. There remains, however, the problem of trying to convert these percentages into reliable figures.

For the period 1776-1815, for which it has been suggested that there was an Ulster contribution of up to 80%, Connell's estimate of the numbers who emigrated extends to 140,000, a figure which includes emigration to Britain as well as to North America.[6] Maldwyn Jones suggested that 100,000 made the passage to America in the period to the end of the Napoleonic Wars.[7] It is likely that each of these estimates is inflated. Connell's conclusion was based on a multiplication of an estimated annual average of 3,500 for each of the 40 years in question but it is clear that there was no constant stream of emigration on anything like that scale. Hanson reckoned that 'with eight years of American Revolution, ten years of political uncertainty from 1783-93, 19 years of European turmoil and three years of American involvement, these years comprised a period during which immigration was scarcely more than a trickle'.[8] In point of fact there appears to have been emigration from Ulster at every opportunity on a considerable scale between the end of the War of Independence and the outbreak of hostilities in 1812. The *Belfast News-letter* estimated, and provided a detailed account of the estimate, that up to 10,000 emigrants had arrived in colonial America each year from 1771-1774.[9] This pattern was resumed in 1783: John Moore, agent to the Earl of Annesley's estate in Co Down, writing in May 1783 even before the Treaty of Paris and formal British disengagement had begun, commented: 'The moment the preliminaries of peace came over, a ship was advertised at Belfast to carry over merchandise, passengers etc to Philadelphia. In three days after, a linen draper went to the owners and engaged a passage for his own and 30 other families around him'.[10] And Phineas Bond, the British consul in Philadelphia, observed in 1789 that Irish emigration in 1784 may well have exceeded 10,000.[11]

These independent sources convey an impression that the War of Independence had been a temporary if lengthy hiatus in a stream of emigration which was resumed at the earliest opportunity. There was a number of further interruptions such as the closure of American ports from December 1807 to the middle of 1809, and the Passenger Act of 1803 by the Westminster parliament which attempted to regulate, for the first time, the number of passengers the tonnage of each ship could carry. At most, therefore, there were 25 calendar years when emigration was feasible between 1776 and 1815. A crude formula for arriving at a figure for emigrants could be the annual average of 3,000 which is that used by R. J. Dickson, K. H. Connell and Maldwyn Jones. (It is also worth mentioning in passing that this is the basis of Dickson's suggestion of 250,000 as the total for emigration from Ulster to America before 1776, a figure which finds wholehearted support neither in the first census of the United States in 1790 nor in the eyes of recent historiography.[12])

The same degree of uncertainty characterises any attempt to ascertain the true rate of emigration from Ulster in the period 1815-45, although the problems of interpretation are different. Adams's estimate of one million for the number of emigrants from Ireland to North America in this period still finds general acceptance (or, at least, has not been challenged). The most comprehensive statistics available which range over most of the period are the statistics prepared by Imre Ferenczi for the National Bureau of Economic Research.[13] These provide data for immigration into the United States from 1820 and Canada from 1829. American immigration in the period 1815-45 included, according to Ferenczi, 449,000 Irish men and women.[14] The Irish quotient in Canadian immigration for 1829-45 was 281,887.[15] As far as the pre-1829 Canadian figures are concerned, no breakdown by nationality is given but it is possible to arrive at a realistic figure for Irish immigration to Canada by extrapolating from the 1829-45 data which show that 60% of all immigrants to Canada were Irish. Ferenczi's estimate for Canadian immigration during 1816-29 is 120,000 of which 60% (some 72,000), it can be assumed with some confidence, were Irish. The population of Ontario increased from 150,000 to 500,000 in the period 1825-45: 'the majority of immigrants were Irish and the bulk of them Protestant Ulstermen'.[16] This leaves the period 1815-1820 unaccounted for.

Emigration was quickly resumed on a substantial scale and Connell's estimate is for 20,000 in 1818 alone.[17] He suggests an annual average of 8,000 for these years which, when added to the immigration data for USA and Canada 1820-45, points to a total of 800,000 Irish immigrants to the USA and Canada from 1815-45. These immigration statistics are generally regarded as underestimating the true flow of immigration and their reliability is further jeopardised by the unknown factor which dogs all data relating to embarkation from Ireland: the extent of Irish emigration via Liverpool.

Irish Immigration To North America 1815-1845

Irish immigrants to United States 1815-19 (estimated)	20,000
Irish immigrants to Canada 1816-28 (estimated)	72,000
Irish immigrants to Canada 1829-45	255,701
Irish immigrants to United States 1820-45	448,927
TOTAL	796,628

Estimate of Ulster emigration 1815-45
(as 40% of total from Ireland): 320,000

However, regardless of whether the true number of emigrants is closer to 800,000 or one million, each of the totals serves to demonstrate the extent of pre-famine emigration and as a forceful reminder that nineteenth century emigration did not emerge as an immediate consequence of the Famine. Indeed, much as recent historiography has shown the Famine not to have been such a watershed in Irish agricultural, social and population history,[18] in terms of numbers who emigrated the Famine might be more soberly represented as an acceleration in the volume of emigration which had been gradually and significantly increasing for 30 years. As far as Ulster is concerned there is a further significance: the passenger lists for New York for the period 1820-46 show almost 40% of emigrants to be of Ulster origin.[19] This converts to a total of 320,000 which may be regarded as a modest estimate of the number of emigrants from Ulster to North America between 1815 and 1845.

This consideration of how many emigrated from Ulster is instructive at least in an evaluation of the sort of evidence available and the problems of its interpretation. And these difficulties are not endemic to statistics: the same overall lack of certainty relates to the basic questions, who emigrated and why? With regard to the former, it would appear that, in the period between 1776 and 1820, the typical emigrant was, as described by E.R.R. Green:

> A young man of around 20 years of age with a good family background, of industrious and prudent small or medium farmer stock, who has been given a fair education and who already has some idea of where to go and what to do in the United States. Even more important he has a sizeable number of contacts in America.[20]

The emigrants referred to in John Moore's letter of 1784, when he talks of the linen draper leaving with 30 families, are reminiscent of the group or corporate migrations which featured not infrequently in emigration to colonial America, particularly to the Carolinas in the 1760s and Georgia in the 1780s. The post-1783 migration saw an appreciable decrease in the number of families and the number of indentured servants on board emigrant ships. Phineas Bond observed that 'few redemptioners or servants have recently arrived from Ireland; the passengers from thence have been chiefly as such as have paid their passage money before they embarked'.[21] The decline in the 1780s and early 1790s in indentured servants and redemptioners has no obvious explanation but it does indicate that ships were able to make up a full complement with passengers of some substance, able to pay the full fare of about £3. 10s. 0d. per head. The *Belfast News-letter* as early as 1773 had commented on the decline of indentured servants and observed that some of those now going were 'people employed in the linen manufacture, or farmers and of some property'.[22]

There is evidence in the pre-1776 period in support of a case for both individual and family being the predominant unit of emigration. After the resumption of emigration in 1783 there is proportionately more evidence for unmarried individuals being the dominant unit. The 1803 Passenger Act, by introducing restrictions on the number of passengers on board ship, had the effect, even though it was not rigidly enforced, of raising the fare to a prohibitive £10-£12. In the 1803-06 passenger lists just under 40% of the passengers of Ulster origin who arrived in America were unaccompanied. This does not take into account single members of the same family who travelled together.

The Ordnance Survey emigrant lists from Counties Antrim and Londonderry show that, by the 1830s, the proportion of unaccompanied adults had been substantially reduced. Instead, there is a preponderance of identifiable family units, whether they are nuclear or extended to include a third generation or, more frequently, unmarried adult brothers and sisters, is not clear. Family emigration on this scale was made more feasible by the reducing fare for a direct sailing from the Ulster ports of Derry and Belfast, particularly to Canada, the fare to which, by the 1840s, was around £3. 10s. 0d. per adult. By the 1830s, in addition, there had reappeared the opportunities for sponsored family emigration, this time to Canada, which had not been uncommon to some states in colonial America and, in the later 1780s, to New Hampshire. In Ulster as well there was always the possibility of the realisation of Tenant Right to provide the capital needed to support family 'root and branch' emigration, although there has not yet been any serious attempt to show the true extent of the sale of Tenant Right as seed capital for individual or family cases of emigration.

As far as Ulster is concerned the basic capital to be invested in family emigration appears to have come largely from Tenant Right. Witnesses to the Devon Commission frequently testified to a tenant right value of up to £20 per acre but more usually in much of Ulster it was £8-£10. Posnet, agent to Lord Dungannon, deprecated Tenant Right on the ground that 'the tenant, in some instances, sells at an enormously high price and ... puts the money in his pocket and emigrates to America'.[23] The post-famine Chelmsford Committee on Tenant Right pointed out that:

> The Ulster tenant is more independent ... than the other tenants throughout the country; he will not squat on a small portion of land, he would rather emigrate, and generally does emigrate, to Canada. And by the sale of his tenant right, he has the means of going and taking his family with him whereas in the poorer parts of the country one member of the family emigrates first and then sends money to bring another ... the Ulster tenant in consequence of having the price of his tenant right can emigrate in a favourable way with his family altogether.[24]

Scattered evidence from the papers of Ulster estates indicates a willingness among landlords to grant-aid intending emigrants. In the eighteenth century landlords' agents were often beset by the problem of having to prove that one of the three lives cited in a lease, and who had subsequently emigrated, was still alive.[25] The general reduction in estates' leasing policies after 1820 from three lives to one, or for a shorter fixed term of years, may have helped landlords view intending emigrants in a more favourable light. There is evidence from the cash disbursement books of well-populated estates such as the Caledon estate in Co. Tyrone of landlord willingness to assist emigrants financially.[26] It has to be said however that, when balanced against the full extent of emigration from Ulster pre-1845, such documented examples are infrequent, and the fact that they were often loans rather than outright gifts means that assistance is best interpreted as a sign of landlord attitude to emigration rather than a significant practical measure.

The resumption of emigration in 1815 was as quick and in such numbers as it had been after the cessation of hostilities in 1783. Connell estimates that 6,000 emigrated in 1816 and this had risen to 20,000 by 1818.[27] Young single tradesmen, denied the opportunity for work in Ireland, figured prominently. Thomas Clark wrote to his mother in Limavady in 1817 asking her to send on his chest of tools and to 'thank Mr King for encouraging me to leave that poor and wretched country'.[28] But the dearth of opportunities faced every occupation after 1815 particularly in agriculture. The prolonged period of prosperity enjoyed by Irish agriculture since the 1760s, and particularly during the Napoleonic Wars, rapidly went into decline. The equally rapid increase in population which had been a corollary of this prosperity and 'the biological carry-over from the years before 1815[29] meant that in the period after the Napoleonic Wars there was an excess of supply over demand for employment in an agricultural system which swung from tillage to animal husbandry. This dramatic change in circumstances, which Crotty has called 'the cauldron of social and economic pressure which characterised Ireland in these years,[30] is the background against which emigration from Ulster post-1815 must be viewed.

By 1825 approximately 10,000 a year were emigrating to the United States and Canada; by 1830 this had risen to 20,000 and in 1831 a total of 45,000 are estimated to have emigrated from Ireland. Of the 800,000 emigrants computed to have arrived in North America from Ireland between 1820 and 1845, over 300,000 arrived in Canada. This represents over 40% of the entire migratory movement to North America in the 30 years before the famine. There are a number of reasons for this sudden and intensive concentration of emigration to that country. The most immediate lies in the lower port entrance charges levied by Canadian ports. This meant that it was cheaper not only to go to Canada but that it was also cheaper to go to the United States via Canada: the two journeys, from Ireland to Quebec and from Quebec to Boston or New York, cost less than the journey from Ireland direct to the United States. Many of the emigrants refer to and describe their entry to the United States via Canada, overland or by ship to Boston, in letters to their families in Ireland. John McBride, writing from upstate New York in 1819, having travelled there overland from Quebec, refers to his travelling companion 'James Hunter who left me at Quebec to go to Boston'.[31] And A.C. Buchanan, giving evidence in 1828, considered that 'an average of two thirds of all the emigrants arriving [in Quebec] in these years (1815-28) passed into the United states'.[32]

The connection between Ulster and Canada in the post-Napoleonic period was exemplified, and certainly propagated, by the appointment of A.C. Buchanan as Emigration Agent at Quebec in 1828. A member of a prominent shipping family in the port of Londonderry, Buchanan found in the hinterland served by it a plentiful supply of the small-farmer class which he preferred, of all the classes of emigrant which found their way to Canada. His most effective method of attracting the attention of prospective emigrants was by the insertion of notices in the Londonderry newspapers which recommended, in philosophical as well as practical terms, opportunities for advancement in Canada. Of particular attraction to the agricultural community in Ulster were the advertising features placed in the local press by Buchanan on behalf of the Canada Land Company which offered 'great encouragement to industrious farmers, labourers and mechanics in Canada'. In modern terms a package deal, of travel to and accommodation in Canada, was on offer, aimed specifically at the farming sector in the northern and western counties of Ulster.

These press advertisements appeared particularly in the newspapers which served counties Londonderry, Antrim and Tyrone in the late 1820s and until the mid-1830s.[33] In these counties landlords and land labourers, as well as having to face the problems of falling prices and the general agricultural depression encountered throughout Ireland, found that their only other source of income, which was based on the domestic spinning of linen, was competing despairingly against the growth of the mechanised linen industry which spread after 1825. The situation in which agricultural labouring families who supplemented their income through linen was summarised by a witness to the Devon Commission in 1844:

> Formerly the most industrious of this class were weavers, leaving only a necessary supply for agricultural work. Now a superabundance is thrown upon the land for employment, which makes the supply of labour much greater than the demand ... the contrast between the present and former state of these people is indeed melancholy.[34]

It was this class of tenant farmer, attracted by the opportunities to continue a farming life who, having emigrated to Canada, ultimately settled there. By the 1830s the Ordnance Survey Memoirs record that just over half of emigrants from County Londonderry are listed as having Quebec or St John's (New Brunswick) as their destination.[35]

The problems facing small landholders and agricultural labourers with sizeable families in a period of dwindling incomes and employment outlets, as well as poor harvests, generated a process of emigration in the 1820s and 1830s which has been more usually associated with the post-famine period. This entailed the staging of a family's emigration so that the passage of the rest of the family might be earned and supported by one member, usually a younger son, going out in advance. Tenant Right, if it was to be of practical assistance at all, was most useful to a small landholder with a young family of manageable size. Those whose families were larger and more mature did not, however, have the same mobility and their position is best represented in a 'reverse emigrant' letter written in 1836 from James Smyth in Moycraig, County Antrim, to his brother in Philadelphia:

> Robert [his son] expresses a strong desire to go to America in the Spring and indeed I am sorry to say that I am not fit to send him ... but James Patterson of the livery and his family are going out in the spring direct to Philadelphia and we are thinking of speaking to them to take him to you and that you would be so far a friend to him to answer his passage ... until such times as he would earn it and repay you ... This has been the severest season ever I experienced in my life. Our summer was almost like winter and our harvest in November. And this 4th day of December a great deal of grain in the field and likewise a poor crop of potatoes, which has the appearance of a hard summer in Ireland.[36]

Later in the letter James refers to the size of his family 'which is in number ten' and of these at least two brothers – first Robert, assisted by the uncle with whom he lives when he arrives in Philadelphia, and then Jonathan, helped in turn by Robert who sent him his fare – emigrate in

1837 and 1839. This type of extended family emigration must have been, as the logistics of emigration in a period of economic depression would suggest, at least as common a category as the two into which Irish emigration is usually divided, emigration by single individuals or by nuclear families, each making a clean, irrevocable break from Ireland. But the emigrants' letters are only one source which make it clear that it was implemented in a large number of removals prior to 1846. The Ordnance Survey Memoir for the parish of Faughanvale in 1833-4 noted that 'it is a usual system in this, as in other parishes, to send out the younger members of a family first to act as pioneers for the older. A constant correspondence is kept up and each emigrant is generally furnished with his outfit by another who has gone before him'.[37] The Canada Land Company also contributed practically to the assisted scheme by arranging passages for the dependants and family of pioneer emigrants to Canada.

The extent of correspondence from emigrants, and more particularly from emigrants who were from an artisanal or agricultural background in early- and mid-nineteenth century Ulster, does shed some further light on who exactly it was who emigrated. It becomes clear that regardless of the socio-economic reasons for propelling them, or the opportunities in America which served as attractions, a general level of literacy was central in enabling intending emigrants to, in the first instance, make the decision to emigrate and subsequently to conduct their passage to and arrival in America. Just as importantly, it was essential in keeping in contact with their immediate family and relatives in providing moral and financial support to the rest of the family's emigration intentions.

The level of literacy evident in the emigrant letters has something to contribute to the 'brain drain' aspect of emigration: did the people whom Ulster could least afford to lose, go? Demographers constantly warn of the inaccuracies and infidelity of literary evidence and there can be little doubt that the letters of Ulster emigrants are a generally unreliable sample (even if only on the obvious ground that it is hard to find letters of illiterate emigrants). Indeed, the more representative the letters are of the level of education in the Ulster population, the less they can say whether the 'best' (i.e. best educated) were emigrating. What can be said about the considerable quantity of emigrants' letters that remain as evidence of the movement from Ulster to North America in the first half of the nineteenth century is that they formed an essential link in the process of chain migration of families and friends.

The letters have an additional value in that they contain enough accounts of individual emigrants' experiences from which generalisations might be made about Ulstermen's assimilation into American society. The single status of so many Ulster emigrants encouraged in them a remarkable degree of mobility, both geographical and occupational, in America. The letters of Robert Wray of Coleraine,[38] the Kerr Brothers of Newpark (Antrim)[39] and the Smyth Brothers of Moycraig near Ballymoney all contain accounts of their odysseys in search of work (and, in the case of the three Kerrs who all died in the 1840s from tuberculosis, a healthier climate). John, William and David Kerr travelled to and worked in New Orleans, Cincinatti and a number of smaller towns in Pennsylvania trying their hands at a variety of jobs – bookbinding, millwriting and, when these jobs dry up and there is no choice open to them, they fall on teaching, by their own admission, as a last resort.

Rather paradoxically the letters of Ulster emigrants reveal, in addition to the tendency and ability to travel widely in the quest for work, that many eastern seaboard ports and towns had an Ulster 'urban village' akin to that characteristic of European national community nuclei in cities such as Boston, New York, Philadelphia and Pittsburgh. Letters from the emigrants regularly contain a list of names of fellow Ulster emigrants and news about them which is for the benefit of acquaintances of the writer's family in Ireland. The information is more often than not gossip; 'Joseph Crawford gave me a letter from James Burnside [and] I forwarded it to him immediately about 20 miles in the country. Joseph Crawford is well. Joseph Chestnut and wife are well ... I can inform you that Hugh Boyle is well and all his family. I see him every day, he drives a cart. All the people that are in the city or county from our part are all well, as I know them all'.[40] The County Antrim community in Philadelphia, as portrayed in the letters of the emigrants, displays many of the 'home-from-home' characteristics usually associated with post-famine Irish and European migrant settlements in American cities.[41]

Ulster emigrants also show a general tendency, traditionally associated with Irish emigration later in the nineteenth century, to move from a rural to an urban environment although, when the migration to farms in Canada is taken into account, the overall proportion of Ulster emigrants ultimately residing in urban America is probably the lowest of the four provinces of Ireland. And, regardless of whether their eventual location was urban or rural, there is evidence that first-generation Ulster settlers experienced varying degrees of assimilation into American society. Robert Smyth, writing in 1840 about the diplomatic unease between London and Washington, comments on the prospect of war: 'if we thereby could get our necks from under the yoke of the most ruthless of despots, the money power of London ... as for my part I will take to arms against Great Britain and Ireland of whom I was heretofore a subject but have denounced that for ever and become a citizen of the United States'.[42] John Kerr, writing in 1844 of the Nativist riots in Philadelphia says: 'the object of the "Natives" is to prevent foreigners from being naturalised until 21 years in this country. This the Irish do not like – for my part I care not a straw whether they pass this law or not. I am very well contented of still remaining a subject of your little queen'.[43] Both John Kerr and Robert Smyth in their respective accounts of the anti-Irish riots assume the role of a detached commentator and make it clear that they are not regarded, nor do they regard themselves, as being wholly Irish. So there is in the emigrants' letters a sense of being Ulster-Irish though there is implicit a belief that American society is more acceptable and libertarian than that in either Ulster or the rest of Ireland.

This portrait of a classless society was indeed the view of America widely held in Ireland but it is clear that the attractions of moving there were more practical than philosophical. It is also clear that these considerations, which included advice on financial assistance and the dependability of familiar faces on arrival, played as much a part in galvanising emigration from Ulster as did the 'push' factors of agricultural depression, decline in domestic linen income and pressure of population. These were all evident in pre-famine Ulster and swelled the stream of 300,000 emigrants, but there remains the conclusion that the migrations to America in the later colonial and Napoleonic periods had generated a momentum of their own and that the pre-famine migrations from Ulster contained, as a consequence, many of the characteristics of the post-famine exodus.

Notes

1   The exceptions to this are W.F. Adams, *Ireland and Irish Emigration to the New World* (Yale, 1932); Oliver MacDonagh, *A Pattern of Government Growth* (London, 1961); C. O'Grada in 'Across the Briny Ocean: Some Thoughts on Irish Emigration to America 1800-50' in *Comparative Studies in Scottish and Irish Economic and Social History* (Edinburgh, 1983); Kerby A. Miller, *Emigrants and Exiles: Ireland and the Irish Exodus to America* (Oxford, 1985) and, most recently, Donald Harman Akenson, *The Irish Diaspora: A Primer* (Toronto, 1994).

2   Census of Ireland 1901, Vol iii, province of Ulster HC 1902 CXXVI, CXXVII.

3   As listed in C. O Grada, 'Across the Briny Ocean'. They include: 1803-06, to Boston (PROL) and PRONI T521); 1830-39 to USA and Canada (Ordnance Survey Memoirs, R.I.A.); 1822-39 to Boston (US Immigration Archives); 1820-48 to New York (US Immigration Archives).

4   C. O Grada, ibid.

5   Ibid.

6   K.H. Connell, *The Population of Ireland* (London, 1950), p. 38.

7   Maldwyn A. Jones, 'Ulster Emigration to Colonial America 1783-1815' in *Essays in Scotch-Irish History,* edited by E.R.R. Green (London, 1969).

8   M.L. Hanson, *The Atlantic Migration,* p. 79.

9   *Belfast News-letter,* 26 November 1773, PRONI MIC 19.

10   PRONI D2309/4/4, published in *Letters from an Ulster Land Agent,* edited and with an introduction by W.H. Crawford, (Belfast, 1976).

11   Phineas Bond to Duke of Leeds 10 Nov. 1789, F.O. 4/7.

12   For example, David N. Doyle, *Ireland, Irishmen and Revolutionary America* (Dublin and Cork, 1981).

13   Imre Ferenczi, *International Migrations. Volume I, Statistics* (Washington, 1929).

14   Ferenczi, pp. 99, 380-1.

15   Ferenczi, pp. 360-1.

16   Cecil Houston and William Smyth, 'The Ulster Legacy', *Multiculturalism,* vol 1, no 4 (1978).

17   K.H. Connell, *Population of Ireland,* p. 28.

18   Most notably, R. Crotty, *Irish Agricultural Production* (Cork, 1966).

19   O Grada, 'Across the Briny Ocean'.

20 E.R.R. Green, 'Ulster Emigrants' Letters', in *Essays in Scotch Irish History.*

21 Phineas Bond 10 November 1789 F.O. 4/7.

22 *BNL*, 26 Nov. 1773.

23 *Report of Inquiry into the Occupation of Land in Ireland* (1845), vol 1, p. 799.

24 Report from Select Committee of House of Lords on the Tenure (Ireland) Bill 1867, Cmd 518, vol XIV.

25 P. Roebuck, 'The Lives Lease System and Emigration from Ulster: an Example from Montgomery County, Pennsylvania', *Ulster Historical and Genealogical Guild Newsletter*, vol 7 (1981).

26 PRONI Caledon Estate records, D266/377.

27 K.H. Connell, *Population of Ireland*, p. 28.

28 PRONI D3127/1.

29 R. Crotty, *Irish Agricultural Production*, p. 39.

30 Ibid.

31 PRONI T.2613/3.

32 C. O. 42/223, Buchanan to Aylmer, 7 May 1831.

33 Particularly the *Londonderry Sentinel* and *Londonderry Standard.*

34 Devon Commission Vol I.

35 I am very grateful to Ms Deirdre Mageean for this information, based on her work.

36 PRONI D.1828/4.

37 *Ordnance Survey Memoir, Parish of Faughanvale, Co. Londonderry.* Originals in Royal Irish Academy, Dublin; published by Institute of Irish Studies, The Queen's University of Belfast, 1992.

38 PRONI, T.1727.

39 PRONI, MIC.144. See also

40 PRONI, D.1828/

41 Herbert Gans, *The Urban Villagers* (Chicago, 1962).

42 PRONI, D.1828/

43 PRONI, MIC.144/

TWO NEGLECTED BELFAST MEDICAL PROFESSORS: JAMES LAWSON DRUMMOND (1783-1853) AND JAMES DRUMMOND MARSHALL (1808-1868)

PETER FROGGATT

ON 8 OCTOBER 1835 the 'Board of Faculty of the Medical Department' of the Royal Belfast Academical Institution (hereafter RBAI) met for the first time. I have told its story elsewhere.[1,2,3,4,5, 6,7] There are adequate biographical memoirs on three of the five foundation 'professors' viz. Thomas Andrews – professor of chemistry,[8,9] Robert Little – professor of midwifery and diseases of women and children,[10,11] and John Macdonnell – professor of surgery,[12] the younger son of the redoubtable Dr James Macdonnell.[13] Drummond – professor of anatomy and medical physiology (1818-49) and also of botany (1835-36) – to George Benn '... an able promoter of all scientific and literary matters in Belfast'[14] – has received only very brief notices;[15,16,17] while his nephew, J. D. Marshall – professor of materia medica and pharmacy (1835-49) – has received none.

Drummond's neglect is puzzling. It may be that 'his life was not marked by any startling incident, nor was the world enriched by any important scientific discovery as a result of his individual exertions';[15] but he also lacked glamour and reaches us as a colourless if worthy academic. Also, there is no repository of personal papers to flesh out or challenge this image, and no direct descendants to foster an interest. He deserves better: as well as Benn's accolade (above) he played the pivotal role in inspiring and founding the joint RBAI/Belfast Fever Hospital medical school, one of the leading contemporary provincial preparatory schools.[2] (The Fever Hospital later became the Belfast General Hospital in 1847, the Royal

74

Belfast Hospital in 1875, and the Royal Victoria Hospital in 1899.) Drummond was foundation 'president' (i.e. dean) of the medical faculty board, was an able educationalist, was far-sighted with clear and prescient views on a medical course, and 'by his assiduous and unremitting zeal the intellectual life of Belfast was considerably advanced during the first half of the nineteenth century'.[15]

In this paper I outline Drummond's life and achievements though I omit much to do with the medical school, since I have already fully described it.[1-7] I also add a short biographical note on his nephew, Professor J. D. Marshall, to save him from his present obscurity.

James Lawson Drummond: early life and career

Drummond was born in Larne probably in late 1783[18], the youngest of the daughter[19] and two sons[20] of a naval surgeon, William Drummond RN, and Rose Hare. Drummond *père* was paid off in 1783 and entered surgical practice in Ballyclare but died of fever on 18 May 1787[21] leaving his straitened family to decamp to Belfast where his widow started a 'circulating library' in Castle Street.[22] The two brothers attended the Belfast Academy then in Donegall Street[15,16,23] but lack of means forced the elder, William Hamilton, into a menial commercial job in England and later compelled him to withdraw from Glasgow University without a degree;[24] while James on leaving school had to earn a living and enrolled (on 27 December 1799) as an apprentice apothecary.[25] Nothing is known of his indentureship but he sought self-improvement and joined the Linen Hall Library in December 1804 impressively being able to find the £2. 18s. 6d. combined admission fee and subscription for the first six months![26] He also joined the Belfast Literary Society in March 1806, read a paper in May and so impressed his colleagues that in June he was elected secretary/treasurer for the following session aged only twenty-two![27]

In 1804 or 1805 he joined his future brother-in-law, Andrew Marshall, in practice in 51 High Street.[28] To his family's dismay,[29] however, he decided to follow his father's and Marshall's career[28] and on 7 October 1806 he was appointed assistant surgeon (a rung above 'surgeon's mate' but not then a commissioned rank) to the ex-French *La Nereide* in the Mediterranean under Lord Colling-wood, and on 14 February 1810 was commissioned as surgeon to the ex-Spanish *San Juan Nepomaceno*.[30] He

75

was paid off on 21 May 1813, returned briefly to Belfast,[31] and then set off for Edinburgh where on 24 June 1814 he graduated Doctor of Medicine[32] with a thesis 'De Oculi Anatomica Comparativa'.[33]

He returned to a receptive and vibrant Belfast[34] and set up in practice at 5 Chichester Street.[35] His advancement was rapid due partly to his patrons the Rev Dr Bruce (to whom he dedicated his thesis), his brother William (now minister of the Second Belfast Congregation) and his brother-in-law, Andrew Marshall, now attending surgeon at the Belfast Fever Hospital.[36] On 24 July he was appointed a physician to the General Dispensary and 'soon afterwards' attending physician to the Fever Hospital then in West Street, was attached to the Belfast Charitable Society, and in October 1816 was appointed to the newly founded 'Belfast Institution for Diseases of the Eye', next to 1 John Street, 'to give advice to the poor every day at noon',[37] all non-stipended but crucial career posts. During this period work with his practice was broken only by some six months in Dublin (from December 1815)[38] probably extending his clinical knowledge. Fate now took a hand. On 28 September 1818 the Fever Hospital committee recommended that attending medical staff be stipended.[39] After all from 1807 the hospital was receiving at least £400 p.a. from the grand jury.[40] Drummond and S. S. Thomson were the main supporters: they argued that the doctors were spending their time (and risking their lives!) beyond any reasonable charitable obligation. The board of subscribers backed by Doctors S.M. Stephenson and James Macdonnell, did not agree and 'controversy was only closed by the final retirement ... of Dr S.S. Thomson and Dr J.L. Drummond'.[39] The matter rankled for years. Thomson later returned to the staff but Drummond never did and thereafter his only connection with the hospital (other than through the RBAI medical school) was to subscribe annually one guinea, the minimum necessary to qualify as a voting 'subscriber', and only after the medical school opened in 1835 and then irregularly,[41] a parsimony at odds with his generosity to RBAI and others.[42]

By now Drummond had reached a career cross-roads. By inclination a scientist and teacher rather than a clinician or practitioner, he was attracted increasingly to the study of the basic medical sciences – anatomy, physiology, biology and chemistry – which were to be his life's interests. He increasingly withdrew from practice[43] and was only a very fitful member of the Belfast Medical Society.[44] The exclusive local forum for science was then the Belfast Literary Society – despite its name it listed 'literature, science and the arts' as its interests[45] – and after returning from Dublin in the summer of 1816 he was an active member attending 21 of its next 36 meetings,[46] reading five papers all in the natural sciences,[47] continuing as curator of the Society's growing specimen collection,[48] and only resigning in May 1821[49] on founding the Belfast Natural History Society (hereafter BNHS) as a more exclusive vehicle for his interests (see below). He also rejoined the Linen Hall Library.[50] His resignation from the Fever Hospital staff and withdrawal from practice freed him to develop these interests and his ambitions now became clearly focused on five objectives: (i) teaching basic medical sciences (which he did); (ii) founding a natural history society and museum (which he did); (iii) establishing public botanical gardens (which he helped to do); (iv) creating a preparatory (i.e. non-licence-awarding) joint medical school (which he did); and (v) expressing and disseminating his scientific *credos* (which he also did). Altogether a formidable agenda which he largely completed, as I address below.

First, however, I complete Drummond's biography. From 15 December 1818 until he retired through ill-health on 30 September 1849,[51] the pivot for his activities was as professor of anatomy and medical physiology at RBAI.[52] In January 1849 'by an accident ... he broke one of his thigh bones and is thereby completely disabled'[53] and he retired on a pension equal to his salary of £150 p.a.[54] He died on 16 May 1853[55] at his residence, since 1824, 8 College Square North.[56] He married three times: none produced issue. His first wife, Jane, was the only daughter of John Getty of Donegall Street, a leading orthodox Presbyterian layman.[57] She died on 8 February 1831.[58] On 13 October 1834 he married Catherine, daughter of the late Alexander Mitchell of Newgrove, a member of the Church of Ireland.[59] She died on 27 December 1848.[60] On 10 May 1850, now 67 and physically disabled, he married the 45-year-old Eliza,[61] second daughter of the late Daniel O'Rorke of a prominent Catholic family of Ballybollan near Ballymena.[62] She outlived him by forty-three years dying on 27 November 1896 aged 91. They are buried in the O'Rorke plot in the 'old' burial ground in Ahoghill[63] and have adjacent memorial plaques in nearby St Colmanell's Church.[64]

What kind of man was Drummond? Without personal papers I can only view him skeletally through his deeds and professional writings. As a man of his time and place, however, his religious beliefs require comment. He was raised in the non-subscribing church, his brother William Hamilton became a leading 'new light' divine and his sister Isabella married into the staunchly 'new light' Marshall family. Drummond probably conformed but on marrying Jane Getty he joined her (orthodox Presbyterian) Church through custom, prudence or possibly belief. Eighteen months after this marriage he averred 'I am a Presbyterian: I attend Dr Hanna's house [the Third Belfast 'orthodox' Congregation]: I am of orthodox principles'.[65] Perhaps so but he was latitudinarian enough to wed twice subsequently under Church of Ireland rites. He was not prominent in the affairs of 'Dr Hanna's house'[66] nor was he a member of St George's after his marriage there to Catherine Mitchell.[67] In the broader sense he held, in his science, stout Christian, or at least deist views, lauding 'the great and Almighty God whose offspring the works of nature are ... [which] gives us the most exalted conceptions of power, wisdom and beneficence of the Deity',[68] and much more in like vein. He differed if at all only in degree from the bulk of the pre-Darwinian deist scientific *cognoscenti*.

Later career

With an exquisite irony and a coincidence unlikely to be chance, on the very day (6 October 1818) when the board of subscribers of the Fever Hospital rejected his case that staff be stipended, Drummond wrote to RBAI offering himself for the chair of anatomy without any stipend at all, only the student class fees:[69] 'Let me be nominated Professor and I will give you my service *gratis* so long as you honour me with the title'.[70] After some negotiation[71] and a narrow defeat of a motion to defer,[72] he was appointed to start classes on 1 February 1819 (with £50 p.a. salary),[73] and gave these at 2.00 p.m. daily until the end of April and then throughout each session (November – April inclusive). He taught 'a very wide field of natural history and a good deal of natural theology; there is scarcely a fact in Paley's *Natural Theology* which is not explained and illustrated ... [also] a little human dissection' mainly to students preparing for the ministry 'for which I think the classes must be of great importance' but also 'to a number of medical men, apothecaries, apprentices and others'.[74] The embryo medical school had been conceived. In 1819 he was empowered to buy textbooks,[75] in 1820 he became 'curator' of the zoological and botanical sections of the RBAI 'museum',[76] in 1822 he started classes in botany,[77] and when in 1823 he co-ordinated these with Professor Stevelly's course in 'elements of chemical science' the embryonic pre-clinical syllabus was shaped.[1,2] His letter to RBAI and the Fever Hospital suggesting a joint 'school of medicine and surgery, useful and important to the medical youth of Ulster' which he made public on 7 November 1826,[78] was the seminal catalyst, and after nearly a further decade of negotiations and resource procurement the faculty of medicine with Drummond in the chair was born on 8 October 1835 and survived until the opening of Queen's College Belfast in 1849. It was to be of great benefit to Ulster, to some 600 of its youth who enrolled in it, and to the local profession. It was an achievement for the institutions concerned but a triumph, although one largely unsung, for Drummond's foresight, faith and perseverance.[1-7]

Drummond's appointment to RBAI, his resignation from the Fever Hospital, and his withdrawal from practice gave him the opportunity and the obligation to write, research, teach, and further the medical school's development. He used his time well. A keen prosector, he played an important role in creating a public botanic gardens (which opened in 1827),[79] but his main achievement of this period was as leading founder of the BNHS (in 1821) and its associated museum (in 1831). These have been fully described and need little comment here.[80] Drummond was the driving force. He convened the meeting which founded the Society (on 5 June 1821) and it met in his house fortnightly for sixteen months; his seven foundation 'apostles' elected him first president; it was he who scheduled the annual presidential address for 24 May 'the anniversary of Linnaeus' birth'[81] (his botanical mentor) and delivered the first two,[82] made the first donation to the embryo library[83] and was curator for 'botanical specimens' in the developing museum.[84] He was president (1821-22; 1827-42) or vice-president (1822-27) until his sudden resignation as president on 30 November 1842 on the grounds of long tenure and other commitments [85] – at face value reasonable enough, if somewhat abrupt, although after the first few years he had been anything but a regular attender.[86] (Drummond was not a great 'committee man' other than in RBAI where he rarely missed a faculty meeting. He was on the committee of the Linen Hall Library for two years, February 1825-27, but could manage only four of the 24 meetings![87] Despite this he gave 32 papers to the Society from 1821 to 1842 and the opening address of the Museum Building (in College Square North) on 1 November 1831,[88] was an active fundraiser[89] and subscriber for the museum project[90] and was especially pleased with the role it came to play in the science courses at RBAI,[1-2] and he encouraged the 'Juvenile Natural History Society' formed by 'two or three boys' in 1826 led by his nephew William Marshall, brother of J.D. Marshall, and which met in the Society's rooms in the Commercial Buildings.[91]

Drummond's main activities were the professorial ones of teaching and writing. We know little of his pedagogic and educative abilities except through his books, but his syllabi were progressive, his classes in the faculty of medicine were well-attended,[92] he discharged his duties conscientiously – as the faculty of medicine minutes attest – and his hold on his offices was durable without undue tenacity. As already noted, his teaching load was heavy and included marking holiday (summer) prize essays,[93] but he rarely evaded it.[94] As well as the works already cited as read to various Societies, he wrote in 1820 an anonymous monograph on the basics of a natural history curriculum;[83] a primer in botany on Linnaean principles (1823);[95] a collection of essays on the study of nature (1831) in which he adduces his educational strategy of a museum, lecture-room and library in each town or village '... to display the works of God in the great subjects of natural theology',[96] which he followed successfully in Belfast; a primer in anatomy with some progressive thoughts on the education of medical students (1845);[97] a further botany text (1849);[98] a handful of articles mainly on Irish marine life and entozoa;[99,100,101,102,103,104] and possibly some others.[105] A talented draftsman, he illustrated many of these himself. As a whole the books are educative, well-ordered, and in places philosophical: the articles are of descriptive morphology except one which reflects 'spontaneous generation'.[103] For his reading he borrowed extensively from the Linen Hall Library who allowed him 'to have such books ... as he may have occasion to consult' and 'any of the restricted books he may want'.[106] Some idea of his lecture material may be gleaned from one published in a short-lived students' magazine.[107]

Drummond's life now revolved around RBAI, the museum and BNHS, his writing mainly at his home at 8 College Square North, and the Linen Hall Library (then in the White Linen Hall), all within a bare three minutes' walk, and what domestic life his childless marriages and extended family provided. The medical school increasingly absorbed his attention which turned to concern as, from 1845, it became increasingly clear that it would give way to the proposed Queen's College Belfast which, despite much lobbying, would not incorporate collegiate RBAI. There is no evidence in his teaching load or writings of declining energies or health until severely disabled in January 1849 when he became virtually housebound, his later years being eased by the care of his third wife Eliza whom he married in 1850. The two institutions he had vitalised and loyally served were represented at his funeral as 'his remains were followed to their final resting place in Ahoghill ... by the members of the Natural History and Philosophical Society and by those of the Joint Boards of Managers of the Royal Academical Institution'[55] but the Fever (now General) Hospital was not, continuing in death a certain estrangement begun with his resignation in 1818 and discernible if not in the end obstructive during the long gestation and short life of the joint medical school.[1,2,6]

How justified are the judgements of Benn[14] and Millin[15] above? Drummond was unquestionably an 'able promoter of all scientific matters in Belfast' but hardly of 'literary' ones also. He abandoned the Literary Society in 1821, his borrowings from the Linen Hall Library are scientific with an occasional travel memoir,[108] his writings, lectures and addresses are exclusively scientific, the flavour of his non-technical comments in his books are philosophical rather than literary. Admittedly, like many of his background he was highly literate, liberally sprinkling his earlier work with literary citations, much of it poetry.[68] Nevertheless, Benn was generous with his 'literary' accolade; Millin's opinions are more to the point. Through his writings and achievements, however, there dimly emerges a man of intellectual and moral substance keen to popularise and promulgate science though not vulgarise it, an educator especially of youth for the betterment of society and themselves, a man of principle and sincerity, perhaps a man genuinely 'in private life amiable and affable',[55] who certainly enjoyed the trust and confidence of his scientific colleagues, a man of vision above all in the need for a medical school for Ulster's youth, open to all, and the way to achieve it. The apparel of personality and the more private man must await the unearthing of personal papers. He has been overshadowed in the Belfast medical coterie by more flamboyant contemporaries, and the fame of Thomas Andrews, but none did more to promote science and a medical school in Ulster, very much to Ulster's and Ireland's benefit.

James Drummond Marshall

James Marshall was a son of Andrew Marshall, attending surgeon to the Belfast Fever Hospital, and James Lawson Drummond's only sister Isabella.[19] He was born in late 1808 or early 1809[109] at 94 High Street,[110] eldest in a sibship of five (three girls; two boys).[111] He entered the 'writing class' at RBAI on 7 November 1815 and between February 1818 and May 1825 attended classes in arithmetic, geography, mathematics, classics and French.[112] In November 1821, aged 13, he also enrolled in the RBAI extramural section for two sessions of 'junior mathematics', sat the general RBAI collegiate entrance examination in 'Greek and Latin exercises' in November 1824 and until 1826 studied these languages with 'Logic' and 'Senior Mathematics'.[113] These were evening classes and at the same time, on 19 December 1823 when at most 15, he and his brother William (who was even younger) were accepted as licensed apprentices by Apothecaries Hall, Dublin,[114] doubtless indentured to their father.

James resolved also to become a physician and following the then frequent practice first took the LRCS of Edinburgh (28 April 1830) on the ground that funds may not stretch to taking the Edinburgh MD which could be expensive.[115] Funds however did stretch and he graduated on 12 July 1832 with a thesis 'De Pertussi'.[116] He now returned to join his father Andrew, and in 1834 also his brother, in surgical practice at High Street before moving to establish an independent practice and druggists at 8 High Street at first also with his brother.[117] James however had academic leanings. While still an apprentice apothecary he had joined the BNHS[118] and was an active member presenting specimens when only 17,[119] reading two papers while still at RBAI, two while an undergraduate, and a total of 12 in all.[120] He was a Belfast Museum curator from its foundation in 1831, gave a lecture on the BNHS 'public night' in 1832, served on the council 1832-50 (except for 1842-43), was joint recording secretary (with Robert S. McAdam) 1834-37, and unlike his uncle, J.L. Drummond, was a good

82

attender and 'committee man'.[121] He also joined the Belfast Literary Society (on 6 October 1834), attended regularly, read one paper, but disappears after May 1836.[122] In June 1834 he spent some weeks surveying Rathlin's natural, human and biological features wandering 'with gun, gun-belt and botany box' which produced his main publication[123] and he attended the British Association meeting in Dublin in 1835 as an annual subscriber and contributed a paper.[124] He appears as a young, energetic surgeon also engaged in retail pharmacy with his brother as 'surgeons and chemists' and with the naturalist's interests and the energy and enquiring mind of his family. He was not, however, unlike his father and uncle, a member of the Linen Hall Library.

The foundation of the medical school at RBAI gave Marshall an opportunity for his academic ambitions and he was one (of the three) applicants for the chair of materia medica and pharmacy. He was appointed on 29 September 1835 against the opinion of the moderator of the Ulster Synod (the 'orthodox' Presbyterian body).[125] He was elected secretary of the faculty of medicine at its first meeting and remained so throughout its 14-year life adding the treasurership after 1840.[126] Throughout he handled the faculty business with skill, was a member of numerous *ad hoc* faculty committees, was a 'medical attendant' at the RBAI 'College Hospital' during the fever epidemic in 1837, wrote succinct minutes and reports in a legible hand, and did much more worthwhile work besides. He was also dutiful: from 8 October 1835 to 13 February 1846 (after which the number of meetings fell as did morale due to the certainty of closure) he missed only eleven of the 124 faculty meetings. In 1838 he was a medical attendant to the General Dispensary but only for a year and he was never appointed to the Fever Hospital staff.[127] Like his uncle his interests lay elsewhere and like his uncle also he was niggardly in his hospital subscriptions giving at most 7s 6d annually up to 1847 and thereafter usually the minimum one guinea necessary to be a voting 'subscriber'.[128] He did not join the Belfast Medical Society until 1843,[129] was a poor attender and book borrower,[130] and his main achievement was to act as a 'steward' for the annual dinner![131] He 'retired' from the Society in 1853[132] as he increasingly withdrew from practice.

Marshall was as conscientious, active, and committed to RBAI as was his uncle, though he had less teaching duties.[133] His professional interests however lay more in his professional practice and the retail pharmacy which he ran with his brother than in more academic activities.[134] He also had a growing family: he had married the 22-year-old Jane, eldest daughter of the author, playwright and actor James Sheridan Knowles, on 22 April 1837[135] and soon had a son and daughter.[136] His affairs prospered during the next decade and in December 1848 he applied for the foundation chair of materia medica at Queen's College Belfast.[137] Events now moved against him. His application was unsuccessful and though his affairs enabled him to live in Holywood from 1852, his wife died on 4 April 1854[138] by which time he had started to sever his connections with his various scientific and medical societies and in 1856 dropped his name from the *Medical Directory*[139] and did not apply to be registered under the 1858 Act.[140] He read a paper at the British Association meeting in Belfast in 1852 but this is his last recorded scientific foray.[141] In 1861 he is listed as at 13 Shore Street, Holywood,[142] but by then had disposed of his Belfast business[143] and ceased any meaningful practice. He died at home on 27 March 1868 aged 59, of 'heart disease of several months, uncertified'[144] and was buried as were his wife and father in the New Burying Ground, Clifton Street.[145]

Marshall was not as significant as was Drummond but he was not unimportant. As secretary and treasurer of the RBAI faculty of medicine he ably supported his uncle throughout the school's existence, was successful in practice and business, and was chemist-in-ordinary to the Queen in Ireland. He comes through even more dimly than Drummond because as well as leaving no personal papers he had no corpus of writings and has attracted no biographical note. When the brilliant Thomas O'Meara resigned the chair of materia medica at Queen's College Belfast in 1849 before taking it up, it was offered not to Marshall but to H.A. Stewart, then only 29, who had applied for the chair of surgery and 'was very well thought of as a surgeon but does not appear to have had any particular qualifications in the subject of his chair'.[146] This was an undoubted disappointment to Marshall who in his application stood on his record, named the new vice-president of Queen's College Belfast (his RBAI colleague Thomas Andrews) as his referee,[137] and numbered among his family circle the first registrar of QCB, his brother-in-law W.J. Campbell Allen. But it should not be seen as an unequivocal adverse professional judgement since Stewart had strong professional and family connections and Queen's would not have been comfortable with Marshall's extensive commercial activities in a senior member of staff.

Epilogue

Drummond left no issue; Marshall none of note. Through Drummond's brother they were, however, connected with three generations of noteworthy Unitarian clergy, while through Marshall's sister Margaret and her husband Rev J. Scott Porter they were connected to the distinguished liberal Ulster legal and clerical family of Porter including Scott's brother, William, the famous liberal attorney-general of the Cape Colony, 1839-65, the subject of a recent biography,[147] whose memory and colour-blind Cape franchise are now much revered in the new Republic of South Africa. Scott's son, Sir Andrew Marshall Porter, MP, was former attorney-general and master of the rolls, and Scott's brother-in-law Frank Dalzell Finlay was founder of the *Northern Whig*, the voice of Ulster liberalism. Drummond especially, and Marshall in his own way, bridge the gap between the intellectually vibrant days of the early nineteenth century so crucial to the development of Belfast and which is the subject of much comment and research, and the mid-century when Belfast was set in its Victorian (and later Edwardian) mould which carried it to great wealth and prominence but also to a social and political structure which many of their early contemporaries, and perhaps they themselves, would have deplored. But as educationalists they would have applauded much which came later and would have taken pride in being among that coterie which laid the foundations for our liberal educational system and a medical school which for much of its life has ranked with the best in these islands. How, why, and in what ways their heritage has flourished is an absorbing story which I have touched on elsewhere,[4] but a story still requiring to be told.

Notes and references used in the Notes

BLS	Minutes, Belfast Literary Society (Linen Hall Library, Belfast), 1801-50.
BMS	Minutes, Belfast Medical Society, 1822-1862 (Belfast Medical Society rooms, Whitla Building, QUB).
BNHS	Minute Books of the Belfast Natural History Society, 1821-50 (PRONI. D 3263/AB/1-3).
Directory	*Belfast Directory* e.g. Smyth's, Henderson's, Martin's, Belfast Street Directory etc.
DNB	*Dictionary of National Biography*. London: Smith, Elder, 1888.
FA	Minute Book of the Faculty of Arts of the (Royal) Belfast Academical Institution (PRONI. SCH 524/3C/1).
FM	Minute Book of the Faculty of Medicine of the Royal Belfast Academical Institution, 1835-49 (PRONI. SCH 524/3C/5).
JB	Minute Books of the Joint Boards of Managers and Visitors of the (Royal) Belfast Academical Institution, 1807-64 (6 vols) (PRONI. SCH 524/3A/1-6).
Lett. Bk.	Letter Book of the Institution (RBAI), 1807-79 (4 vols) (PRONI. SCH 524/7A/1-4).
LHL	Minute Books of the Linen Hall Library, 1812-55.
NL	*(Belfast) Newsletter* (Linen Hall Library, Belfast).
PRONI	Public Record Office of Northern Ireland (66, Balmoral Avenue, Belfast).
Rep. Fev. Hosp.	*The Annual Medical Report of the Dispensary and Fever Hospital of Belfast*. Belfast: Alexander McKay. The year is 1 May – 30 April for 1817-29; 1 April – 31 March thereafter (Archive office, Royal Victoria Hospital Belfast).
SPOI	State Paper Office of Ireland (Now amalgamated with the Public Record Office of Ireland as the National Archives, Bishop Street, Dublin).

Acknowledgements

I am grateful to the Deputy Keeper of the Records, Public Record Office of Northern Ireland, and the Keeper of the Irish National Archives have kindly allowed me to consult and cite extensively from their archives.

Notes

1   P. Froggatt, 'The Foundation of the "Inst" Medical Department and its Association with the Belfast Fever Hospital', *Ulster Medical Journal*, 45 (1976), 107-145.

2   P. Froggatt, 'The first Medical School in Belfast', *Medical History*, 22 (1978), 237-66.

3   P. Froggatt, 'Medicine in Ulster: the Belfast School', in *A Portrait of Irish Medicine: an Illustrated History of Medicine in Ireland*, edited by Eoin O'Brien, Ann Crookshank, and Sir Guy Wolstenholme (Dublin, 1983), pp. 183-213.

4   P. Froggatt, 'The Distinctiveness of Belfast Medicine and its Medical School', *Ulster Medical Journal*, 54 (1985), 89-108.

5   Peter Froggatt, *The Belfast Medical School in the Context of Irish Medicine: Past and Present* (Belfast, 1985).

6   P. Froggatt, 'The Early Medical School: Foundation and First Crisis – the "College Hospital" Affair', *Ulster Medical Journal (suppl.)*, 56 (1987), S5-S14.

7   P. Froggatt, 'The People's Choice: the Medical Schools of Belfast "Inst" (1835-1849) and the Catholic University (1855-1908) Compared',*Journal of the Irish Colleges of Physicians and Surgeons*, 20 (1991), 49-59.

8   P. G. Tait, A. C. Brown, *The Scientific Papers of the Late Thomas Andrews MD, FRS, with a Memoir* (London, 1889).

9   H. Riddell, 'Dr. Thomas Andrews: the Great Chemist and Physicist', *Proceedings and Reports of the Belfast Natural History and Philosophical Society for the Session 1920-21* (Belfast, 1922), pp. 107-38.

10   P. Froggatt, 'The Resignation of Robert Little from the Chair of Midwifery at Inst', *Ulster Medical Journal*, 48 (1979), 19-31.

11   P. Froggatt, W. G. Wheeler, 'Robert Little MA, MD, LAH, LM, Professor of Midwifery and Diseases of Women and Children, Royal Belfast Academical Institution, 1835-1840: a Biographical Note', *Ulster Medical Journal*, 52 (1983), 58-66.

12   P. Froggatt, 'MacDonnell, Father and Son. James (1763-1845), Physician of Belfast; John (1796-1892), Surgeon of Dublin', *Journal of the Irish Colleges of Physicians and Surgeons*, 13 (1984), 198-206.

13   P. Froggatt, 'Dr James MacDonnell MD (1763-1845)', *The Glynns*, 9 (1981), 17-31.

14   George Benn, *A History of the Town of Belfast from 1799 till 1810 together with Some Incidental Notices on Local Topics and Biographies of Well-Known Families* (London, 1880), vol. 2, p. 232.

15   S. Shannon Millin, 'James Lawson Drummond MD', in *The Belfast Natural History and Philosophical Society: Centenary Volume, 1821-1921*, edited by A. Deane (Belfast, 1924) pp. 72-3.

16   *DNB*, vol xvi, pp. 33-4 (by Rev Alexander Gordon).

17   H. G. Calwell, 'The Drummonds of Larne', *The Corran*, 25 (1982-3), 2-3.

18   *NL*, obit. 20 May 1853. Or perhaps 1784 (memorial plaque, St Colmanell's Church, Ahoghill – see note 64 below). The baptismal records of the 'old' Larne and Kilwaughter (Non-Subscribing) Church, where most of the Larne and Ralloo Drummonds worshipped, are missing for 25 December 1767 to end-1796 (PRONI. MIC 1B/6A/1A,1B; Misc 1B/6A/2). No relevant records are extant for other Presbyterian churches in the area.

19   Isabella (born 15 September 1776) married the surgeon Andrew Marshall on 24 December 1807 (*NL*, 1 Jan. 1808). There were two sons (James Drummond and William) and three daughters: Margaret who married Rev John Scott Porter on 8 October 1833 (*NL*, 11 Oct. 1833) and had eleven children; Isabella who married the banker, lawyer, and first Registrar of QCB, W.J. Campbell Allen on 14 August 1838 (*NL*, 17 Aug.

1838) and had three children; and Rosa who married the artist Richard Rothwell on 6 December 1842 (*NL*, 9 Dec 1842) and had eight children (*Old Belfast Families and the New Burying Ground from Gravestone Inscriptions with Wills and Biographical Notes*, edited by Richard Clarke (Belfast, 1991), p. 199.) See also 'Register of marriages 1790-1930 and of births 1757-1977, Rosemary Street Non-Subscribing Presbyterian Church (Belfast first congregation)' (PRONI. MIC 1B/2/1) for baptismal details of the progeny.

20 The elder, William Hamilton, poet, controversialist and prominent divine, was minister of the (Non-Subscribing) second Belfast congregation, 1800-15 and of Strand Street church, Dublin, 1815-65 (*DNB*, vol xvi, pp. 52-4).

21 *NL*, 22 May 1787.

22 Her daughter, Isabella, helped her before marrying Andrew Marshall (*Directory*, 1807 and 1808).

23 Records are incomplete and do not reveal the Drummonds. I am grateful to Mr W. M. Sillery, Headmaster, Belfast Royal Academy, for this information. See also 'Minutes, the Belfast Academy' (PRONI. T 3l01/1).

24 He matriculated at the University of Glasgow in 1794 and withdrew in 1798 (*Matriculation Album of the University of Glasgow 1728-1758*, transcribed and annotated by W. Innis Addison (Glasgow, 1913), p. 174).

25 At Apothecaries Hall, Dublin. I am grateful to Dr Malachy Powell for uncovering this record in the Hall's archives.

26 He resigned in January 1806 rejoining in February 1819 ('Register of Members of the Linen Hall Library 1792-1829').

27 He attended as a guest as early as 14 January 1805. The paper (in May 1806) was 'Spontaneous generation of plants and animals' (BLS, under dates).

28 S. Shannon Millin, *Sidelights of Belfast History* (Belfast, 1932), pp. 141-42. There is no extant record of Drummond obtaining his licence and he never described himself as 'Lic. Apoth (LAH)' or 'LSA (Irel.)' (*Medical Directory for Ireland* (London, 1852); H. Croly, *The Irish Medical Directory for 1846* (Dublin, 1846) though he is described in BLS as 'an apothecary'. Marshall is entered as 'surgeon, chemist, apothecary and practitioner in midwifery' (*Directory*, 1807). The following year the address was 94 High Street (*Directory*, 1808).

89

Marshall was a former naval assistant surgeon, 1802-1804, who re-enlisted in 1807 as surgeon on HMS *Brunswick* sailing from Yarmouth on 6 July with Admiral Gambier's Baltic fleet but was back in time for his wedding in December! He served again in 1808 before finally retiring.

29   His brother wrote to his sister 'could you bear to see your dear James a prisoner in the cockpit, at the mercy of winds, and waves, and cannon balls ... No, No James, thou deservest a better fate' (*DNB*, vol xvi, p. 33).

30   Sydney Allison, *The Seeds of Time: being a Short History of the Belfast General and Royal Hospital, 1850-1903* (Belfast, 1972), p. 78, n. 4.

31   He attended the Belfast Literary Society on 4 October and 1 November (BLS, under dates).

32   Drummond's naval career earned him course exemptions and he enrolled only for materia medica and the theory and practice of medicine ('Institutions of Medicine') for one session. I am grateful to Mrs Jo Currie, Assistant Librarian, Special Collections, University of Edinburgh, for identifying Drummond's course records. Also see *Edinburgh Medical Journal*, 10 (1814), 511.

33   He read part to the Royal Society of Edinburgh on 2 May 1814 (J.L. Drummond, 'On Certain Appearances Observed in the Dissection of the Eyes of Fishes', *Transactions of the Royal Society of Edinburgh*, VII (1812-15), 377-85). The thesis is dedicated to Rev Dr William Bruce, so important a family patron that his brother William's first-born was called William Bruce Drummond! ('Register', note 19 above, 18 Sept. 1804).

34   He returned before 24 July on which date he was appointed a physician to the Belfast General Dispensary (Andrew Malcolm, *The History of the General Hospital Belfast and the other Medical Institutions of the Town* (Belfast, 1851), p. 67).

35   *Directory*, 1819; 1820.

36   William Drummond and Bruce were also members of the hospital committee (Malcolm, note 34 above, App. III, p. iv).

37   Ibid., p. 67; R.W.M. Strain, *Belfast and its Charitable Society* (London, 1961), p. 246; *NL*, 18 Oct 1816.

38   He was elected president for 1815-16 (BLS, 1 May 1815) but in December stepped down 'in consequence of [his] removal to Dublin'

(BLS, 4 Dec. 1815). He attended on 4 November 1816 and thereafter. He might have stayed with his brother recently called to Strand Street Church, Dublin.

39 Malcolm, note 34 above, p. 77; *NL*, 6 and 10 Oct. 1818.

40 Under 47 Geo. III, c. 40 (1807). These monies were, strictly, exclusively for 'fever' cases but this was not enforced until 1839 (*Rep. Fev. Hosp.*, 1839-40, pp. 9 *et seq*).

41 Drummond annually subscribed £1-1-0 in 1835-7, 1839, 1841-8, 1851-2; 15/- in 1838; £2-2-0 in 1840 and 1849; nothing in 1850 (*Rep. Fev. Hosp.*, 1835-52).

42 Drummond for example subscribed £216-13-4 in 1832 towards the total cost of the RBAI 'medical buildings' of £871-4-0 (Froggatt, notes 1 and 2 above), and voluntarily passed up his salary for two years (1823-5) when RBAI was straitened.

43 In 1845 Drummond said 'I have not practised as a general practitioner [i.e. in clinical practice] for the last 20 years'. 'List of persons examined in Belfast [for the siting of the 'northern' college of QUI]', pp. 277-83 (SPOI. CSO Unregistered Miscellaneous Papers, 1846, No. 2, OP 1846/2.)

44 4 Dec. 1826 – 1 May 1828, 1 Feb. 1836 – 1 May 1837, 5 Oct. 1846 – 1 May 1847. He attended no meetings during the last session (BMS, 1822-28). See also 'A list of subscribers to the Belfast Medical Library re-organised on the 8th June 1822' (BMS, 1842-52).

45 Regulation III of the Belfast Literary Society (BLS, 23 Oct. 1801).

46 From 4 Nov. 1816 to 3 April 1821 (BLS).

47 On 6 Jan. 1817, 3 March 1817, 6 Oct. l817, 1 Nov 1819, 6 Nov. 1820. He also offered another paper (on 2 Dec. 1816) which he did not read ('The circulation of the blood illustrated by the anatomy of the heart and arteries'). These are additional to the four papers read before his Dublin sojourn (5 May 1806, 1 Nov. 1813, 2 Jan. 1815, 2 Oct. 1815) and two exhibits viz. 'a monstrous foetal calf' (6 Feb. 1815) and divers 'Mediterranean natural artefacts' (6 March 1815) (BLS, under dates). *Belfast Literary Society 1801-1901: Historical Sketch* (Belfast, 1902), p. 163, has a summary list though it is not complete.

48 BLS, 7 Oct 1816.

49 By letter (BLS, 7 May 1821).

50 LHL, 1812-25, p. 113 (meeting 4 Feb. 1819).

51 His last quarterly payment of salary (in arrears) was on 30 September 1849 (Lett. Bk. 1846-79, pp. 71-2),

52 He was also lecturer (1822-35) and professor (1835-6) of botany, was twice dean of the faculty of arts (1823, 1831) and three times dean of the faculty of medicine (1835, 1836, 1844) (Froggatt, note 2 above).

53 Secr. RBAI to Chief Secretary of 17 Sept. 1849 (Lett. Bk., 1846-79, p. 71). *DNB* erroneously suggests the accident was in 1848.

54 Lett. Bk., 1846-79, p. 74. Drummond was permanently tenured; the medical professors had nominally five-year terms ('List of Persons ...', note 43 above, pp. 300-322, evidence W. J. C. Allen, Secr. RBAI).

55 *NL*, obit, 20 May 1853.

56 Ibid. Also *Slater's Irish Directory*, 1846; Noel Nesbitt, *A Museum in Belfast: a History of the Ulster Museum and its Predecessors* (Belfast, 1979), p. 9. *Pigot's Irish Directory*, 1824, has him at 36 Donegall Street. He was earlier at 5 Chichester Street (note 35 above).

57 Married 30 March 1824 (*NL*, 2 Apr. 1824). Rev S. Hanna officiated. Two of his nieces, Margaret and Rosa Marshall, both children, attended, but not his 'new light' brothers, sister, or brother-in-law! 'Rosemary Street Presbyterian Church, Register of Marriages', 'c' 2 (PRONI. T 654/4).

58 *NL*, 11 Feb. 1831.

59 In St George's Belfast, Rev Thomas Drew officiating (*NL*, 17 Oct. 1834).

60 *NL*, 3 Jan. 1849.

61 In St Anne's, Belfast, Rev T.F. Millar officiating (*NL*, 14 May 1850; 'St Anne's Parish Records' (PRONI. MIC 1/178B/4)). Eliza is entered as 'lady' and her late father Daniel as 'gentleman'.

62 Daniel O'Rorke died on 22 September 1829. The O'Rorke menfolk remained in the old religion; the women were often raised in the Church of Ireland.

63 Under a cross inscribed 'IHS' with the legend 'In memory of the O'Rorkes of Ballybollan, linear descendants of the O'Rorkes (Breffni), of Dromahaire Castle, County Leitrim, 1884'. The plot is to the left of the main (Church Street) gate. I am grateful to Dr Eull Dunlop, Ballymena, for drawing my attention to these memorials.

64 The larger reads: 'Sacred to the memory of James L Drummond, MD, surgeon RN, professor of anatomy in the Royal Academical Institution and founder of the Natural History Society of Belfast. After serving his

country with distinction in the fleet under the command of Lord Collingwood, by whom his talents, zeal, and professional skill were highly appreciated, he dedicated the close of his life to science which he enriched by his discoveries and illustrated by many able, eloquent and ingenious writings. He died 17 May 1853, aged 68'. The smaller reads: 'To the glory of God and in memory of Eliza wife of the above James Drummond LLD [sic.] and second daughter of Daniel O'Rorke, Ballybollan. Died November 27th, 1896, aged 91 years'.

65 *Fourth Report of the Commissioners of Irish Education Inquiry.* H.C. 1826-27 (82) xiii, pp. 101-2.

66 'Records of Rosemary Street Church (third congregation)' (PRONI. MIC 1P/7/2-8).

67 St George's parish records (PRONI. MIC 1/116).

68 J.L. Drummond, *Letters to a Young Naturalist on the Study of Nature and Natural Theology* (London, 1831).

69 JLD to RBAI of 6 October 1818 (PRONI. SCH 524/7B/12/54; JB, 1814-21, p. 353 (6 Oct. 1818)). The chair was agreed but was unestablished for lack of endowment. The fees were £1-1-0 per session, sons of clergymen (of the Synod of Ulster) were exempt, so that 'my expenses fully counterbalance them'. From 1817 he had given a course 'chiefly upon osteology ...' (*Fourth report* note 65 above, pp. 101-2).

70 JLD to RBAI of 2 November 1818 (PRONI. SCH 524/7B/12/57).

71 PRONI. SCH 524/7B/60, 62; JB, 1814-21, pp. 354-60; FA, p. 16 (31 Oct. 1818).

72 By ten votes to seven with two abstentions (JB, 1814-21, p. 361) (15 Dec. 1818).

73 Ibid., pp. 359-60 (17 Nov. 1818).

74 *Fourth Report* note 65 above, p. 102. Numbers prior to the medical school (1835) were as low as five (JB, 1821-8, p. 129 (13 May 1823)) and as high as 26 (JB, 1828-36, p. 36 (5 July 1829)).

75 FA, p. 42 (11 Dec 1819).

76 FA, p. 52 (7 July 1820).

77 At first a 'popular course' to as many as 50 students (Lett. Bk. 1818-33, p. 147 (19 Feb. 1822), p. 174 (18 Feb. 1823); *Fourth report*, note 65 above, p. 102).

78 *NL*, 7 November 1826.

79 Eileen McCracken, *The Palmhouse in Botanic Gardens, Belfast* (Belfast, 1971), p. 16. The first curator was the naturalist, Thomas Drummond, of Forfar, Scotland, who went to America in 1831 and died in Havana, 1835. Another curator was James Drummond who died in Belfast in November 1855 (*NL*, 17 Nov. 1855). Neither was related to JLD. See also D.J. Owen, *History of Belfast* (Belfast, 1921), pp. 319-20.

80 Nesbitt, note 56 above; Deane, note 15 above.

81 BNHS, 1821-30, pp. 1-3.

82 On 19 July 1821 ('Botanical characters of the roots of plants') and 29 May 1822 ('Closing the session') (Deane, note 15 above, p. 126).

83 His 'Thoughts on the Study of Natural History' written anonymously to the proprietors of RBAI, 1820 (BNHS, 1821-30, 5 July 1821).

84 Ibid., 29 May 1822 and 28 May 1823.

85 BNHS, 1840-50, 28 Dec. 1842.

86 From 8 June 1826 to 9 November 1831, after which only the number present is recorded, Drummond attended only 15 of the 94 scientific meetings. He read papers at six, presented specimens at two, took the chair for his nephew J.D. Marshall at two, and presented the Templeton medal at two (BNHS, 1821-30; 1830-40).

87 LHL, 1825-38.

88 Deane, note 15 above, p. 126. There are some errors in dates and the paper in September 1827 should be titled 'Respiration of insects'.

89 Drummond was one of the 15-man group who collected subscriptions from (five) Belfast districts. He served 22 December 1830 until replaced by his nephew, J.D. Marshall on 21 March 1831, but served again from 19 September 1833 ('Belfast Museum: Committee Minutes Book and Subscription Lists of Building Fund.' PRONI. D3263/AD/1). He also wrote to prospective patrons e.g. letter JLD to Viscount Ferrard of 26 Sept. 1830 (PRONI. D562/ 3333).

90 Nesbitt, note 56 above, p. 11.

91 William Marshall to Natural History Society, undated, probably 1826 (PRONI. D 3263/BB/1/3). Also *Magazine of Natural History*, 1 (1829), 86.

92 Fifty-five enrolments by 1845 (FM, 5 Dec. 1845). His average student fee income, 1844-49, was £132-5-0 p.a. (Lett. Bk. 1846-79, p. 71).

93 FM, 28 Apr. 1838.

94 Drummond was personally giving up to 140 lectures and 100 demonstrations (though for a while he had an assistant) each six-month session as well as supervising dissections (FM *passim*).

95 J.L. Drummond, *First Steps to Botany, Intended as Popular Illustrations of the Science Leading to its Study as a General Branch of Education* (London, 1823). This went through four editions in 12 years.

96 Drummond, note 68 above. This went through two editions and was well received (*Magazine of Natural History*, IV (1831), 421).

97 J.L. Drummond, *First Steps to Anatomy* (London, 1845).

98 J.L. Drummond, *Observations of Natural Systems of Botany* (London, 1849).

99 J.L. Drummond, 'On certain Effects produced by Fresh Water on some Marine Animals and Plants', *Magazine of Natural History*, II (1829), 121-7.

100 J.L. Drummond, 'On a new Oscillatoria, the Colouring Substance of Glaslough Lake, Ireland', *Annals of Natural History*, I (1838), 1-6.

101 J.L. Drummond, 'Notices of Irish Entozoa', *Magazine of Natural History*, new series, 2 (1838), 515-24, 571-7, 655-62.

102 J.L. Drummond, Ibid., 3 (1839), 63-71, 227-30, 353-5.

103 J.L. Drummond, 'Thoughts on the Equivocal Generation of Entozoa', *Annals of Natural History*, VI (1841), 101-8.

104 The article by 'James Drummond' 'Cork Tree (Quercus Suber) at Summerstown', *Magazine of Natural History*, II (1829), 91) is by the curator of the botanic gardens in Cork, a brother of Thomas Drummond, the Scottish naturalist appointed to the Belfast Gardens in 1829 (see note 79 above).

105 *DNB* refers to articles by Drummond in 'the *Belfast Magazine*' which I have been unable to trace and also 'at the time of his death he had nearly ready for the press a work on conchology and another on the wild flowers of Ireland'.

106 LHL, 1825-38, 1 Apr. 1830, 2 Apr. 1835 and elsewhere.

107 *New Belfast Magazine conducted by the Students of the Royal Academical Institution 1833-1834* (Belfast, 1834), pp. 48 *et seq*; 253-7. This monthly journal survived for only one session.

108 E.g. W.J. Burchell, *Travels in the Interior of Southern Africa, with Map and Engravings*, 2 vols (London, 1822) (LHL, 1812-25, 3 Apr. 1823).

109 Andrew Marshall and his daughters were married in Belfast Non-

Subscribing Presbyterian (First Congregation) church and most of his grandchildren were baptised there, but seemingly not his five children ('Register' note 19 above). J.D. Marshall's death certificate enters him as '59 years' at death on 27 March 1868 (see note 144 below).

110 *Directory*, 1808.

111 See note 19 above for the sisters. The brother William, became LSA (Irel.) in 1833 and LRCS (Edinb.) in 1834. He was in surgical and commercial practice for a time with James but also had his own concern at no. 100 and from 1854 also at no. 67 High Street (see note 134 below). He married Letitia Bernard on 15 October 1844 (*NL*, 18 Oct. 1844), third daughter of Adderley Bernard RN, completing an impressive Drummond/Marshall naval connection!

112 J.R. Fisher, and J.H. Robb, *Royal Belfast Academical Institution: Centenary Volume, 1810-1910* (Belfast, 1913), App. xv, p. 246. For course dates see 'RBAI School Album, (PRONI. SCH 524/lA/1, p. 12).

113 Marshall is 'student no. 317'. His entry against 'Presbytery' is 'nil'! He did not enrol for divinity, Hebrew, or moral or natural philosophy nor, surprisingly, for his uncle's anatomy classes. His brother William is student no. 554: he *did* attend the anatomy classes 1826-7, 1828-9. 'RBAI, College Album, 1815-38' (PRONI. SCH 524/lA/6).

114 'Minutes, Court of Directors, Apothecaries Hall Dublin', for 19 December 1823. I am grateful to Dr Malachy Powell for uncovering this document. William was licensed on 14 May 1833 (Ibid.) but James not until 'about 1840' (*Medical Directory*, note 28 above; Croly, note 28 above, pp. 155 *et seq.)*

115 I am grateful to Miss A.M. Stevenson, Archivist, Royal College of Surgeons of Edinburgh, for this information.

116 *Edinburgh Medical Journal*, 38 (1832), 469.

117 Andrew also traded as a 'druggist, oil and colourman' (*Directory*, 1832, 1835). See also *Directory*, 1836-40.

118 Elected 4 January 1826 aged 17 on proposal by his uncle (Drummond) though he had been a visitor on 7 January 1824 and 7 December 1825 (BNHS, 1821-30 under dates and p. 11).

119 Ibid., 18 Jan. 1826.

120 Two of the papers listed by Deane, note 15 above, p. 138 (for 30 Apr. 1834 and 17 Feb. 1836) are by another 'J. Marshall'. One paper is omitted:

'Some remarks on the adaptation of the structure of birds to their situation and modes of life', read on 1 December 1830 (BNHS, 1830-40, 3 Nov. and 1 Dec. 1830) .

121 BNHS, 1830-40, 24 May 1831, 26 Dec 1832, 28 May 1834 and elsewhere; Ibid., 1840-50, 20 May 1841, 12 May 1842, 17 May 1843, and thereafter annual meetings.

122 He had been a visitor on 2 December 1833 and 5 May 1834. His paper (5 Jan. 1835) was 'A sketch of the life and character of Linnaeus' (BLS, under dates).

123 J.D. Marshall, 'Notes on the Statistics and Natural History of the Island of Rathlin off the Northern Coast of Ireland', *Transactions of the Royal Irish Academy*, (antiquities): 17 (1832-37), 37-71. Also published separately in Dublin by Dixon Hardy, 1836. It is illustrated by the author.

124 J.D. Marshall, 'Observations on the Zoology of the Island of Rathlin off the North Coast of Ireland (abstract)', *British Association for the Advancement of Science: Report of the Fifth Meeting held in Dublin 1835 (Transactions of the Sections)* (London, 1836), pp. 68-9.

125 By 13 votes to six for Dr Ninian Hall, the Moderator's choice (JB, 1828-36, p. 345 (29 Sept. 1835)). Marshall had given *ad hoc* classes in RBAI during 1834-35 (Ibid., p. 295 (4 Nov. 1834)).

126 This was after the resignation of Dr Robert Little who had served as treasurer (Froggatt, note 10 above; Froggatt and Wheeler, note 11 above).

127 *Rep. Fev. Hosp.*, 1838.

128 Ibid., 1840 to 1853.

129 BMS, 1842-52, 5 June 1843. His brother joined at the same time.

130 Ibid., 1842-52, 1852-62 *passim*.

131 Ibid., 1842-52, 1 June 1846 and elsewhere.

132 'List of Members on and from 1st October 1852'. In ibid., 1852-62, pp. 1-4.

133 He gave 12-15 lectures per month during the six-month session and set holiday essays. His average class fees were £16-16-0 p.a. as against Drummond's £132-5-0 (Lett. Bk., 1846-79, p. 71).

134 They practised as 'surgeons and chemists' in the Northern Medical Hall, 8 High Street, opposite Cornmarket, which advertised extensively. William also ran his father's former wholesale 'drug, oil, colour and

spice merchants' business from the Belfast Medical Hall, 100 High Street, seemingly quitting no. 8 in the early 1840s (*Directory*, 1839, 1840-1, 1842-3, 1843-4. Also *Slater's Irish Directory*, 1846, 1856). From 1840 they are described as 'chemists in ordinary to the Queen in Ireland', an accolade which stayed with James. By 1858 James had vacated no. 8, while William's premises (nos. 67 and 100) were entered as 'vacant' by 1865 (*Directory*, 1854-65).

135 In St Giles's, London (*NL*, 2 May 1837). Knowles lived in Belfast, 1811-16, but in Britain thereafter. He toured Ireland with his plays when presumably Jane and James met (*DNB*, vol xxi, pp. 297 *et seq.*) He was related to Richard Brinsley Sheridan.

136 Sheridan Knowles (baptised 22 Feb. 1838) and Isabel (baptised 25 Nov. 1839) ('Register' note 19 above).

137 Letter JDM to Chief Secretary of 28 December 1848. Marshall gives Thomas Andrews MD as a sole referee. He gives his credentials as his knowledge gained 'over the last thirty years' and 'the satisfaction and trust of all the [RBAI] professors' (SPOI. CSO Registered Papers 1848/124, filed under 012312 incorrectly as 'J. D. Marsh'). There were 25 applicants (Ibid., 1849/125).

138 'After a very short illness' (*NL*, 7 Apr. 1854).

139 *Medical Directory for Ireland*, 1856, (note 28 above).

140 *Medical Register*, 1859.

141 J.D. Marshall, 'On Some Fowl Shot in the Neighbourhood of Belfast Lough (abstract)', *British Association for the Advancement of Science: Report of the Meeting held in Belfast, 1852 (Transactions of the Sections)* (London, 1853), p. 77.

142 The 'house, yard and small garden' were rated on a valuation of £18 – above average for the street but not the highest (£23). Marshall is the 'immediate lessor'. (R. Griffiths, *Union of Belfast (part of): Valuation of the Several Tenements in that Portion of the Union outside the Municipal Boundary of Belfast and Situate in the County of Down* (Dublin, 1861), p. 32.

143 In 1856 or 1857. In 1858 the occupant of no. 8 High Street is 'Alex Forrester, grocer' (*Directory, 1858*).

144 'Certified copy of an entry of death'. General Register Office, Belfast.

145 Clarke, note 19 above, pp. 199-201.

146 T.W. Moody, and J.C. Beckett, *Queen's, Belfast, 1845-1849: The History of a University* (Belfast, 1959), vol. 1, p. 119.

147 J.L. McCracken, *New Light at the Cape of Good Hope: William Porter, the Father of Cape Liberalism* (Belfast, 1993).

THE BELFAST HISTORIC SOCIETY, 1811-1835

W. A. MAGUIRE

THROUGHOUT THE BRITISH ISLES from the latter years of the eighteenth century, the growth of towns, the development of an urban middle class and the spread of enlightenment culture led not only to the foundation of new schools and academies in provincial towns and to the spread of circulating libraries and reading rooms, but also to the formation of a wide range of voluntary societies whose members aimed at the practice and propagation of self-improvement. The Manchester Literary and Philosophical Society, one of the earliest, was established in 1781; by the end of the century Glasgow, Liverpool and Birmingham had similar bodies. Growth of population alone did not ensure their appearance, however. Someone remarked of Leeds in 1817, when its population of 70,000 was more than twice that of Belfast: 'Philosophical researches are not much cultivated [in this town]; still less do literary pursuits engage the attention of its inhabitants'.[1]

In most cases the first step on the road to self-improvement was the formation of reading societies and subscription libraries. In Belfast a Reading Society, founded in 1788, developed into the Belfast Library and Society for Promoting Knowledge, better known as the Linen Hall Library. Though the town may never have deserved the title of 'the Northern Athens' on cultural grounds (the name was actually bestowed by an enthusiastic local patriot in the 1790s for its supposed love of liberty, rather than culture), it was nevertheless in the early nineteenth century the scene of a remarkable outbreak of intellectual activity. Two of the bodies then established, the Belfast Literary Society (1801) and the Belfast Natural History Society (1821), have happily survived continuously – and in pretty much their original form – to the present day; one might also mention the Medical Society (1806) which, with the help of trans-plant and transfusion – and even resurrection – still exists in the shape of the Ulster Medical Society. Other societies founded during those years were not so fortunate, or so necessary, or so well-conducted. The Society for Acquiring Knowledge, started in 1806, soon had 'an extensive library of well-chosen books and an excellent pair of globes';[2] its members met quarterly, paid £1.5.0 for admission and subscribed 1s.1d. (an Irish shilling) a month. In 1811 some of the more zealous members of that society formed the Cosmographical Society, 'with a view to render familiar to them the important sciences of Astronomy and Geography'; the members met fortnightly, each in turn giving a lecture.[3] A Galvanic Society was formed about 1805. Despite its name, it seems to have transmitted a feeble impulse and soon stopped twitching altogether; instead, some of its members who 'wished to extend their views into the wider and more general field of philosophical research' formed the Philosophical Society. They claimed to have a 'valuable apparatus' which enabled them to perform 'curious and interesting experiments'.[4] Even this inducement did not help it to attract support beyond 1813. The Belfast Historic Society lasted some-what longer than any of these but in the end fared no better. Founded in 1811, it did not meet for some years after 1819; revived in 1826, it finally disappeared in 1835. It had, therefore, two distinct manifestations.

The First Society

The Historic Society had its origin in September 1811 in the meeting of 'a few young men, strongly impressed with a sense of the pleasure and improvement arising from the cultivation of the mind', whose purpose was 'investigating and discussing subjects connected with useful knowledge'.[5] The notice in the *Belfast Almanac* for 1813 gave the objects of the Society as 'the investigation and discussion of Historical, Moral, and Literary subjects, particularly those connected with Ireland', but this is the only reference (in what is admittedly a scanty collection of evidence) to specifically Irish concerns. We should know almost nothing about the first Historic Society were it not for the *Belfast Monthly Magazine*, the liberal periodical published between 1808 and 1815 whose chief promoter was the old radical Dr William Drennan. There appear to have been no notices in the local press (the *Belfast News Letter* was hostile, the *Commercial Chronicle* indifferent), while the *Almanacs*, not very informative at the best of times, merely advertised the existence and aims of the Society in the years 1813 and 1815, without giving the names of office-bearers. The *Belfast Monthly Magazine*, on the other hand, prints the rules adopted in 1811, the addresses delivered by three early presidents (which describe, among other things, how the Society functioned or was intended to function), an address by John Templeton (an honorary member), and one or two letters about the Society from correspondents. The entry in the 1815 *Almanac*, however, though uninformative about membership and organisation, does in its statement of the Society's purpose give the flavour of earnest self-improvement that was the ideal. 'The study of History', said the writer, appeared to the young men who founded the Society 'particularly calculated to expand and invigorate the intellectual power; combining as it does, instruction with amusement, and almost serving to form the moral principle of action, by exhibiting the virtues and vices of human nature, divested of the colouring they receive from prejudice or interest'. The study of English Laws and Constitution was expected to make them better members of the community, 'when they understood the rules by which their conduct was to be governed, and the principles on which the duties of man in society are founded'.[6]

The rules of the Society allowed for two classes of member, ordinary and honorary. To be an ordinary member, one was simply required to be of good character and to have the desire and determination to advance in knowledge; honorary members were drawn from those already distinguished in learning (the only two known were Templeton and Dr Robert Tennent). The work of the Society was organised on very practical lines. All new members had to attend the History class for at least one session and had to pass an examination at the end of it. They then proceeded to a session in the Constitution class, where the set text was Blackstone's *Commentaries on the Laws of England*. In both classes a silver medal was awarded for the best answering in the examination. The third and principal class was Oratory, where members were trained for public speaking, with the practical intention of enabling them to speak effectively at town meetings and on local committees. The Society met weekly at first, then fortnightly, in a variety of unsatisfactory places before eventually settling on the Lancasterian School.

Meetings began at half-past seven. The first half-hour, till eight o'clock, was devoted to the study classes in History and Constitution. Then, after a recess of ten minutes, the proceedings of the last meeting were read and signed, examination successes announced, new members proposed and voted on, committees appointed, and the subject for the debate in a fortnight's time selected. Thereafter, till eleven o'clock, the evening's debate proceeded, led by a speaker on either side. The hour in all cases was 'determined by the watch of the regulator, set by the town clock'. Under the rules, theology and 'observations injurious to any private character in this kingdom' were forbidden, as was any question 'which is under, or stands for discussion in the then session of Parliament'.[7]

On being admitted to the Society, each member had to pay a guinea and had then also to pay a subscription of half-a-crown for the first session, 1s.8d. for the second, and 1s.3d. for the third, after which he was allowed to attend free of charge (unless fined for misconduct). Members who completed two sessions were excused from all offices but had to attend the debates or be fined 10d. each time. Those who completed three sessions were no longer obliged to attend meetings or to be subject to any pecuniary contributions except fines for misconduct; neither were they eligible for the 'best speaker' and other awards (silver medals). The number of members in 1813 was said to be above thirty, 'all respectable and well conducted young men'.[8] Attendance could be swelled considerably on occasion by visitors: the closing session in June 1813, when William Neilson delivered his presidential address, was attended by 19 members and no fewer than 41 'strangers', perhaps in anticipation of what his successor as president, Robert Grimshaw, described as a 'brilliant display of eloquence and youthful talent'. There are no lists of office-bearers for this period, and the minutes of the Society have not survived. The only names we know, apart from the two honorary members already mentioned, are those of William B. Neilson, president 1812-13; Robert Grimshaw, president 1813-14; Henry William Tennent, president 1814-15; and two prize medal winners, Randal Robinson (1812) and Robert McAdam (1814). We do know, however, from the information printed in the *Belfast Monthly Magazine* in June 1812, that as well as a president the Society had a 'regulator', a treasurer and a secretary, the regulator apparently organising and keeping the time at debates.

Though half a dozen names may appear to be very little to go on, they tell us a good deal about the social background and political views of the Society. Neilson (or Nelson as his name is spelt in a Society pamphlet) was the son of Samuel Neilson, proprietor of the *Northern Star* and United Irishman in the 1790s, who, when released from a long period of imprisonment in Scotland, was exiled to Holland and made his way thence to the United States by way of Ireland; he died in America in 1802. His eldest son, William, had shared his imprisonment in Fort George, where the father superintended the son's education. Young Neilson died of yellow fever in Jamaica early in 1817 at the age of twenty-two, which means that he was no more than eighteen at the time he presided over the Belfast Historic Society.[9]

His successor, Robert Grimshaw, a Belfast merchant, was one of the nine children of Nicholas Grimshaw, a cotton spinner from Lancashire whose mill at Whitehouse near Belfast, established in 1784, pioneered the town's thriving cotton industry. If his background was less radical than Neilson's, he was certainly a man of very liberal political views and was later prominent in radical politics. Along with one of Neilson's fellow-inmates of Fort George, William Tennent, he was active in the public life of Belfast in encouraging such things as the Mechanics' Institute in the late 1820s. Grimshaw was also closely involved with the troubled affairs of the Academical Institution. When the government grant to the Institution was withdrawn in 1816 on the grounds that some of the managers and staff had been present at a St Patrick's Day dinner where anti-government toasts had been drunk, and the managers concerned had offered their resignations in order to reassure the authorities, Grimshaw spoke vehemently against letting them resign. He was later active in banking and in the Chamber of Commerce, among other things, and reappears in our story.

The third president, Harry Tennent, was one of the nine illegitimate children of the Belfast merchant and banker William Tennent. Born in 1791, he was sent by his father to board at Green Row, a well-known dissenting academy in Cumberland, and then to university in Dublin. At Trinity College, where he attended lectures between 1807 and 1809, he was an active member of the undergraduate debating club, the Historical

Society. After Trinity he enrolled at the Middle Temple in London and became a barrister. His brief career was cut short when he died in 1815, shortly before his twenty-fourth birthday.

Of the two known honorary members of the Society, John Templeton (1766-1825) was a noted amateur naturalist. In a life 'void of incident' he became 'the Gilbert White of Ireland', though his great project for a natural history of the country, illustrated by his own drawings, never got beyond the manuscript for Hibernian Flora. Though a scholar rather than an activist, Templeton counted many radicals among his friends. One of them, in the early 1790s, was Thomas Russell, whose journals record a walking tour he and Templeton took to the Mournes in 1793, in search of mineralogical specimens. Templeton was one of the founders of the Academical Institution, which was very much a liberal project. He was also a regular contributor to the *Belfast Monthly Magazine*, the liberal organ which reported the Historic Society's doings. The other honorary member, Robert Tennent (1765-1837), was a more obviously political figure. A brother of the banker and former United Irishman William Tennent, and of John Tennent, who fought in Napoleon's Irish Legion and was killed at the battle of Löwenberg in August 1813, Robert Tennent became a doctor and spent some time in the Royal Navy as a ship's surgeon, before returning in 1799 to Belfast. A pious and charitable man with a strong sense of justice and a deep interest in public causes, he retained the strict Calvinist faith in which he had been brought up (the father of the Tennents was minister of the Presbyterian Seceder congregation at Roseyards near Ballymoney, County Antrim). Apart from the Sunday School and Bible Societies in which he was deeply involved he was also by conviction a supporter of Catholic emancipation and parliamentary reform and in general an anti-establishment figure – all the more detested by the conservative elements in Belfast because he was fearless in opposing them in public.

In 1813 he was involved in an interesting fracas which reveals something of the political tensions which existed in Belfast despite the total absence of normal political activity in the town (till 1832 a close borough controlled by the Donegall family, whose members or relations invariably represented it in parliament, with the inhabitants having no more to do with the choice of them, as someone remarked, than if they had been sent over ready elected from Botany Bay). On the 12th of July, 1813, some Orangemen from Belfast assembled at the White Linen Hall and marched to Lisburn. Returning in the evening at seven o'clock, they marched to Thompson's public house in North Street, through a crowd of watchers, many of whom were apparently hostile, and the pub was soon surrounded by a large crowd. Emerging from the building, some of the Orangemen fired shots into the crowd and two people were killed as a result – a lad of fourteen named Graham and a man named McNarry who with his dying breath identified one David Morgan as his murderer. Morgan and four others were subsequently arraigned for murder at the County Antrim assizes at Carrickfergus, where two of them were found guilty of manslaughter and sentenced to six months' imprisonment – the same sentence as was given to a man who had thrown stones at them.[10]

Dr Tennent and other liberals (among them Robert Grimshaw) were outraged both by the Orange processions and by the outcome of the trial, and demanded a town meeting to discuss the matter. The sovereign of Belfast, Thomas Verner, at first refused but later gave way and a meeting was summoned for the 28th. It turned out to be a very rowdy affair, at which the sovereign and his brother-in-law Edward May (a magistrate, and vicar of Belfast and also a brother-in-law of Lord Donegall) came into conflict with Tennent and his supporters, in the course of which May made some slighting remark about Tennent's brother. Tennent took this to be a gibe about his brother William's revolutionary past, though May later claimed he had been referring to another brother, Samuel, who was dodging a bench warrant at the time, accused of having been involved in the Twelfth riot. Robert Tennent approached May and grasped him by the arm (apparently he had the habit of doing this to everyone he spoke to), whereupon May said, 'Sir, you have assaulted me, and I will commit you to the Black Hole [the town prison]'. Tennent was then seized and taken through the streets and lodged in the Black Hole, whence he was bailed. May sub-sequently prosecuted him for assault and, despite the evidence of reputable witnesses, Tennent was found guilty, fined £50 and sent to gaol for three months. When released he sued May for unlawful imprisonment, but without success. There was a strong element of personal as well as political antipathy in relations between Tennent on the one hand and May and Verner on the other. In the interval between the fracas at the Town Meeting and his trial early in October, Tennent became involved in helping a poor Catholic woman named Barnes to bring a case against Verner, whom she had accused of assault and attempted rape. At the trial in Downpatrick on 5 October 1813, where Verner was acquitted, the defence alleged that Tennent had funded a malicious prosecution.[11]

These stirring events did not fail to cause a ripple in the Historic Society of which Dr Tennent was an honorary member. A letter to the *Belfast Monthly Magazine* of October 1814 urged the members not to confine 'all their ideas of patriotism within the walls of their own room'. 'I sincerely hope', the writer went on, 'when they are discussing questions relative to the sacred cause of liberty in the days of Cato and Aristides, they will recollect that there are occasions in their own times which would require them to act as Cato, and to resist the rapid downfall of liberty'.[12] A motion put forward at a meeting of the Society for an address of thanks to Robert Tennent as an honorary member had apparently been negatived, which seemed astonishing to the writer. The political questions of the day – parliamentary reform, Catholic emancipation, Orangeism – though forbidden as subjects of debate, could not be altogether avoided and even at this early stage tended to divide the more radical members from the more cautious.

The three presidential addresses printed in the *Belfast Monthly Magazine* reveal something of their authors' ideas. Neilson remarks that, 'in admitting new members, we require from no man in what manner he worships that God we all adore: here the foul Demon of Bigotry dare not enter!' One would expect this sentiment to have been well received by his hearers. Rather less palatable, one suspects, was his view of commerce:

> Beneficial as an institution such as this [the Historic Society] must be, wherever it may be established, it is in a large commercial town such as Belfast that it is truly indispensable. With all the eminent advantages that accompany the pursuit of commerce, if the habits it produces are not checked in their progress, they have a tendency to smother all that is noble, generous, and candid in the breast of man.

Then, warming to his theme, he went on:

> Commerce is an enemy to virtue, she is the parent of distrust
> and suspicion; she calls into action the vilest passions of
> human nature, sordid avarice and selfish interest; under her
> baneful influence the finest sensibility becomes callous, the
> heart that once beat warmly to every noble and generous
> sentiment, is cold and contracted, and the high sense of
> honour, the only bond of confidence among men, is deadened
> or destroyed.

It is perhaps not surprising that Neilson later failed in business in the
town. Like his successors in the chair, Neilson was obliged to chide the
members for lack of zeal in fulfilling their duties: 'The necessary information
on the subject of debate has been neither acquired nor communicated to
the proper extent, too frequently indeed it has been grossly neglected;
while upon several occasions a degree of apathy has appeared, which
cannot be viewed without the deepest regret'.[13]

In his address Robert Grimshaw made no secret of his sentiments on
the question of Catholic emancipation, which he supposed was about to be
achieved by steady constitutional pressure on parliament. 'Let us look
back to their cause in the days of Lord George Gordon', he said, 'when it
was dangerous even to mention the subject in the House of Commons, and
look now at the change of sentiment, when they are within a few votes of
having their rights restored them'. The tribulations of Dr Tennent too
were not ignored, though his name was not mentioned:

> In town meetings we have seen the inhabitants of this
> respectable town browbeaten and insulted, their opinions
> treated with contempt, and even told they have no right to
> express them... Truth is called violence, and opposition to an
> intolerant faction termed disloyalty. For we never can erase
> from our memory the feeble support experienced by one of
> our most valuable citizens in his struggles against oppression
> and tyranny.[14]

Harry Tennent traced the origin of the Society to the character of
Belfast – her knowledge, enterprise and literary exertion, 'her eagerness

in the cause of religious freedom, her ardour in the cause of political liberty... the existence of strong independent public feeling, of deep reflection, and sound principle amongst all classes of her inhabitants'. To him, the lesson history inculcated was that 'the more political liberty any nation enjoys, the happier and more respected it will become'; America was 'the refuge of liberty', Henry Grattan 'the generous assertor of our country's independence, now alas! buried in the demoralizing Act of Union' who still, even in a foreign land, battled for the good of his country by his exertions for Catholic emancipation. Like a true Tennent, however, he defended the character of the Belfast merchant against the low opinion of those who, 'in the little pride of college education', forgot that the basis on which such character was formed was even more extended than any of the so-called learned professions – and therefore suitable material for an enlightened body such as the Historic Society.[15]

Apart from what they tell us about the organisation of the Society and about the supposed advantages of studying history and practising oratory, the addresses and letters printed in the *Belfast Monthly Magazine* give us some interesting and amusing glimpses of the unregenerate citizens of Belfast whom the Society hoped to transform. 'It is impossible not to feel the most poignant regret', wrote 'Theocritus' in July 1813,

> that such a praiseworthy institution should be now nearly of two years standing, and that it should be confined to such a small number... Well would it be for many thoughtless dissipated young men in this town, were they to attach themselves to such pursuits, instead of ruining their constitutions in the tavern, or debasing their minds at the card-table: in the one place, nothing but noise and nonsense is to be heard, and in the other, the utmost extent of their knowledge is whist, loo, Pope Joan, or the technical terms attached to such games.

The writer went on to give a depressing picture of the salons of Belfast:

> At present, in many companies, if by any chance the conversation should be turned to any object above the fashion,

the weather, or the unimportant occurrences of the day, a large proportion of the company become dumb, some whispers about pedantry circulate, and the person who is hardy enough to introduce a literary subject has it all to himself, and is sneered at by the party as a person who wishes to make a vain display of his superior knowledge.

Worse still:

At one of those numerous parties which so much prevail in this town: to witness a crowd of well-dressed people huddled together in a room, where the whole of the conversation consists of common-place observations, without a single remark worthy of being remembered after it is expressed; and when the uninteresting chit-chat begins to lag, to observe the anxiety of countenance of every individual, for the appearance of the card-tables, and the avidity with which the cards are taken up by the parties.[16]

This view of card-playing as the death of improving conversation was echoed by John Templeton: 'Gaming with its mild insidious grace captivates the unwary victim'. He wished he could impress upon the minds of his bearers, and on that of every Irishman, that 'engaging in serious pursuits was the true means of enjoying happiness'.[17]

One final piece of evidence about the early Historic Society is the address delivered to the members by the president at the close of the sixth session in June 1817, and subsequently published.[18] Who the president was we do not know, and the speaker provides no clues to his own identity. He does, however, say some revealing things about the attitudes and aspirations of the Society, and about its decline. 'The course of our particular study', he said, 'is the knowledge of history, and the English laws, with the cultivation of written composition and oratory'. The reasons for adopting English history in the Historic Class were obvious: it was 'the duty of every man to be well acquainted with the history of his own country (and the affairs of unfortunate Ireland have been so long connected and mingled with those of Britain, that to know the one, you must study the other)'; and no history afforded 'more valuable materials to convey instruction to the reader, than that of England'. It was the history of a people 'placed at the extremity of Europe, inhabiting but a small island, yet by their industry and civil institutions, surpassing almost every other in sciences, arts, and arms, and, at one period, in liberty'.[19]

In adopting Blackstone's *Commentaries on the Laws of England* as the course of study for the Constitution Class the members of the Society were fulfilling a sacred duty both to themselves and to the community. Every free man had a duty to be well acquainted with his own rights and the laws that governed him – not to know every law in the statute book or 'become what is termed lawyers' but to 'be instructed in those general rules that bind society, and a knowledge of what is usually termed the constitution…', besides 'an intimate acquaintance with the extent of the powers and duties of the several constituted authorities of the state'.[20] In the circumstances of the time, this was radical talk. And most of the orators whom the members were urged to admire and if possible emulate – in ancient times Demosthenes ('who by the magic of his voice stayed the setting sun of Grecian liberty in its course'), in later times Mirabeau, Fox, Burke and Sheridan, 'in our own days' Grattan, Curran and Phillips – were liberal heroes.[21]

The president went on to expatiate on the benefit arising from 'the frequent discussion of moral, historical, and biographical questions', considering the Society 'a strong preventative of foolish, bad or vicious habits'. He deplored the young men who received all the advantages of a liberal education and showed great abilities when at school but who afterwards became coxcombs – 'frittering away their time and existence in dress, horses, and parties, totally useless to themselves, their family, and the community', or sinking into the selfish pursuit of gain, or 'early falling into habits of dissipation and folly'.[22] On the contrary, any young man who joined the Society entered on 'a continuation of his studies, without the wearisomeness or irksomeness of the Schools'. The Rousseauesque premiss of all this self-improvement was boldly stated: 'No human being is born with a propensity for folly or vice; it is education, that is, the education of circumstances, that makes him either virtuous or vicious'.[23] It was impossible, thought the speaker, that the opinions and principles imbibed in the Society should not influence the conduct of its members, and recalled with pride that it was two members of the Historic Society who dared, almost alone, in the hall of the Academical Institution 'to maintain the sacredness of the right of private judgement; and who put to the blush men who, in earlier years, in other times [presumably the radical 1790s], would have reiterated their sentiments, and honoured the hearts that gave them utterance'.[24] This was a reference to the affair of the St Patrick's Day dinner the previous year.

Before ending with a review of the proceedings and progress of the Society during the session, the president devoted some time to refuting the 'often refuted assertion' that the Society was a political one. It did not meet to discuss the leading state questions of the day or to meddle in party politics or to be 'operated upon by the bickerings and feuds of men in or out of power'; but if by political was meant 'the inquiry into the general principles of the rights and privileges of man, the admiration of every thing that is great and noble in our nature; the love of liberty, and of those principles that formed the British constitution, which we here study' – then the Society was indeed political and proud to be so. 'Let our calumniators attend', he concluded, 'and they shall find that the politics of Greece and Rome are much more frequently discussed here, than those of more modern states'.[25]

For some ardent souls, that must have been a disappointment. It was more prosaic reasons, however, that had reduced the membership of the Society during the past year by ten, nearly one-third of the number who had attended the closing night of the previous session. Some had emigrated, 'in the pursuit of that independence denied to their industry at home'; one had died abroad; others had been 'justly expelled for irregular conduct' (they had apparently not paid the fines for non-attendance that the rules stipulated). So attendance had been smaller than usual, while some of those most active in the early days of the Society had forsaken it because of pressure of business.[26]

The Revived Society

Whatever the reason – political divisions, the apathy of members, the insidious attractions of the tavern and the card-table – the Historic Society waned after 1815 and petered out in 1819. There is no sign of it again in the *Almanacs* until 1827. We have more names associated with this second manifestation but less information: the *Almanac* gives lists of all the officers from 1827 to 1835, but there do not appear to be any press reports of the Society's proceedings and the *Belfast Monthly Magazine* had long since expired. One of the few sources of information is an address delivered by Robert James Tennent (son of Dr Robert Tennent) to the opening meeting of the second revived session, on 6 September 1827, a date which tells us that the first revived session began a year before.[27] Tennent refers to 'deep rooted and unconquerable hostility' in several minds to the re-establishment of the Society, and of the impossibility of entirely destroying 'the polypus vitality of prejudice'. The original founders of the Society, he thought, had had much greater difficulties to deal with. 'They were the first adventurous colonists of an unknown land. Feeble in number, scanty in resource, undirected by experience, and uncheered by sympathy, they were impelled by a kind of intellectual famine to encounter and to vanquish every obstacle'. It was not only in Belfast during those years that the authorities saw any kind of intellectual independence in young men as jacobinism. As Tennent remarked, the Dublin Historical Society was expelled from Trinity College (in 1815) and subsequently persecuted almost to destruction as 'the spirit of corporate infallibility took the alarm'. In his view, the existing systems of school and college education almost totally overlooked the important topics of history, morals, jurisprudence, elegant literature and general politics which were the Historic Society's subjects of debate.

He went on to say:

> There is no more common, and perhaps pernicious, mistake than that the discipline of the School or of the University is the completion of Education. It is, on the contrary, only a part, and a very subordinate part, of that preparatory training, which is necessary to form a useful, an intelligent and a virtuous member of society.

With Tennent, thought led to action: he concluded by bidding the Society farewell, being about to set off to Greece with his then friend and fellow-member James Emerson (James Emerson Tennent as he was later to call himself when he married William Tennent's daughter Letitia) to take part in some real history. The Ulster Museum has the silver medal awarded to him by the Historic Society in 1827 for his skill as an orator. If his address was delivered as well as it was written, he was a worthy prizewinner.

The first president of the revived Society was Robert Grimshaw, one of the survivors of the original body. There were now two vice-presidents, in this case John McAdam and R.J. Tennent. McAdam may have been the druggist and manufacturing chemist of that name listed in the 1835 directory with an address in Donegall Street; he became president in 1829. The office of treasurer was held until 1831 by H. McDowell – Henry McDowell, commissioner for taking affidavits and agent for the County Insurance Company, whose addresses in 1835 were the Belfast Bank and 19 College Street. McDowell was followed as treasurer by Samuel Archer junior, a son of the bookseller and stationer in Castle Place. Archer had entered the Academical Institution as pupil in 1815, along with his brother William, who became a vice-president in 1832. It was probably the younger Samuel Archer who was also secretary of the Belfast Mechanics' Institute in 1833 (the older had been on the committee of the Lancasterian School as far back as 1811) and one or other of them sat on the committee of the United Society for the Promotion of Christian Knowledge in the 1830s. The last known treasurer, in 1835, was Francis C. Haddock, who is listed as an architect at 10 Hamilton Place.

The Society's secretary throughout its second existence was Maurice Cross, clerk to the Belfast Savings Bank. Cross is an interesting character, with interesting connections. For many years master of the boys' side of the Lancasterian School, he was later secretary of that admirable institution, an office earlier performed by Dr Robert Tennent. Cross was also active in liberal politics in the 1830s, along with Robert Grimshaw, R.J. Tennent and other members of the Historic Society. He left the Savings Bank, and Belfast, in the late 1830s to take up a post with the Poor Law Commission. The half dozen letters from Cross to R.J. Tennent in 1827, preserved among the Tennent papers in PRONI, reveal him as a meticulous man, very keen on debating, admiring of his young friend's talents as an orator and writer, firmly devoted to the Glorious Revolution, and not without a sense of humour.[28] One communication is a summons to the end-of-session meeting on 7 June 1827, at which Tennent was awarded the prize for oratory. From this source we learn that the Society met on Thursday evenings in rooms in the Commercial Buildings rented from the Belfast Natural History Society. The motion for debate at that meeting was an anodyne one – 'Are early marriages desirable?' – proposed and opposed by William Pirrie and Marcus Patton respectively. Other letters mention the names of Emerson, Finlay, Brice, Magennis, Morgan, Dunlop, McEwan, John Galway, John McAdam, Harrison, Hyndman and J. Black. Of these, John Morgan (flax dresser and dealer, 188 North Street in 1835) and Bartholomew Magennis (manufacturer in the linen and cotton trade, with an office and warehouse in Donegall Lane and a house in Donegall Street) were vice-presidents in 1829, when McAdam was president. Another vice-president was Robert Alexander, who lived at 4 College Street in 1835. Hyndman was mentioned as having decided to resign.

The president in 1828 was Conway Blizard Grimshaw, another of the Grimshaw family, 'agent to the Atlas Fire and Life Assurance Company', whose office in 1835 was in the Piazza of the Commercial Buildings, his residence Linnfield. Like Robert Grimshaw, Dr Tennent, John McAdam and others, Conway Grimshaw was closely associated with the Academical Institution. He was also a member of the town's Police Committee in 1833, and thereafter secretary for many years of the Chamber of Commerce. His vice-presidents were John McAdam and Robert Alexander.

New men appear in 1830: B.J. Shannon as president [John B. Shannon, Laganvale, was proprietor of the vitriol works at Ballymacarrett in 1835]; Dr J.E. Kidley (Donegall Street 1835, York Street 1841), prominent in Liberal politics in the 1830s as a supporter of R.J. Tennent, and John Stewart (a linen merchant in Arthur Street in 1835) as vice-presidents. Kidley was president in 1831 and again in 1832, B.T. Stannus and David Patton vice-presidents. Of the two last named, Bartholomew Teeling Stannus was lecturer in elocution at the Academical Institution 1828-31; his address to the Society on 9 September 1830, subsequently published, is full of elegant rhetorical flourishes but is otherwise thin stuff – and pretty uninformative about the Society and its affairs. Patton seems to have been a son of the Mrs Patton who had a silkmercer's and haberdasher's business in High Street. He and his brother Marcus had both been entered by their father Isaac (a wholesale printed calico merchant) at the Academical Institution in 1815. David Patton was the senior vice-president in 1832 and 1833. He appears to have worked for George Ash, a wholesale grocer and general merchant in Waring Street.

The president in 1833 was Thomas O'Hagan, another and rather younger product of the Academical Institution.[29] Born in 1812, O'Hagan was the son of the Catholic merchant Edward Hagan (the son re-adopted the O prefix). O'Hagan was to have a glittering career in the law – he became Solicitor-General, Attorney General, a judge and eventually Lord Chancellor of Ireland – but as a young man in Belfast he edited the Catholic *Northern Herald*, later marrying the daughter of its proprietor, C.H. Teeling, and was an enthusiastic supporter of Daniel O'Connell and repeal of the union with Britain. The officers listed for 1835 (O'Hagan; Patton and William Archer; Samuel Archer junior and Cross) were the same as for 1834 and 1833, except that Samuel Archer was replaced as treasurer by Haddock in 1834. There is no mention of the Society in the almanacs and directories after 1835, and since no other reference to its activities is known we can assume that it ceased to exist.

The fact that, for the only time in its existence, its committee remained virtually unchanged for three years suggests that the Society had been in difficulties for some time. One would guess that the reasons for its collapse had partly to do with its peculiar nature and partly to do with the temper of the times. As to the first, any society which encouraged its members to progress through active membership in three years needed a constant supply of young recruits, which seems to have fallen off in the 1830s (the total in the early years of its revival was said to be about fifty); while like any debating society it might succumb to an overdose of hot air from young orators (an anonymous lampoon of its activities, published about 1830, suggests as much).[30] As to the temper of the times, the Society appears to have flourished between 1826 and 1832, during a period when the two great questions that had occupied reformers for many years – Catholic emancipation and parliamentary reform – came to a head. The latter question in particular united the opposition to the established order – one feature of which was the lack of any political voice for the citizens of Belfast.[31] Real politics appeared in Belfast only in the 1830s, but parliamentary reform was publicly aired and argued with increasing force from the mid-twenties onward (the Liberal paper the *Northern Whig* was established in 1824). The passing of the Reform Act in 1832 divided the reformers, however, and led to increasing friction between those who accepted it as adequate and the more radical who demanded a further extension of the franchise. Then O'Connell's campaign to repeal the Act of Union, which began to gather momentum from the mid-thirties, further agitated the political scene and divided Protestant and Catholic Liberals. The 1835 elections in Belfast (there was a general election in January, followed by a by-election in August) were particularly acrimonious. In these circumstances, a society based on debate proved unable to survive.

Attempts to replace the Historic Society fared no better. A new body, the Belfast Oratorical Society, whose modest purpose was 'the mental improvement of its members' and which also excluded politics and religion, made its appearance in 1835 but it too did not survive long. The contrast between the fate of the Historic Society and that of the Literary Society and the Natural History Society is instructive. The relatively non-controversial, and coherent, body of knowledge which formed the subject matter of the latter two bodies provided a better recipe for longevity in a community that was already well on the way to being deeply divided along sectarian and political lines.

Notes

1   The Leeds Philosophical and Literary Society was established in 1819.
2   *Belfast Almanac* for 1811.
3   Ibid.
4   Ibid.
5   *Belfast Almanac* for 1815.
6   Ibid.
7   *Belfast Monthly Magazine*, vol. VII, no. 47 (June 1812), pp. 512-13.
8   Ibid., vol. XI, no. 60 (July 1813), letter of 'Theocritus', pp. 16-19.
9   See R.R. Madden, *The United Irishmen, their Lives and Times*, second series, 2 vols. (London, 1843), vol. 1, pp. 340-44, for a useful brief memoir of W.B. Neilson.
10   See J.J. Monaghan, 'A social and economic history of Belfast 1801-25' (Ph.D. thesis, Queen's University, Belfast, 1940), p. 586.
11   For a detailed account, see W.A. Maguire, 'The Verner Rape Trial 1813: Jane Barnes v the Belfast Establishment', *Ulster Local Studies*, 15, 1(1993), 47-57.

12 *Belfast Monthly Magazine*, vol. XIII, no. 75, pp. 351-52.

13 Ibid., vol. XIII, no. 73 (Aug. 1814), pp. 111-16.

14 Ibid., vol. XIII, no. 74 (Sept. 1814), pp. 194-99.

15 Ibid., vol. XIII, no. 75 (Oct. 1814), pp. 299-306.

16 Ibid., vol. XI, no. 60 (July, 1813), pp. 16-19.

17 Ibid., vol. XIII, no. 74 (Sept. 1814), pp. 189-194.

18 *Address Delivered to the Belfast Historic Society, on the Closing of the Sixth Session, June 5, 1817, by the President* (Belfast, printed by Francis D. Finlay, 1817).

19 Ibid., p.4.

20 Ibid., p. 6.

21 Ibid., p. 8.

22 Ibid., pp. 8-9.

23 Ibid., p. 9.

24 Ibid., pp. 11-12.

25 Ibid., p. 12.

26 Ibid., pp. 13-15.

27 R.J. Tennent, *Address Delivered to the Belfast Historic Society, Published at the Request of the Society* (Belfast , 1827).

28 PRONI, D1748/C/131/1-6.

29 See J.R. Fisher and J.H. Robb, *Royal Belfast Academical Institution Centenary Volume 1810-1910* (Belfast, 1913), appendix XV, for information about those of the Society's members who had attended the Institution.

30 *Noctes Minores*, printed by Henry Lanktree, (Belfast, n.d.) unfortunately gives no clues sufficient to identify the characters it calls Boreall, Bridlegoose, Master Tommy Absolute and so on. The last-named was possibly O'Hagan.

31 See W.A. Maguire, *Belfast* (Keele, 1993), pp. 41-46.

COUNTRY LETTERS:
SOME CORRESPONDENCE OF ULSTER POETS
OF THE NINETEENTH CENTURY

B. M. WALKER

THE EARLY NINETEENTH CENTURY was a time of considerable cultural activity in Ulster. It witnessed not only the founding of reading clubs, debating societies and other cultural and educational bodies, but also the appearance of a flourishing school of rural poets. Mainly based in the north east of the province, these poets were weavers, farmers or teachers, who wrote poetry, often in the local dialect, for and about their own communities. John Hewitt's *Rhyming Weavers and other Country Poets of Antrim and Down* (Belfast, 1974) was the first modern work to give serious attention to these writers. Since then Ivan Herbison, Philip Robinson, Linde Lunney, Don Akenson, W.H. Crawford, Jane Gray and Ronald Adams have written on this subject. With the exception of a recent article by Linde Lunney, however, little in the way of original correspondence by or between these poets has been produced. This essay contains extracts from an important collection of the poets' letters which have not been available before to those interested in the subject.

Most of the letters were written between the poets and one John Rea Semple. Semple was a toll-gate keeper, responsible for collecting tolls from travellers who used his road. He was based at the turnpike gate, first at Antrim, then at Ardoyne and finally at Edenderry. John Semple was a friend of many of the poets and these letters give an interesting perspective on their lives and work. Through them we can learn something of the problems of publishing, of their views of each other and of their opinions of their own and others' poetry. Besides this, the letters reveal some of the human problems and anxieties faced by these people. Semple not only encouraged their work and helped sell their volumes: he was also a good friend who assisted them in times of need and gave helpful advice which was much appreciated.

These letters were eventually given in the 1870s by Semple to his friend, William Fee McKinney of Carnmoney. McKinney was a farmer of considerable learning and inquisitiveness who took a deep interest in local history and culture. He had a special concern for these poets, partly because of his own love of poetry and partly because many of the poets came from his area. He collected their published works and preserved this collection of their letters and other unpublished writings.

The grandson of W.F. McKinney, Dr Joe Dundee, kindly allowed me access to this material when I was writing *Sentry Hill: an Ulster Farm and Family* (Belfast, 1983, reprinted 1993). Besides the letters to Semple, the material at Sentry Hill also included original ballad sheets, newspaper cuttings and correspondence between several of the poets. There were also letters between some poets and members of the McGaw family from Ballyvesey, Carnmoney, County Antrim, who were related to the McKinneys. A typescript of all the letters can be found in the John Hewitt archive in the library at the University of Ulster in Coleraine and the originals, along with all the Irish books at Sentry Hill, are now in the Linen Hall Library.

Our first letter is from Andrew McKenzie to Semple and relates to the problem of publishing and distributing poetry. These local poets usually arranged publication themselves, finding subscribers willing to take copies so as to finance the project in advance, and arranging with friends to distribute other copies. On 26 November 1832 McKenzie wrote to Semple:

My Dear Friend,

On account of some unforeseen misfortunes I have been prevented from sending you the copies of the *Masonic Chaplet* until now. Indeed I feel rather ashamed at not getting them sent sooner; but I am confident you will do the best for me you can.

Let it always be understood, that any copies which cannot be readily disposed of, may be returned to me; as I do not consider your honour in any degree pledged to get off all which I send you. I hope to be able yet to see you at the place, and be introduced to Mr Crowe. I am surprised at never seeing any of his production. I send 18 copies. I am your Sincere Friend. And^W. McKenzie

McKenzie was born at Dunover on the Ards, Co. Down, the son of a small farmer. He became a weaver and in 1810 produced his first collection of poetry entitled *Poems and Songs on Different Subjects*. He fell on hard times, however, and was forced to move to Belfast. The *Masonic Chaplet* (1832) mentioned here was a small volume of poems, including several addressed to Masonic lodges and brethren and one describing his cottage's contents. In a letter of 9 July 1832 to Semple, Andrew McKenzie began with an apology:

My Dear Sir,

I have seen your letter to T. Beggs; and tho I was highly gratified to see that you were capable of expressing your ideas in such an able, and even elegant manner: yet the reflection which you glanced at me, rather wounded my sensibility; and the more so, because I knew it was deserved. It is long, very long since I promised to write to you. My word I should have kept; and feel myself highly blameable in breaking it: but the reason of my procrastination was this - I could not bear the idea of troubling you with an epistle which would so ill repay the trouble of reading it. I am happy to understand that you are pleased with your situation. I feared that it would be irksome to your feelings at first, but in any situation, however strange, if we only possess sufficient perseverance to pursue its duties for a certain period, we will at last discover some part of it not so unpleasing - "See some strange comfort every state attend".

McKenzie then continued with some pert comments about Belfast poets:

You seem to believe that I have much correspondence with literary characters; but in that you are mistaken. Belfast is not the place where a man compelled to work for his living, will be admitted into the company of those who possess high literary attainments. They generally move in a higher sphere of society and would think themselves disgraced by noticing a poor serf though gifted with genius. I am sufficiently pestered with one class who think themselves men of literature, but none among those I can place on a footing with Thomas Beggs.

When I think on some young men in your own neighbourhood - namely Williamson, Walker, Crowe and yourself, I cannot refrain drawing a comparison rather disgraceful to the Northern Athens.

I take the liberty of enclosing the prospectus of a little work which I am about publishing. Tho' the title is a Masonic one, I hope many will encourage me who are not belonging to that order. I trust that you and Mr. Crowe will do what you can; and I have no doubt of Mr. S. Walker of Shanes Hill doing all he can to assist you. I would like to hear from you in a few days, from your situation you cannot want opportunity of sending direct to Andw. McKenzie, No. 14 George's Place - to be left at Messrs. McMurtry's, Great Patrick Street.

May you be happy! I am etc.
Andw. McKenzie

Besides helping to distribute the poets' work, Semple's aid was sought in other areas. In February 1843 Robert Huddleston from Moneyrea, Co. Down, wrote to Semple for advice concerning employment prospects:

My brave friend Semple,
Would you make me acquainted if a man could better life in any kind of a tolerable way by any of the tollgates that are now to be let in suburbs of your grand town - the conditions they are let on - which one would be best in your opinion to make application for - or if you would advise me to any of

122

them at all, knowing that the keeping of Tollgate is no sinecure office, but dearly earned all the emolument you receive ...

My dear Semple, a hint to a man of your taste, talent and intellect is enough. Please give me in as full a scope as possible the details for my welfare or my woe: and as I expect this note to reach you on Friday evening, 10 inst., if you could convey the answer any way to Cruther's Yard, Ann Street, before Saturday evening for Bann's Car it would be a laudable exertion on your behalf for the benefit of an humble well-wisher who would inscribe himself

your obliged and thankful servant

Robt. Huddleston.

In a second undated letter, Huddleston raised another matter with Semple:

My dear Semple,

I wish information concerning widow Brown's family and circumstances, at the foot of the mountain across the Forth Water. All the intelligence you can give me of them ... will be agreeable to me. I shall tell you my reason for this the first time I shall see you. Do you think I could court the daughter? She is not a perfect heiress. Keep it secret - all that I require of you. Post yours as soon as possible mentioning the townland they live in and I shall pay the postage.

Directions care of postmaster,

Ballygowan.

Robert Huddleston, Moneyrea.

Huddleston published a number of volumes of verse in the 1840s, after which he was a contributor to local newspapers. Several of these newspaper poems were on political matters including one entitled 'How changed are the times', published in the 1870s, and included in the Sentry Hill material. Some of these poets, or their fathers, had been strong United Irishmen, and had taken part in the 1798 rebellion, but this was to alter as this extract shows: as in Huddleston's case they became staunch liberals.

How changed are the times
(Air - 'Oh, name not his name')

How changed are the times since Wolfe Tone was your chief!
Oh! Erin, remember, remember with grief,
By mountain and glen, when your hopes were but low,
You vowed ne'er to rest while the land held a foe.
Ah! well you remember, and bravely have done -
Now bursting out brightly is liberty's son -
The days of the robbers and rebels are past,
By might of the mind you have conquered at last.
Reforms great and many good governments grant -
With Church Bill and Land Bill, what more do you want?
Does itch of the devil 'gain drive you astray?
Reflect, bully boys! who the reck'ning must pay.
'Repeal of the Union' no more let us hear;
For the rose and the thistle and shamrock loud cheer.
These islands united with freedom on par -
Be ye brothers in peace and brave allies in war.

Semple encouraged the poets. An example of the guile he sometimes employed can be seen in this amusing piece of writing by Samuel Walker of Shane's Hill, Templepatrick, Co. Antrim. Walker wrote for the *Dublin* and *Belfast Penny Journals*, but his work was not published in a single volume. On 6 October 1832 he wrote to Semple:

> It is recorded in the History of England that when Robert Bruce was in London, a conspiracy was formed against his life by King Edward I and that the Earl of Gloucester, who was Edward's son in law and Bruce's friend, had no other method of apprising Bruce than by sending him a purse of gold and a pair of spurs: Bruce took the hint, mounted horse and was in Scotland before the conspiracy was ripe for execution. I suppose you in like manner sent me the present of white

paper in order to apprise me that I should write to you. So much for that, I now proceed to thank you for your paper which I do in manner and form following...

Accept my thanks (I've naethin cheaper)
For sen'in me sae muckle paper
Lash man but I was fidgin fain
To think that it was a my ain
An' then 'twas gratis I had got it
Whilk pat me ay' mair glad about it
Ye need na ferly that I vaunt
But gifts are now-a-days sae scant
That for this town and back I vow
I gat nae gifts, but this frae you
Then there's sae much, (and I'm delighted)
Twad tak amaist a week to write it
But (figs), if I hae life remainin
Afore December's hin' most e'enin
I'll write jokes upon yer paper
The whilk to read, wad make ye caper
For whan the writin maggot bites me
There's nought on earth sae much delights me

And so he continues. In the same letter Walker also enclosed a poem entitled 'The maid's lament' which tells the sad story of a luckless maiden deserted by her lover. The poem begins with the following three verses:

The maid's lament

When rude October's howling blast
Proclaim'd the winter near
I wander'd out one moonless night
The raving storm to hear.

A grove upon the mountain's brow
Was stretched out far and wide
To which my steps I quickly bent
And gain'd its shelter'd side.

125

As here I mus'd in thoughtful mood
A voice came on the gale
Which prov'd when I to it gave ear
A hapless maiden's wail.

As the poem continues we hear all about this poor woman deserted by her rascally lover. In a covering note to Semple, Walker explained how the idea for the poem had come to him:

Do (my dear Semple) place this in contrast with some of your amorous ditties on the groves, it is my latest production, and though mournful yet I am fond of it, its history is as follows. There is a young woman in this neighbourhood with whom I am intimate (that is to say as far as friendship goes but no further) and she had a suitor who at their last meeting promised a speedy return, and had already treated with her on the subject of marriage but 6 weeks are past and she has heard nothing of him since, she sent for me to consult with her about sending him a letter which she wished me to write for her. She appointed our place of meeting at the side of a grove near her father's house. Wednesday evening last was the time and a stormy wet evening it was. When I went to the place she had been waiting nearly half an hour, exposed to the rain and wind. We stood half an hour longer and by that time you may depend she was neither dry nor warm. The recollection of this circumstance so wrought on my mind that I composed this poem on it which I finished this evening. Some of her tale is embodied in it and more of my own imagination. Her 6 weeks I extended to 6 months, the rain I kept out of the poem as it would not seem likely that a young woman would take a rainy night to wander by a grove on such an errand.
Yours faithfully
Samuel Walker

Another poem sent personally to Semple came from Joseph Carson, a

126

weaver from Kilpike. It is dated May 1842. An extract from it reads:

T'other night when the sable of nature was spread
And your Poet and spouse had got nestled in bed
With a book in my hand and light at my nose
As my wont is to learn and encourage repose
In sleep the profoundest was closed every eye
And (infantile) nurture had stilled the last cry
When a voice at my side like the chirp of a cricket
Says Joseph, my dear, did you buy me a ticket?
A ticket, says I, yes, a ticket, says she,
Sure all the mens wives will be at the Soiree.
And tho' I may not be as splendidly dressed
I can see and drink tea just as well as the rest
All I want to be decent's a single half crown
To buy a respectable cap in the Town
With nine pence or ten pence for ribbon or lace
And I'll pick up my head with the best in the place
As calm as I could to persuade her I tried
That the cash for the cap might be better applied
For instance I told her the money would buy
Some checkers for slips for our own little fry
Or else it would pay as she very well knew
As part of the Bill to the grocer was due.
Well, well, never mind she replied with a frown
But I wish you were always as thrifty in town
The cash would not last very long on your sprees
At 3 pence the pint double X in Magees
At this critical (juncture) the child gave a squeal

— — —

But the very next morning to Arnolds she sped
And yonder's the cap that she bought on her head
But stop she's not here, like old puss stole away
For she knew very well I had something to say.

127

Two other rural poets of the early nineteenth century were James Orr of Ballycarry and Samuel Thomson of Crambo Cave, Carngranny. In a letter of 4 January 1806, Orr expressed his regrets to Thomson that they did not meet more often:

My good Friend,
 I will not deny that I duly rec'd two letters from you, and if you can forgive my negligence in not acknowledging them sooner, I promise to you I will not be guilty of a similar offence. My correspondents would be respectable indeed, if I had any that I preferred to you. I wish we liv'd near other - we would pass many an agreeable hour together, for I'm proud to think that there is a congeniality in our tastes and tempers - we wou'd read sometimes - we would rhyme sometimes - 'the joy of the [skill] should go round' and we would enjoy 'the feast of Reason and the flow of soul'. If you are lonely I am equally so; honest fellows in abundance I can associate with; but such conversation! Their wit is ribaldry or scandal, their serious discourse is on the bloody gazettes of the day; their religion is damning all men and their song is Nancy Vernun - but I must change the subject, else you'd think me as splenetic as any of them.

Orr then continued with information about his work:

In reply to your question how I succeeded with my publication - you have read the subscription list, and the printers were not immoderate in their demands: in one of your letters I think you have overated the merits of my effusions; but in a note you formerly sent you and I are just agreed concerning them, namely that 'with some of them you were quite pleas'd, and with others of them the reverse' - I wish Ballycarry fair in particular had never been written.
 I have lately published some essays in the *Belfast Commercial Chronicle* (for I have no intention of abandoning the society of the Muses). I am told that they have been

favourably rec'd. by the public and if you are not a reader of that paper I will enclose one or two of them in my next letter - I approved so much of your poem 'Gloaming' that I sent it to a friend in Belfast, that he might share in the pleasure it afforded me.

I acquiesce in your scheme of us exchanging scrawls monthly. Direct yours to the care of George Thomson, Muckamores Stores, Waring St., Belfast. He'll be punctual in sending them and I'll reply with promptitude.

I am your sincere friend and brother Poet,

James Orr

Orr, the bard of Ballycarry, was born in 1770 and he died in 1816. He wrote several volumes of poetry and was a frequent subscriber of verse to local newspapers. Examples of his work have recently been brought together in a book by D.H. Akenson and W.H. Crawford. *Local Poets and Social History: James Orr, Bard of Ballycarry* (Belfast, 1977). They cover many interesting topics, including the '98 rebellion, emigration and fairs.

In a letter of 24 May 1807 Orr made criticisms of Thomson's latest work.

Dear Sir,

You want to know my opinion of your last publication and I shall readily give it. The epistle to Lamont, as published in *Microscope* was excellent; but you have added some stanzas which have somewhat impaired its beauty. Your 'address to the Cuckoo' and 'grateful thanks' are very good indeed! In the address to 'his guardian angel', you at once breathe the spirit of true repentance and of genuine poetry. Of the Gloaming you already know my opinion. The 'Fragment' is poetically descriptive of your situation and sentiments. Your address to the rising is far superior to the one to the setting sun and were it not for a tincture of calvanistic Divinity that makes some of the verses displeasing to my taste, w'd call it the best in the miscellany. Of your sonnets I will only observe, that, what speaks dim of composition appears to be your forte.

And now permit me to mention a few that I would rather you had suppressed. 'the Contract', 'to my Boortree' and the address to Capt. McDougall, have not, I believe, met with public approbation and in '[Willy sings Grizzy's Awa]' there are two or three lines which are no honour to the company among which they mix. You'll excuse the freedom of my cursory remarks and do me the justice to believe that where I have been incorrect the error did not originate in my heart.

Concerning the books I have not as yet the price of them all; but that will be no loss to you. I seldom see or hear Mr. Paul; but as I understand he holds his sacrament in C'money I will (if health permit) call at C. Cave on the Saturday before it, and punctually pay you.

Yours fraternally

James Orr

Orr's verse includes a lengthy poem on the value of tea, but it seems that it was not his favourite drink. The *Belfast Penny Journal* of 20 December 1845 remarked: 'Orr was never married, he was low in stature with ruddy cheeks and lively expressive eyes and sometimes indulged in the pleasures of the intoxicating cup far too freely'.

Samuel Thomson of Crambo Cave, Carngranny, was the author of *Poems on Different Subjects Partly in the Scottish Dialects* (Belfast, 1793) and *New Poems* (Belfast, 1799). Linde Lunney has recently reprinted extracts from an important book of his original letters, now in the library of Trinity College, Dublin. Among the Sentry Hill material is a letter to him from Henry Montgomery of Ludford Lodge, dated 4th July 1808. Montgomery later became famous as the leader of liberal opposition to the Reverend Henry Cooke. This letter of 1808, which contains an apology from Montgomery to Thomson for a mix up over distribution of his books, ends with the words 'you see that I value and esteem you. For I would not thus yield to a man whom I considered as unworthy of attention. Let bye gones be bye gones, and let me see you soon subscribed my friend, as I am, yours truly, Henry Montgomery'. This reflects an interesting connection between poets such as Thomson, and members of the Ulster academic and intellectual élite, such as Montgomery.

While these poets corresponded frequently with each other and passed comments on each others' work, they were also aware of literature and poetry elsewhere. On 21 May 1836 David Harbison, who was a weaver and small farmer from outside Ballymena, and was known as the bard of Dunclug, wrote to Semple:

Dear Sir,

I think by this time you have given up all hope of ever hearing from me but believe me when I tell you that it was only want of health prevented my writing you. I send you now Byron's select works which I promised, his English bards and scotch Reviewers. Perhaps you have seen, if not, you will find the poem worth the reading, the two would bind together and make a volume of no ordinary merit. I would not part with them had I not his whole works except a fragment of prose which you have here. I did not like to break the volume or indeed I would have taken it out. Should you think the volume too dear of the 2 shillings return it to me and for the English bards I feel myself happy in presenting them to you as a gift of friendship. Hoping to hear from you soon.

I remain yours truly,

D. Harbison

N.B. Excuse this scrall as I am just going out to the market.

Harbison, and many of the other poets, often addressed poems to individuals. This practice, however, met the disapproval of another Ballymena native, John Fullarton, whose book, *Wanderings in the British Isles* (1853) was a large-scale poetic tour of the British Isles. At the same time he could be critical of his own work. Writing to Semple on 6th August 1837 he remarked about his poetry.

You will find in the volume before you far too much of that spiritless juvenile talk of leaves and trees and flowers, of dew and stream and moonshine, which however they may touch the eye or ear fail to affect the head or heart. Still he has done

131

his best and we must not be too severe. He has not stooped to base flattery and for this he should be respected. We do not find many whining elegies or those despicable odes addressed to individuals a few degrees above him in point of wealth. There is no thing so mean as a high-minded man especially the child of the muses crouching at the steps of another man's door except writing verses for one whom we despise.

I remain

yours

J. Fullarton

The letters which we have seen so far show how Semple acted as distributing agent, adviser and confidante to the poets. In the case of Thomas Beggs, however, he was something more. He helped Beggs and provided friendship when his morale was very low. Beggs was born at Glenwherry, Co. Antrim, in 1789. The son of a small farmer, he went to sea for a time, worked as a labourer and then was employed as a worker at the bleachworks at Mallusk. Between 1819 and his death in 1847 he was responsible for seven volumes of verse. The most famous work of his was *Rathlin* (1820), a poetic account of the island and its history. A short extract from it reads:

But now the wintry gust is o'er
And heaven is filled with wrath no more!
The azure seas and skies again
Are calm as minds of holy men,
To whom the sum of soul is given
To light them on their way to heaven.
What beauties now the bard descries,
When evening shuts her languid eyes,
And lights her lonely beacon star
To cheer the pensive pilgrim star.

A letter of 5 November 1820 from Beggs to William McGaw, Ballyvesey, comments on this poem.

132

Dear Wm

I suppose you will think when I plead want of time and opportunity for not answering your favour before this, that it is a very silly excuse; but I can assure you with truth, that it was in a great measure owing to the want of both - I intended to have paid you in rhyme, but my thoughts were so much in confusion, some time past, that I could not bring them to be stationary so long as to enable me to complete the design in a manner that would have pleased either you or myself - So that in consequence I know you will be so good natured as to take the will for the deed - Your favourable opinion of Rathlin was very gratifying to me, for two reasons, the first, that I value your judgement; and the next, that I believe you would not say what you do not consider to be truth.

The length of the poem makes all other pieces I have ever published appear as trifling, in that respect; so that it must embrace a share of matter which otherwise would have been omitted and the nature of the subject, with the scenery to be described, must make the expressions more sounding, and the imagery more varied. But I believe that considering the titles, and topics of some pieces in my former publications, that they are equal if not superior to anything I have every written, or ever will write. I must ask your pardon for troubling you with so much about my own writings, which was only meant to give my opinion with yours.

There is a weekly pamphlet about to be published every Friday in Belfast, under the title of *The Gleaner* with the printer and publisher of which I am engaged; the matter will be selected from the newest, the best, and most curious works extant; and the originals shall undergo the investigation of a Committee appointed for the purpose. Each number shall contain twelve pages, printed with a good type on suitable paper so low as three half pence; the cheapest periodical work, I suppose, ever published. I will send you a copy of the proposals, and plan on which we intend to bring it forward.

133

If it meets with your approbation I hope you will oblige us with your influence, and interest in its support. What I mean is that you will lend your assistance to introduce it into notice. After which we have every reason to hope, and believe, that cheapness, and chastity will keep it from sinking - Remember me in friendship to your father and mother, and believe me to be with sincere friendship and esteem, truly yours,

Thos. Beggs

Another letter from Beggs to William McGaw is dated 15 Feb 1821 and was written in Lambeg.

Dear William,

I have been determined to write you every day this fortnight past, but has been so much hurried that I could scarcely get so much time.

I suppose you have heard of my removal from Belfast - I saw the situation was not likely to be productive of any profit to me, and in consequence I am here. I stop in the house of the Clerk whose wife tells me she is related to your family, her husband is a very nice man, and seems inclined to favour me with his friendship; indeed I feel myself tolerably happy in their society. Do you send any thing to the *Gleaner*? Your piece on Sunday schools I have read with a good deal of attention, and think there are some very beautiful lines in it, my memory does not at present supply me with the poem, or I would point out what I like, and dislike most. I have been doing something in the poetical way of late, but not since I came here - the subject is a new one, I may venture to say, and one that ought to have been handled before this, - you shall know what it is if I had it completed.

I wish you would write me as soon as possible, and send me a copy of any thing you have lying past, as I am always anxious to hear or see any thing produced by a friend, and particularly by a friend of poetical talent and taste. I am just as it were beginning the world anew, and the prospect before me gloomy enough but I shall endeavour to bear up with fortitude, as I am inclined to believe that there is virtue in bearing well and that virtue I am sure is in some degree mine - and [no worse] adversity is become very familiar to me, we are old companions - you will excuse this egotism and give my best wishes to your father and mother, and John, and believe me sincerely yours -

Thos. Beggs

I hope you will write me soon as I shall be impatient - direct to me at Mr. [Gremmell's Green.]

Among the Sentry Hill material is a ballad broadsheet by Beggs entitled 'New taties - corn laws'. Internal evidence suggests that it was written in the early 1840s. An extract reads:

Wi' gladsome heart, and blithesome e'e,
Thou precious root, I gaze on thee;
To mony a starv'ling wilt thou be
A rare delight,
An' weel I wat thou art to me
A welcome sight!

Thou art the poor man's frien' in need;
To him thou art the daily bread;
An' wantin' thee how wad he feel?
Lord only knows,
But sally forth in hungry greed,
An' buy wi' blows.

Beggs then proceeds to give a prophetic warning of danger should the potato fail:

But should the 'tatie fail us noo,
What shall we then, pair bodies, do?
Our warld has sic a motley crew
Wha canna want it;
'Twere better far we never knew
The way to plant it.

May ill befa' the heartless loon,
An' strip him baith o' sark an' shoon,
An' lea' him but an empty spoon
In but or ben,
Wha wad withold the rightfu' boon
Frae honest men.

May plenty be the gude man's lot,
An' warm his castle or his cot,
Aye biggit on a bonny spot,
To please himsel';
An' may his 'taties never rot,
No' ...ye gae yell!

A letter from Beggs to Semple, on 8 July 1837, mentions some personal problems of the former:

Dear John,

You will no doubt think that all friendship and obligations are forgotten by your humble friend and servant - but to my tale and my task - I am in the hope of being settled and would need try to be so - after long wandering, and pain and poverty in the extreme - I would be almost ashamed to state to you the particular of my pilgrimage these 12 months past. Indeed my own follies had an ample share in the making of my ill fortune and if I had any share of Genius I began to think, and every other person, to say that it was an evil one. I am resolved however that if misfortune will continue to persecute me it will not be owing to my own imprudence any longer - I will not drink any strong drink for a long time to come and am determined to let it be along with yourself the first that I do take in the way - but I must keep it at bay for many a month yet, I have not swallowed spirits or beer these 15 weeks past, and I am begun to work at Cottonmount with Mr Bragg once more. I am standing at the desk in the Lapping room while I write this.

He then proceeded to thank Semple for his help:

> I hope you are happy and prosperous - I will never forget your real friendship to me while memory has existence - I need say no more on that head. I would wish to have a line of introduction to Dr Keenan if you would be so good as to let me have it. I have not seen Mr McComb since I was with you, but will as soon as I can - he has not been pleased with me for some time past - your piece I have still in preservation.
>
> Thomas Beggs

It was probably at this point in time that Beggs wrote a street ballad in protest against drink which is among the Sentry Hill material. This was printed on a single piece of paper and hawked around the streets at the price of one penny. It was obviously a parody of a well known poem by Byron:

The fiery fluid - a parody

The alcohol poison, by cunning men plan'd
Come down like the lava and smote the fair land;
The peace and the pride of our being to wreck -
For madness and murder were found in its track.

Then the old and the young, and the wealthy and poor
Were caught in its way, and were happy no more;
For the drunkard was made - and the mild and the good,
And the wicked and weak, were immersed in the flood.

And so it carries on for twelve verses, telling of the destruction caused by alcohol, the rise of a temperance movement and the eventual defeat of the alcohol poison. However, in Beggs' own case the story ended rather differently. In May 1841 he wrote to Semple:

My dear Friend,
    The storm has blown past for a time and I hope the last time. I am like the dog in hot weather, I must be both muzzled

and cloged - perhaps it is best, at least it must be so taken - I have erred and the penalty has to be paid. I need not say how much I am obligated to you for the deep interest you took on the trying occasion - God forbid that thee or thine may be ever so tried.

The last day of jeopardy in the same way, is come, and past with me. I may well damn the whisky for it has nearly damned me - and yet withal I love it not. I would be glad to know of the little piece that I sent to the *News-letter* or if you had called on Mr. Sanson, please let me know by the Bearer.

As Colridge says a wiser and a sadder man I have been since I saw you - But the mind will not be for ever depressed and the old even temper will prevail at the last - and now I say farewell, a long farewell to all intemperate habits. I hope to see you soon, and often too - my best wishes to Mrs. Semple and D. Clyde, while I remain in truth and sincerity Dear John, ever yours,

Thomas Beggs.

Whether or not Beggs kept to his temperate ways we do not know. But it is appropriate to end with this small verse which Beggs wrote in honour of his old friend and comforter, John Rea Semple:

Lord bless ye for your kind desert,
And mak' ye hale an' well at heart,
And keep it in ye'r mind to be,
The guid man, ye has been to me.
And gie ye in your time o' need,
A bumper, and a loaf o' bread,
A cozie room, and free o' fleas,
A wallet fu' o' cash an' claes,
A trusty frien' a bonnie wife
To bring ye a' the sweets o' life,
And tak' ye when y're gone and speed
To Heaven, on better fare to feed.

Acknowledgements

Thanks are due to the following: Dr Joe Dundee who kindly allowed me to study the Sentry Hill material; Mr Wesley McCann who gave invaluable assistance in cataloguing the Sentry Hill books; the Linen Hall Library which now owns the Sentry Hill books and poets' letters; the library of the University of Ulster at Coleraine where a transcript of the letters has been deposited. An earlier version of this paper was broadcast by the BBC.

Bibliography

1.   J.R.R. Adams, *The Printed Word and the Common Man* (Belfast, 1987).

2.   D.H. Akenson and W.H. Crawford, *Local Poets and Social History: James Orr, Bard of Ballycarry* (Belfast, 1977).

3.   Jane Gray, 'Folk Poetry and Working Class Identity in Ulster: an Analysis of James Orr's "The penitent,"' in *Journal of Historical Sociology*, vol. 6. no. 3 (Sept 1993), pp.249-75.

4.   Ivan Herbison, 'A Sense of Place: Landscape and Locality in the Work of the Rhyming Weaver', in Gerald Dawe and J.W. Foster (eds), *The Poet's Place: Ulster Literature and Society* (Belfast, 1991), pp.63-75.

5.   Linde Lunney, 'Ulster Attitudes to Scottishness: the Eighteenth Century and After', in I.S. Wood (ed), *Scotland and Ulster* (Edinburgh, 1994), pp.56-70.

6.   Ernest McA. Scott and Philip Robinson (eds), *The Country Rhymes of Samuel Thomson: the Bard of Carngranny* 1766-1816 (Bangor, 1992); Philip Robinson (ed), *The Country Rhymes of James Orr: the Bard of Ballycarry* 1770-1816 (Bangor, 1992); Amber Adams and J.R.R. Adams (eds), *The Country Rhymes of Hugh Porter; the Bard of Moneyslane* (Bangor, 1992).

BISHOP FRANCIS HUTCHINSON:
HIS IRISH PUBLICATIONS
AND HIS LIBRARY

GORDON WHEELER

BETWEEN 1716 AND 1724 about half of the new appointees to Irish bishoprics were outsiders from Great Britain.[1] Translation had brought the Bishops of Bangor, Carlisle and Bristol to Irish sees. For others of less elevated rank the influence at Court of a powerful patron had secured nomination. To arrive in the entourage of a new Lord Lieutenant as his chaplain was an all too likely route to a mitre. Such a situation was, not unnaturally, far from the liking of the aboriginal Irish clergy. Archbishop King protested in 1718 to William Wake, Archbishop of Canterbury: 'I pray God ... that in time it do not come to that pass, that every obnoxious bishop or worse, who is disliked or troublesome in England be not sent into Ireland to our best bishoprics to be rid of him'.[2] But things were to go from bad to worse. When Hugh Boulter, the Bishop of Bristol, was made Archbishop of Armagh in 1724 he deliberately set out 'to break the present Dublin faction on the bench' by introducing trustworthy supporters of 'the English interest' at every vacancy.[3]

Amongst these imports there had arrived in 1721, as Bishop of Down and Connor, Francis Hutchinson, a Derbyshire man then aged sixty, who had been a vicar in Bury St Edmunds, and a chaplain to George I.[4] 'He is honest and well affected but very narrow minded, imprudent and almost incapable of brotherly advice ... In short ... he shames us all. The Lord Lieutenant disowns him, telling me he is [the Bishop of] Norwich's etc', was the opinion of John Evans, Bishop of Meath (himself an immigrant from Wales) in 1722. Evans went on to report that Hutchinson had so far

140

visited his diocese twice 'and his conduct there was such, that he is (to our great sorrow) in much contempt among them all'.[5] One can only wonder what the Bishop had been up to in so short a time. He had not yet displayed the nepotism so rife among his compatriots but which was eventually to lead to the appointment of his nephew, Samuel, as Dean of Dromore in succession to his son-in-law, a post subsequently held by Samuel in plurality with the Archdeaconry of Connor; and to the appointment of a second nephew, Francis, as Archdeacon of Down.[6] Perhaps he was beginning to show signs of too great an interest in money. An outraged Dean Swift saw the influx of English bishops as grasping marauders in pursuit of lucrative livings which could be enjoyed *in absentia*: 'Ye are in the wrong to blame His Majesty before you know the truth. He sent us over very good and great men, but they were murdered by a parcel of highwaymen between Chester and London, who slipping on their gowns and cassocks here pretend to pass for bishops'.[7]

Hutchinson was, however, to remain a consistent resident in his diocese. Certainly his surviving account books[8] do display a lively interest in financial matters, which possibly may be no greater than that of any other contemporary landlord. There is much dealing in loans, repayments and interest. Indeed Hutchinson was one of only two bishops subscribing to the abortive scheme for a national bank for Ireland which was floated between 1719 and 1721 (his neighbour at Dromore, also an Englishman, was the other).[9] The bank was a further target for an attack by Dean Swift, although he did not name Hutchinson personally during his campaign against it. Within months of his arrival in Ireland the Bishop had, with almost indecent haste, dashed off a pamphlet in support of the bank,[10] which would appear to confirm a tactless interest in matters temporal not altogether seemly for a bishop taking up his pastoral duties. His own estimate in 1736 of the value of his bishopric was £1,379 a year, which he had by then supplemented to £2,111 from income derived from his private land purchases. By 1729 he had been able to acquire an estate at Portglenone at the substantial price of £8,220, a sum put together from his own resources and via a network of loans which were soon repaid.

Not many dioceses in Ireland at this time were as yet supplied with an official bishop's palace. Hutchinson, like his predecessors in Down and Connor, was responsible for his own housing and from 1721 he had lived in a rented house in Lisburn where his Connor cathedral was situated

(Down Cathedral remained in ruins throughout his tenure of the see). It is possible that the Bishop's brother Samuel had already been living in the neighbourhood of Portglenone since early 1720 when the Trinity College Dublin entry books record the transfer of his son from Cambridge to TCD: Samuel is described as 'agricola necnon mercator'.[11] The Bishop's new home was an old castle of the O'Neills, overlooking the River Bann, which had for some time been in the possession of the Stafford family.[12] In the early 1730s it had an immediate demesne of 139 acres, and Hutchinson was paying tax on it for fifteen hearths. Not long after moving there, Hutchinson had installed his extended family in the surrounding townlands which he had also bought; son, brother, nephew and future son-in-law were all tenants. His widowed daughter and her three children were also to live with him for a time in the Castle.

From Wing,[13] the *Eighteenth-Century Short-title Catalogue* and Walter Harris's edition of Ware,[14] it has been possible to compile a bibliography of twenty-six titles attributable to Hutchinson, most of them pamphlets. About half of these were published anonymously but can largely be assigned to the Bishop on the strength of Harris's information, which he said had been conveyed to him by the author himself. Confirmation of Harris's claim is supplied by Account Book D, which contains (pp. 495- 6) a memorandum in Hutchinson's own hand, 'Mr Harris 1736 wrote to me to desire me to send him an Account of the Names of the Books I had publd & the places where I lived at the times that I put them out'. There then follows a list of seven titles, plus a further thirteen 'Since I came to Ireland AD 1720 [i.e.1721]'. Few dates of publication are given; Hutchinson has got some minor details wrong; the titles are not in chronological order (indeed some pre-1721 books are listed in the Irish section); and a pamphlet published in 1738, subsequent to the report to Harris, has been added. When Harris came to publish the Bishop's list, he had expanded it to include two post-1736 publications, an intended new work (eventually never published), and a long editorial note, but nevertheless his bibliography of twenty-three titles was still not complete. The Bishop's list also leaves us with two mysteries: his unqualified claim to *The Many Advantages of a Good Language*,[15] an anonymous work attributed to Thomas Wilson, Bishop of Sodor and Man, in a variety of modern sources;[16] and the as yet untraced, undated title *An English Grammar*.[17]

As a writer Hutchinson's chief claim to fame before he came to Ireland had been his *An Historical Essay Concerning Witchcraft*, first published in London in 1718 and with a second much extended edition in 1720. This had the distinction of achieving a translation into German which appeared in Leipzig in 1726. Hutchinson had been familiar with the tradition of witchcraft in East Anglia during his incumbencies of the parish of Hoxne and of St James's, Bury St Edmunds, and had had the opportunity to gather information from those who had witnessed its suppression. In his history he sought to establish that, while the craft of sorcery might well be practised, there was nothing of substance in it. Lowndes sums it up thus: 'This work contains much interesting matter and developes many celebrated impostures'.[18] It is interesting to find the Bishop still recording in his account and memoranda books local instances of supposed witchcraft in Ireland.

For the purposes of this paper an examination has been made of the content only of Hutchinson's Irish publications. His sermons and other theological works reveal an establishment orthodoxy combined with a burning and blinkered awareness of his mission to convert the misguided Roman Catholic inhabitants of Ireland to the only acceptable Church. The tone is decidedly anti-papist, though an occasional attempt is made to conceal this beneath a veneer of condescending tolerance. In view of the hostility expressed in so many of his publications, it is difficult to accept the 'versatility' of the good relations with both Roman Catholics and Presbyterians with which Hutchinson is credited by his biographer in *The Dictionary of National Biography*.[4] He exhorts his own clergy, churchwardens and laymen to fulfil their duties and obligations to fellow Christians.[19] He stresses the benefits of submission to authority and of a good system of laws and ordinances and attributes Ireland's woes to simple law breaking. A benevolent government can only assist, not obstruct all three denominations.[20] '... modern Papists in this country run after Priests that have been fed out of the Pope's Baskets'. Our greatest duty is 'that of drawing the poor Popish Natives into an Union with that Church and Government which seeks their Good' ... 'There never was a Schism that lasted always; and therefore surely there may be some way or other of putting an End to this by making our Island a Protestant Nation'.[21] Every effort should be made to secure subsistence for converted priests; where possible they should be appointed as curates – 'my own Purse shall never be shut upon such an Occasion'.[22] 'Are not Papists generally courteous, well-bred People, and have not many of their learned Men explained their Doctrines so near to ours, that it is not easy to see where they differ?' ... 'is it not better for us to have our Minds upon these Steps towards Peace, than be always widening the Difference by aggravating those Faults, which many of themselves are ashamed of?'[23]

Hutchinson's partisan and authoritarian attitude even spills over into his social contributions – 'the Protestant Religion is much better suited to a trading nation than the Popish. Popery hath too many Holy-Days, and Monks and Nuns, and expensive Vanities and idle Errands to take them off from their Business; whereas the Protestant Religion, insted of making New Gowns for the Virgin Mary, teaches us to clothe and feed our poor Brethren'. 'Whipping young People for Begging or Pilfering, or Idleness, stops their Vice in the beginning'. The poor should not be allowed to marry (and multiply!) until they occupy a house.[24]

Contemporary comment did not spare the theological short-comings of Hutchinson, the Cambridge Doctor of Divinity. Thomas Hearne, the prodigious historical editor and scholar, wrote in his diary in 1733 of the Bishop's 1731 Gunpowder-Plot sermon: 'Tis a strange immethodical rambling discourse without Divinity, but he hath exhausted his whole stock of Learning (a very small one) in railing. There is one thing, however, that he is right in (and 'tis the only thing of good remark in his Rhapsody), and that is his making the story of Pope Joan a Fiction'.[25] Certainly such a judgement is sadly confirmed by Hutchinson's final theological work of 1738,[26] a jumble of scriptural quotation which reads like the manic diatribe of a fanatic or the feverish meanderings of a man on the verge of dotage in these final months of his life.

One result of Hutchinson's proselytising zeal has, however, earned him a minor place in the history of the study of the Irish language. Amongst the earliest of his diocesan concerns on arriving in Ireland was the creation of a new parish on Rathlin Island by separating it from Ballintoy. In 1721 he circulated a prospectus and appeal[27] for subscriptions printed on the first two pages of a single small folio fold. This indicated that the island's Irish-speaking population of 490 was served by neither Priest nor Minister and had no school; and proposed the building of a church and school and the establishment of a small library to be housed

144

in a parsonage house. Several of those listed as having already subscribed to the project had donated books for the library (including Lord Charlemont and the Archbishop of Dublin). In putting together such a library, Hutchinson was closely paralleling the schemes for setting up parochial libraries pioneered in Scotland by James Kirkwood between 1704 and 1705, and in England, Wales and the Isle of Man by Thomas Bray between 1705 and 1730.[28] By far his most important suggestion was the provision of a series of primers, catechisms, psalters, prayer books and bibles to be printed in parallel columns in both Irish and English. To facilitate this he asked supporters to send him any books or manuscripts which might assist translations into Irish. He was not, of course, the first to attempt to supply cheaply produced liturgical and devotional texts in their own tongue to the native-speaking inhabitants of the more distant corners of the British Isles: between 1686 and 1690, at the instigation of James Kirkwood, Robert Boyle had underwritten the printing of bibles, catechisms and prayer books in the Scots form of Irish then spoken, for distribution to the Scottish Highlands;[29] Thomas Wilson, Bishop of Sodor and Man, produced a catechism in Manx in 1707;[30] and the Reverend John Richardson of Belturbet lost much by personally financing the printing of Irish sermons and catechisms in London in 1711 and 1712.[31]

As it happened, Hutchinson succeeded in publishing only a single catechism[32] for his hoped-for Rathlin flock. This contains a preface, of which the first part, reiterating the aims of the parish venture and setting out the names of managers and subscribers, has been attributed to Hutchinson.[33] The technical part of the preface and the translated catechism itself were by two other unnamed clergymen (one of whom had consulted John Richardson) probably working under the guidance of Hutchinson.[34] The Bishop's purpose was quite clearly not the altruistic one of making books accessible for the Rathlin Irish speakers but rather to rid them of their Irish by teaching them to speak English: '... the Design of this Essay is not to please the Highlands but incorporate this Island Raghlin and other Natives with the English ...', '... we hope it will make them Protestants'. Richardson, unlike Hutchinson, had seen the value of a continuing use of Irish for the purposes of conversion. Linguistically the Rathlin catechism is of special interest because it does not employ an Irish type but instead uses a fairly defective half phonetic spelling to reproduce the sounds of the Scottish form of Irish spoken on the island at that time.[35]

A few years later, in 1724, Hutchinson seems to have been responsible for another parallel text in English and Irish. This appears without date in his manuscript list as supplied to Harris simply as 'An Irish Almanack', but its entry in his library catalogue (see below) is dated. It can only be the Irish-English almanac as described by Edward Evans for that year.[36] There are Irish and English title pages, and the Irish is printed throughout 'in the same common Characters of all Europe', again not in Irish type. The preface speaks of the authors as being a protestant clergyman and a popish priest, but the clergyman ('a diligent Curate with a Wife and several Children') is clearly not Hutchinson, who once more probably acted only as editor. The sentiments and turn of phrase of the preface are all too familiar: 'Irish is what all wise men would take from them; and put English in its place ...', '... if it would teach English in earnest, we must do it by explaining it by their own'. 'If they were but good Christians, good Protestants, and good Subjects, their speaking Irish would do no harm to any body'.

Much of Hutchinson's secular writing displays the same tendency to wander as his theological. He is inclined to use his limited range of material over and over again, discussing the same topics and using the same arguments. This is nowhere more clearly demonstrated than in his remaining contributions on Irish subjects. As a land owner at Portglenone he naturally took an interest in matters of local concern. His pamphlet on Lough Neagh[37] describes how reaches of the lake and the River Bann had ceased to be navigable as a result of silting and the obstruction caused by eel-fishery weirs. He recommends a programme of flood control, bog drainage and land reclamation. Drainage will also employ the poor 'and keep them from running to America', a proposal which he had previously put forward in his 1723 letter on employing the poor. He concludes his discussion of the problems of Lough Neagh with a long and discursive dedication to the Lord Lieutenant in which he extols the dietary virtues of fish and stresses the value of regulating fishery. He finishes with a plea for the establishment of a Company of Fishermen in Ireland. Most of this had already appeared in his letter on the fisheries of Ireland published some nine years earlier.[38]

The most substantial of Hutchinson's Irish works, the *Defence of the*

Antient Historians,[39] is also the best written. In this he set out to review and assess Irish historiography up to his own time. It demonstrates very well his familiarity with the printed sources, most of which were in his own library. A loose sheet inserted after p.528 of Account Book D is a list of other relevant Irish and Scottish history books which he had borrowed from his son-in-law Henry O'Hara of Crebilly. The preface of the *Defence* contains an appeal for information on the whereabouts of surviving Irish historical manuscripts, an early manifestation of the new interest in Irish studies which was to gain such momentum throughout the eighteenth century.

In the remoteness of country livings in Suffolk and Antrim, Hutchinson's library had had to be as self-sufficient as possible for his researches, and we find that its content closely mirrors the interests revealed by his publications. Account Book D contains a 38-page catalogue (pp. 501-38) largely in the Bishop's own hand – 'A catalogue of my Books made after my Removal to Portglenone 1730', further headed (p. 503) 'at Portglenone'. This is preceded (pp. 498-500) by a list of eighty titles – 'Catalogue of such books as I have carryed to or bought in Dublin', later headed (p. 500) 'at Dublin 1736'. That there was a fairly constant traffic between the Bishop's houses in County Antrim and in Bow Lane, Dublin, during the sessions of the House of Lords, can be further seen in the accounts themselves and by the marking of some half dozen titles in the main catalogue as being 'in y Trunk'. Many entries lack date of publication, but an interpolated title dated 1738 shows that the catalogue was being used until the end of Hutchinson's life. Altogether there are 708 titles in 712 volumes. They are catalogued under a dozen subject headings in size groups probably reflecting their physical shelving: sometimes folios, followed by quartos and octavos together; sometimes folios and quartos together, followed by octavos; and sometimes all three formats (or rather sizes) together. There are no shelf numbers.

Divinity (including the Fathers, bibles and commentaries), as is only proper, accounts for 137 titles. These are supplemented by later sections on 'Popish books most of ym controversial' (48) and 'Controversies with Presbyterians & oth Sects' (31). But Hutchinson's real interest, stimulated in his youth by his uncle, the chronologist Francis Tallents, is revealed by the 155 titles in the History and Geography section, the 33 on Irish history, and the 92 titles of his own particular speciality, 'Witches, Conjurers, Devils, Oracles'. The 88 titles listed under Law may seem unduly high, but it was not at all unusual for a bishop, who was also a landowner and member of the legislature, to equip himself as an amateur lawyer for the hazards of litigation with his tenants, and for the necessity to quote statute and precedent in disputes with his clergy. Hutchinson's considerable interest in language, as evidenced in several of his publications discussed above, can be seen in the 51 titles in the Dictionaries and Grammar section. An analysis of the whole catalogue shows that he owned much of what had been printed in Irish and Scots Gaelic, and in Manx during the eighteenth century up to his time, together with a few earlier titles[40] – 'An old imperf Com, pr book in Irish [1608]'; '2 Irish Bibles by Bp Bedel [1681-1685]'; 'The Singing Psalmes in the Com Char for Scotland 1702'; 'Psalms in Irish y Highland translat with several Coll'; 'B of Man's [i.e. Thomas Wilson's] Catechism in Manks in y Com Charact 1707'; 'Tillotson's Serm in Irish by Mr Richardson' [i.e. Richardson and MacBrady's collection *Seanmora ar na Priom Phoncibh na Creideamh*, 1711]; 'Com pr Engl & Irish [1712]'; 'Keiting in Irish charr [1723]'. Hutchinson also owned a manuscript version of Keating in Irish.

The Bishop died in 1739 leaving most of his estates and income to Hutchinson Hamilton, the eldest son of his daughter Frances, who had married as her first husband John Hamilton, Dean of Dromore. 'We hear he has left the bulk of his estate to his grandson, Master Hutchinson Hamilton who is now at Lisburn School'.[41] The Bishop's widow, Anne, was left a life occupancy of the Castle and demesne at Portglenone (with reversion to Hutchinson Hamilton and his heirs) together with the house contents and personal effects.[42] She died in Dublin in 1758 'at an advanced age'[43] having disposed of her husband's library in 1756. A copy of the auction catalogue[44] is in the library of Queen's University, Belfast. This not only provides details of the subsequent fate of a large number of the Bishop's books, but also sheds light on book auction practice of the period. It may well be the earliest known Irish auction catalogue annotated with prices and the names of buyers,[45] but it is certainly a unique survival for its time in that it is the copy actually used by the auctioneer, or his clerk, in the course of the sale.

The octavo catalogue has been separated into single leaves and these have been laid into sections of Fine Demy paper folded in folio format. The interleaves are ruled into columns showing lot number, selling price, name of buyer, and record of payment. Those at the end contain an addendum of some twenty supplementary lots not included in the printed catalogue (largely bulk groups of pamphlets, some of which may have failed to sell the first time round), together with a balance sheet for the outcome of the sale. There are 618 lots in the printed catalogue, but the proceeds from the final eighteen of these (nearly £14 and actually some of the financial high-flyers of the auction) were not credited to the consignor, a good illustration of the unfortunate habit of auctioneers of filling up the tail-end of sales without indicating provenance. After making a reduction for this, the catalogue accounts for some 700 volumes in Hutchinson's library, not much change since his own manuscript catalogue of twenty years before: only a single title of 1746 postdates his death. However, whereas the manuscript catalogue had carefully listed the contents of collections of titles bound together, the auction catalogue notes only the first title of such collective volumes.

The sale was intended to last for seven days, six of them devoted to ninety-one lots each, and the seventh to the residue of seventy-two lots. Each day's consignment is arranged in the usual groups of octavo (and below), quarto and folio. In fact the rate of selling was extremely variable, achieving ninety-one lots on only three occasions and half that on three other days, so that the whole affair extended to nine days in all. Even allowing for the fact that auction sessions at the time rarely exceeded three hours, such a pace is extremely leisurely by today's standards, all the more so when one sees on the interleaves how often the lots were grouped, frequently in pairs but sometimes up to half-a-dozen together.

The printed sale conditions allowed for bidding stages of 2d up to ten shillings, then 6d up to £1; and a shilling beyond that, which make the appearance of $1/2$d here and there in the prices paid seem rather strange. The lowest price achieved for a single lot, and that not uncommonly, was 2d, although the average over the whole sale was about 2s 6d. The total realised amounted to the not very considerable sum of £73.11s. $2^1/2$d, and out of this the Bishop's sole surviving executor, his nephew Dean Samuel Hutchinson of Dromore, had to pay £8. 9s. 9d. to William Ross,[46] the auctioneer, for fees and the hire of the room. There is next to no information in the Bishop's accounts to show what he had paid for his books. Account Book C has an entry under November 1730 for a short list of titles bought by him in Dublin. One of these was John Worlidge's *Dictionarium rusticum* [2nd ed, 1717], an octavo for which he had paid nine shillings: it fetched only 1s 4d at the sale. Hutchinson was putting together his library in England at a time when new octavos normally cost five or six shillings; duodecimos from 2s 6d to three shillings; and folios and quartos from ten to twelve shillings.[47] A median retail price of 2.4d per sheet was typical in London in the 1730s and 1740s.[48] Mary Pollard has established that although Dublin retail prices for books were lower than this in the earlier eighteenth century, they had come nearer to the London prices by the 1750s.[49]

Many lots in the printed catalogue bear manuscript annotations in a shorthand cipher which, after comparison with the names of successful buyers on the interleaves, can almost certainly be taken to be commissions, and it is clear that those leaving bids by no means always obtained what they wanted. The names of forty-six individual buyers are recorded, most of them securing only a handful of lots, but a few achieving large numbers, although the average amount paid per lot probably reflects better the specialist collecting enthusiasms and determination (if not discrimination) of some of these latter. A 'Dr Suthwell' (? Bowen Southwell, MP for Downpatrick) bought twenty-five miscellaneous lots at an average price of 3s 8d. A Mr Matthews spent only £1. 17s. 4d. on thirty-nine lots, almost entirely witchcraft. (He had put in unsuccessful bids for many more: not surprisingly this subject aroused some of the most lively interest throughout the sale). 'Dr Padmor' (? Arthur Podmore) carried off fifty-eight lots of early printing (including a Wynkyn de Worde) and witchcraft at the low average price of 1s 3d. On the other hand a Mr Clements paid a higher average of three shillings for an exceedingly miscellaneous collection of seventy-eight lots. The most considerable buyer of the whole sale was a Mr Rogers who spent £15. 2s. 0d. on no less than 169 lots. The number, low average price of 1s 9d and fairly consistent re-sale appeal of his purchases (dictionaries, historical reference books, standard classics, law and travel) suggest that he may have been a member of the trade. Such an inference is supported by his purchase among the supplementary lots of several of the bulk groups of miscellaneous books and pamphlets, and of a parcel of single sheets. One member of the trade who certainly was present at the sale was Timothy Hinds, the blind second-hand dealer who was active between 1734 and 1767. He paid a respectable average of 7s 3d for his ten lots.[50] William Ross, the auctioneer, himself bought eighteen miscellaneous lots at very low prices, amongst them 120 copies of Hutchinson's Rathlin catechism! Probably the most discriminating purchaser at the sale was the Reverend Mervyn Archdall, the distinguished antiquarian, whose fourteen lots (average nine shillings) included several chronicles, a Bede on large paper, and the manuscript of Keating's history in Irish; he returned Grafton's chronicle of England as imperfect.

As might be expected, the established church was well represented amongst the bidders by names such as Edward Synge, Bishop of Elphin, Henry Smith, Archdeacon of Glendalough, John Owen, Dean of Clonmacnoise, and Richard Wight, Archdeacon of Limerick. Of the better-known book collectors of the period who were either present or left bids, were Lord Charlemont, Richard Terry, John Putland, Christopher Robinson, Richard Cudmore and Michael Kearney, Roman Catholic Archdeacon of Meath.

Several of the lots are marked in the auctioneer's buyers' column simply with the word 'Cash' without a name. It is not immediately obvious what this means, unless it represents immediate payment on the day, without the necessity of presenting an account or preparing further documentation.

Notes

1   Irvin Ehrenpreis, *Swift, the Man, his Works, and his Age*, vol. 3 (London, 1983), pp. 166-186, 'The bench of bishops'.

2   King to Wake 10/05/1718 as transcribed in Ehrenpreis, *Swift*, vol. 3, p. 170.

3   D.A. Chart, 'The Close Alliance of Church and State', in *History of the Church of Ireland*, edited by W.A. Phillips, vol. 3 (London, 1933), pp. 201-3.

4   For details of Hutchinson's life see Alexander Gordon, 'Francis Hutchinson', in *The Dictionary of National Biography*, vol. 28 (London, 1891), pp. 338-9; and *Clergy of Connor ... based on ... Lists compiled by Canon J.B. Leslie* (Belfast, 1993), pp. 34-5.

5   Evans to Wake 12/01/1722 as transcribed in Ehrenpreis, *Swift*, vol. 3, p. 171.

6   *Clergy of Connor*, pp. 401-3.

7   Ehrenpreis, *Swift*, vol 3, p. 170.

8   Public Record Office of Northern Ireland PRONI DI01/22/1-3 (referred to hereafter as Account Books A, B and C); Down and Dromore and Connor Diocesan Library unpressmarked (referred to hereafter as Account Book D). These cover the period 1721 to May 1739, a month before Hutchinson's death. Account Book A, in the Bishop's own hand, contains, in addition to financial transactions, many memoranda such as lists of clergy and parishes, notes of letters sent and addresses. Account Book C is devoted mainly to the Bishop's domestic expenses as recorded by his steward Anthony Kinsly; it has been previously used in J.F. Rankin, 'The account book of an 18th-century bishop', *Lisburn Historical Society Journal*, 5(1984), pp. 6-11, 14-16. Account Book D, which is more fully described in the main text, includes details of various diocesan duties carried out by Hutchinson between 1731 and 1737. Throughout these account books passing reference is made to others – 'the Hilsborow book in quarto', 'the tyed Octavo' – of which the whereabouts remain unknown.

9   F.G. Hall, *The Bank of Ireland 1783-1946* (Dublin, 1949), pp. 25-7. A copy of the printed list of subscribers is in Archbishop Marsh's Library, Dublin. In October 1721 the House of Lords resolved not to let the Bank Bill pass. Hutchinson, who had been introduced into the House only the previous month, was one of six signatories (not surprisingly also including the Bishop of Dromore) who lodged a note of dissent, *Journal of the Irish House of Lords*, 8th October 1721.

10   *A Letter to the Gentlemen of the Landed Interest in Ireland relating to a Bank* (Dublin, printed by and for Aaron Rhames, 1721), 32p. 8vo. Published anonymously. The *Eighteenth-Century Short-title Catalogue* enters this under its title, with a note that it is sometimes attributed to Hutchinson. It further confuses the situation by definitely assigning to Hutchinson a quite different anonymous pamphlet of 1721, *A Letter to a Member of Parliament Touching the Late Intended Bank*. This latter was not printed by Aaron Rhames, Hutchinson's usual printer for the period, and a reading of it quickly reveals that its author was a member of the anti-bank faction, not a supporter.

11   G.D. Burtchaell and T.U. Sadleir, *Alumni Dublinenses: a Register of Students, Graduates and Provosts of Trinity College in the University of Dublin*, second edition (Dublin, 1935). The Bishop's brother had made an earlier visit to Ireland, having fought as an ensign at the Boyne in 1690, *Burke's Peerage* (1897), p.783.

12   Samuel Lewis, *A Topographical Dictionary of Ireland*, second edition (London, 1847), vol. 2, p. 427; J. O'Laverty, *An Historical Account of the Diocese of Down and Connor* (Dublin, 1895- 98), vol. 3, pp. 366-7.

13   D.G. Wing, *Short-title Catalogue of Books Printed in England ... 1641-1700*, second edition (New York, 1982-94).

14   Sir James Ware, *The Whole Works concerning Ireland, revised and improved* [by Walter Harris], vol. 1 (Dublin, 1739), pp. 215-16.

15   *The Many Advantages of a Good Language to any Nation, with an Examination of the Present State of Our Own; as also an Essay Towards Correcting Some Things that are Wrong in it* (London, printed for J. Knapton, R. Knaplock [etc], 1724). 96p. 8vo. Robert Knaplock had been the publisher of Hutchinson's history of witchcraft.

16   For example, S. Halkett and J. Laing, *A Dictionary of the Anonymous and Pseudonymous Literature of Great Britain*, revised edition (Edinburgh, 1926-62); *The New Cambridge Bibliography of English Literature*, vol.2 (Cambridge, 1971), col. 1640.

17   This matches none of the anonymous titles for Hutchinson's date span in R.C. Alston, *English Grammars written in English* (Leeds, 1965); and in *The New Cambridge Bibliography of English Literature*, vol. 1 (Cambridge, 1974), cols. 92-93.

18   W.T. Lowndes, *The Bibliographer's Manual of English Literature*, new edition (London, 1864), p. 1150.

19   *A Sermon Preach'd by ... Francis, Lord Bishop of Down and Connor, at his Primary Visitation, held at Lisburn, May 3, 1721* (Dublin, printed by A. Rhames for E. Dobson, 1721). 16p. 8vo.

20   *A Sermon Preached in Christ's Church, Dublin, on the first of August, 1721. Being the Anniversary of His Majesty's Happy Accession to the Throne* (Dublin, printed by A. Rhames, for E. Dobson, 1721). 23p. 4to.

21   *A Sermon Preached in Christ-church Dublin, on Thursday the 30th day of January, 1723. Being the Anniversary Fast for the Martyrdom of King Charles the First* (Dublin, printed by A. Rhames, for J. Hyde, and E. Dobson, 1723 [i.e. 1724]). 19p. 4to.

22 *Advices Concerning the Manner of Receiving Popish Converts, and Encouraging both Priests and Others to Live in Unity with the Church of Ireland* (Dublin, printed by A. Rhames, [1729]). [1], 22p. 8vo. Published anonymously.

23 *A Sermon Preached in Christ-Church, Dublin, on Friday, November 5th.1731. Being the Anniversary ... of ... the Gun-powder Plot* (Dublin, printed by Geo. Grierson, 1731). 42p. 4to. This achieved a 'third edition' within the same year.

24 *A Letter to a Member of Parliament, Concerning the Employing and Providing for the Poor.* (Dublin, printed by Aaron Rhames, 1723). 16p. 8vo. Published anonymously.

25 Thomas Hearne, *Remarks and Collections*, edited by H.E. Salter, vol. 11 (Oxford, 1921), p. 259.

26 *The Certainty of Protestants a Safer Foundation than the Pretended Infallibility of Papists* (Dublin, printed by R. Reilly, 1738). 44p. 8vo. Published anonymously.

27 *The State of the Case of Raghlin* ([Dublin, 1721]). Published anonymously. This was almost certainly printed by Aaron Rhames for the bookseller Eliphal Dobson, who is mentioned in the text as one of those appointed to receive donations. For detailed summaries of Hutchinson's Rathlin proposals see L.M. Ewart, *Handbook of the United Dioceses of Down and Connor and Dromore* (Belfast, 1886), pp. 103 and following; and H.A. Boyd, 'The parish of Rathlin', *Church of Ireland gazette* (1932), pp. 474–5.

28 Thomas Kelly, *Early Public Libraries ... in Great Britain before 1850* (London, 1966), pp. 104-17.

29 R.E.W. Maddison, 'Robert Boyle and the Irish Bible', *Bulletin of the John Rylands Library*, 41 (1958), pp. 81-101.

30 Alexander Gordon, 'Thomas Wilson', in *The Dictionary of National Biography*, vol. 62 (London, 1900), pp. 139-42.

31 Norman Moore, 'John Richardson', in *The Dictionary of National Biography*, vol. 48 (London, 1896), pp. 228-9.

32 *The Church Catechism in Irish. With the English Placed over against it in the same Karakter* (Belfast, printed by James Blow, 1722). [16], 56p. 8vo. Published anonymously. Account Book A records (p. 52) that Hutchinson paid Blow £15 for printing this. Account Book D

reserves pp. 118-19 for an 'Account of Raghlin'. In it under 16 August 1723 is entered 'Rec for Catechisms now sold £1-2-0. Paid to Mr Blow forgotten in ye Acc 6/3'.

33   Séamus Ó Casaide, *The Irish Language in Belfast and County Down* (Dublin, 1930), p.10.

34   Cathair Ó Dochartaigh, 'The Rathlin Catechism', *Zeitschrift für celtische Philologie*, 35 (1976), pp. 175-233.

35   N.M. Holmer, *The Irish Language in Rathlin Island, Co Antrim* (Dublin, 1942), pp. 13-14.

36   Edward Evans, *Historical and Bibliographical Account of Almanacks, Directories... published in Ireland* (Dublin, 1897), pp. 61-68 (No. XIV): *An Irish Almanack, for the Year of Our Lord, 1724* (Dublin, printed and sold by Mary Laurence, and John Watson, 1724). Published anonymously. Significantly, this carries at the end an advertisement for books printed or published by Aaron Rhames, Eliphal Dobson, John Hyde or James Blow, all of whom appear either singly or in various combinations in the imprints of Hutchinson's other books from 1721 to 1729.

37   *The State of the Case of Loughneagh and the Bann* (Dublin, printed by R. Reilly for J. Smith, 1738). 24p. 8vo. Account Book D has a disappointed note (p.2) 'Medum Mr Smith took nothing of[f] for Printing the State of y Case of Lough Neagh and the River Ban'.

38   *A Second Letter to a Member of Parliament, Recommending the Improvement of the Irish-fishery* (Dublin, printed by A. Rhames, 1729). 30p. 8vo. Published anonymously. Account Book A has an entry in October 1729: 'Mr Rhames printed 750 Bks of 2 sheets about the Fishery for 4 li; paid afterwd 1 li 8s 0'. A more detailed account appears in Account Book B and provides splendid details of current production costs and of the varieties of wrapper in which pamphlets were distributed:

'Printing work done by A Rhames for ye Lord Bishop of Down & Connor

	£	s	d
For printing ye encouraging ye Irish Fishery containing two sheets num 750 Paper & print	4	0	0
For Eight Quires of Dutch Demy at one & eight pence by Quire	0	12	0
For six Quires of Marble Paper at Two shillings ye Quire	0	12	0
For Three Quires of Dutch Blue Paper at ten pence ye Quire	0	2	6
For stiching Folding, Pasting & cutting Four hundred at one & Eight pence ye Hundred	0	6	8
For One Quire of Dutch Demy Gilt	0	1	4
For One Quire of Propatria Gilt	0	0	10
For a Quarter of a pound of Wax	0	2	0
	5	5	4

(Unless there was an extremely hefty discount, Rhames clearly could not add, nor indeed could he multiply; the Bishop's memory would also appear to have been faulty.) Rhames goes on to account for the balance of sheets in his possession: 'I do acknowledg to have in my hande Three hundred & Fifty Pamphlets Entituled a second Lett to a member of Parliament &c: which I promis to be answerable for to ye Lord Bishop of Down or for as many as I have in my hands whensoever your Lordship shall demand them as witness my hand this 26th day of April 1729. A Rhames'.

39 *A Defence of the Antient Historians: with a Particular Application of it to the History of Ireland* (Dublin, printed by S. Powell, for John Smith and William Bruce, 1734). xv, 174p. 8vo. Published anonymously. The *Defence* was also issued in the same year, under a cancel title-page stating authorship, with the addition of two of Hutchinson's sermons delivered before he came to Ireland. In the previous year the preface to the *Defence* was printed on its own and without author by George Grierson, but this may not have gone on public sale.

40 E.R.McC. Dix and Séamus Ua Casaide, *List of Books, Pamphlets, etc., printed... in Irish,... to 1820* (Dublin, 1905).

41 Obituary, *Belfast News-letter*, 26 June 1739.

42 Copy of Hutchinson's will in the Adair papers, Public Record Office of Northern Ireland (PRONI 3860/D/7).

43 Obituary, *London Magazine*, September 1758.

44 *A Catalogue of Books: being the Library of the Right Rev. Dr. Francis Hutchison* [sic], *late Bishop of Down and Connor. To be sold by Auction, by William Ross, at the Coffee-House of ... the House of Lords, on Monday, the twenty-sixth of April 1756. The Sale to begin every Day at eleven o'clock in the Forenoon.* ([Dublin, 1756]). 18[ie.20]p. 8vo.

45 Francis O'Kelley, *Irish Book-sale Catalogues before 1801* (Dublin, 1953), *passim.*

46 The principal place for book auctions in Dublin from about 1698 had been Dick's Coffee House, owned by Richard Pue who was later a successful newspaper proprietor. His son, also Richard, a bookseller, printer and publisher, had conducted book auctions from 1743 until 1746, when William Ross made his first appearance as an auctioneer for the younger Pue. Ross's earliest known sale in his own right took place in May 1748, also at Dick's Coffee House (advertisement in *The Dublin Journal*), and his last known in January 1764. He had a bookshop in Grafton Street from 1755 until his death in 1765. His shop stock was auctioned in March 1766 by Michael Duggan, who seems to have taken on Ross's mantle as auctioneer at the Lords' Coffee House, which was actually within the precincts of the Parliament House. Several of Ross's sales were of libraries of eminent ecclesiastics, including Hugh Boulter and John Hoadley, Archbishops of Armagh, and Robert Downes, Bishop of Raphoe. See further O'Kelley, *Irish Book-sale Catalogues, passim*; and Robert Munter, *A Dictionary of the Print Trade in Ireland 1550-1775.* (New York, 1988).

47 Marjorie Plant, *The English Book Trade: an Economic History*, second edition (London, 1965), p. 245.

48 Philip Gaskell, *A New Introduction to Bibliography* (Oxford, 1972), p. 179.

49 Mary Pollard, *Dublin's Trade in Books, 1550-1800* (Oxford, 1989), pp. 131-35.

157

50 I am indebted to Mary Pollard for making available to me details on Timothy Hinds from the materials for the *Dictionary of the Dublin Booktrade to 1800* which she has in preparation. Miss Pollard has no references to any 'Mr Rogers' in the trade, although it is perhaps just possible that this may have been a *nom de guerre* disguising someone else.

THE ULSTER POETS AND LOCAL LIFE
1790-1870

ALAN GAILEY

FEW WRITERS IN RECENT TIMES have made a more substantial contribution to documenting the realities of local daily life in Ulster's past than Ronnie Adams. His *The Printed Word and the Common Man* (Belfast, 1987) contributed fundamentally to our understanding of the popular culture of the north of Ireland in the eighteenth and nineteenth centuries, drew important conclusions from intractable materials, and has subsequently been widely quoted in similar work in other regions. Ronnie's interest and meticulous work in the elucidation of popular culture continued thereafter. Alongside work at the Ulster Folk and Transport Museum preparing a dictionary of Ulster dialects, he compiled a substantial listing of literary works which draw on the richness of local dialects. Inevitably he was therefore drawn into an interest in the writings of the local poets, both those who wrote in dialect, or with some dialect content, and others whose work was in standard English. This brief article is written in tribute to a much admired librarian, a fine research worker and writer, and a very good friend. It essays to bring together a number of Ronnie's interests, in understanding local popular culture, in local literature and language, and in combining the interests of two institutions which are collections-based, the library and the museum.

Local poetry as documentation of the details of local lifestyles has been a much neglected source for research, particularly in respect of material culture. Sixteen poets have been referred to who provide mainly incidental references to such themes as housing and living conditions, craftwork, agricultural technology, and transport. Their work spans eight decades, onwards from the early 1790s. Mostly they were weavers and farmers, but a few were from well-to-do backgrounds, like the cleric John Anketell, born about 1750, or were from professional backgrounds like Henry McDonald Flecher, a school teacher who emigrated to Texas in 1871 and died there in about 1910.

Some of these poets were not well educated men – and they were all men. Francis Boyle[1] was a farmer at Gransha, to the south of Belfast and not far from Comber, whose *Miscellaneous Poems* were published in Belfast in 1811. He told that:

> My father and my mother dead
> By labour hard I earn'd my bread,
> Without a guardian or a guide,
> In peasants' cots I did reside,
> Whare nane could either read or write –
> Our language rough and unpolite.

Hugh Porter worked as a weaver at Moneyslan in County Down and he, too, protested:

> I naething write by rule,
> For o' the knowledge taught at school
> Mine was a very scanty share,
> I only learn'd the letters there.

The value of the evidence of local life their poetry provides is that these poets were either, like Boyle and Porter, of the common man, or like Anketell, Flecher or the linen bleacher Thomas Stott of Dromore in County Down, people who as a consequence of their professional or commercial work were intimately associated with ordinary folk.

House and home

References to the materials of which houses were built are few. Boyle in 1811 has a fine poem on the death of a local thatcher, and we know that in his time thatch was the ubiquitous roof covering in rural areas.[2] However he was critical of the abilities and attitudes of the younger generation of craftsmen, when compared with the deceased Edward Mills. In frustration he ended his poem:

> But now our thatchers maun hae twa [shillings per day],
> It is weel seen auld Ned's awa';
> Their mornin' tea an' glass o' raw,
> We maun repeat;
> They may gae hing in halters a',
> We'll theek wi' slates.

Slated roofs were still not generally seen a generation later when Edward Sloan, a Conlig weaver, wrote of a money-grasping pub owner, Mrs Sleek, that she kept her road-side drink shop 'In a neat house, two stories and slated'. Statistical evidence for the period shows that only one in four of rural houses had slated roofs, but less than five per cent had two stories.[3] Some poorer houses in Sloan's time, like his own, were built of clay walls, and the remains of a couple like this can still be seen on the roadside midway between Donaghadee and Bangor. Andrew McKenzie, of Dunover, near Ballywalter in the Ards peninsula, in 1810 described his house, which had only one room:

> My mansion is a clay-built cot,
> My house would scarcely load a cart;
> So little straw defends its roof,
> Against the rain it is not proof.

Some details of the interior arrangements of the poorer, smaller houses are recorded. Samuel Thomson was a schoolmaster who lived near Templepatrick, County Antrim and published in 1793 an elegy on a ruined house. He tells of the tenant having had his chair close to the *hallan*, the local word denoting the screen-wall between entrance and hearth in the hearth-lobby house type. This is perhaps the earliest unequivocal reference we have to this vernacular architectural feature. Seven decades later Flecher, another schoolmaster, refers to the previous season's last sheaf of harvest being removed from the *brace*, before the new season's one was brought into the house. The brace was either a beam across the kitchen from the front of the house to the back, and supported on the end of the hallan, or it was a lofted area supported by this beam and the top of the hallan, extending over the hearth area. Thomas Beggs of Glenwherry in County Antrim refers to the *lum*, that is the chimney, as being big enough to hang a lamp within it to light the *ingle-side*. This may well have been a clay-plastered basket-work chimney canopy, although not necessarily associated with a hallan or supported on a brace.[4]

As well as Beggs, Boyle, John McKinley in 1819, Andrew McEwan who worked as an apothecary in Downpatrick in a poem published in 1846, and Sloan, all refer to the ingle. The word is of Scots origin, and means simply the kitchen fire and hearth area; Sloan tells of 'a seat by the bright blazing ingle', McEwan that 'The light beams frae the kitchen-ingle', Boyle that 'A guid seed ingle bleezes bright' in a corn mill, and McKinley evokes the domestic socialising which characterised Irish rural life: 'See roun' the ingle, in a raw, / The rural folks / Sit down and pass the time awa', / In cracks and jokes'. Evidently the word was common usage in the first half of the nineteenth century, but seems to have disappeared from Ulster speech during the following century.

In a bitter poem published in 1848 on the evils of industrialisation and its social consequences for rural folk, David Herbison, 'The Bard of Dunclug' near Ballymena, refers to 'Baith but and ben', the Scots terms for the spaces in a two-roomed cottage. It was lived in by an old woman lamenting her broken teapot. Five decades earlier Thomson refers to '*spence* and *kitchen*' in the 'Cottage in Ruins' near Templepatrick. This is the only known recording of spence in Ulster. The *Shorter Oxford English Dictionary* derives it from late Middle English adaptation from Old French, defining it as a room or separate place in which food is kept; a buttery or pantry; a cupboard; and that in Scots it more broadly refers to an inner apartment of a house, quoting specifically this as a parlour in 1783, only ten years before Thomson published his poem.

Thomson refers to there having been a bed in a corner of the kitchen of the ruined cottage. This might, just conceivably, be an important reference to the existence in the late eighteenth century of a house with bed-outshot in the kitchen on the slopes of Lyles Hill, near Templepatrick,[5] although it may only relate to the overcrowded domestic arrangements of poor people at a time of quite rapid population expansion. Also in 1793

John Anketell records poor people sleeping on bedding of rushes in the north Monaghan district of Stramore. According to Boyle, poor folk sat on seats made of straw bound in some way (perhaps like lip-work) with briars. He refers to such a seat as a *hassock*, a word in more recent times usually associated with ecclesiastical settings. In the 1840s Huddleston refers to stools, when Sloan also notes the 'house-clock' which chimes. This was at a time when, as other evidence suggests, possession of a clock in the home was regarded as something of a rural status symbol.[6]

The poets cited in this article record changing domestic plenishings at the less affluent social levels during the period surveyed. Earlier ones, like Boyle, tell of use of ram-horn spoons, and of stave-built containers. The mill-pout, a poor soul who eked a living around the activities of the corn mill, bequeathed:

> My ram-horn spoons an' noggins three,
> That John the cadger made to me,
> My dishes turn'd by McAfee,
> I lea' them a',
> Wi' a' the thrashtries that ye see,
> To Kate McCaw.

> My chamber-pot, or member-mug,
> My sowen-crock, my guid black jug,
> My sma' hoop'd can, wi' iron lug,
> An' my sma' sark,
> An' my claes-box, sae clean an' snug,
> To Maggy Clark.

Although Flecher in the 1840s suggested that some would 'eat praties and kail to a salt herrin's tail / With devil a fork or a knife', and Flecher then also was recording the continuing use of stave-built noggins in the end-of-harvest rural festival of 'The Churn', by contrast Herbison, as we have seen, wrote his 'Auld Wife's Lament for her Teapot', incidentally telling of use of a table-cloth on the table in this poor house. Much earlier, James Orr of Ballycarry tells of the delft tea-cup used by the local spae-wife to foretell the future.

Three of the poets provide listings of domestic plenishings. Some of the mill-pout's few belongings have already been noted in Boyle's poem of 1811. Thomas Stott in 1825 provides evidence from a different context, in 'A Grocer's List of Goods, for Sale in a Country Town':

> Candles I keep that burn so bright,
> You'd think the sun had risen at night
> ... Horn combs for weavers and for vermin.
> Frying pans, shovels, pots and griddles,
> Tobacco, pipes, and strings or fiddles,
> ... Inkpowder, pencils, quills, and papers,
> For scholars, clerks, and linen-drapers.
> Bibles and Psalters bound in calf,
> And story-books to make you laugh.
> Cards, to amuse the rural gambler,
> Light lanterns for the nightly rambler.

Andrew McKenzie's 'A Poor Man's Petition to the ... Governors of the County of Down', purporting to be from Philip McClabber, of Cabin-comfortless, near Ballywalter, on December 18, 1807, provides the most remarkable of these listings. It is the only inventory of a poor person's dwelling known to exist[7] and provided a basis for furnishing the one-room dwelling in the Ulster Folk and Transport Museum, which, however, as a building, represents social realities some three generations later. McKenzie's lines, almost one third of his poem, are worth quoting in full here, without commentary:

> A spade, by wearing much abus'd,
> A spinning-wheel, but little us'd;
> Three stools, one larger than the rest
> Our table when we have a guest;
> A basket variously employ'd,
> Tho' nearly by old age destroy'd,
> It holds potatoes raw, or boil'd,
> And serves to rock our youngest child;
> A leaky tub, a pot unsound,

With iron hoop encircled round;
A jug, in which we daily bring,
Our humble bev'rage from the spring.
In order, on a shelf of stone,
(For chest or cupboard here is none)
A dish, and three old plates are plac'd;
Three noggins, much by time defac'd;
A mug, from which the ear is parted;
An old knife, by its haft deserted;
Two tea-cups, one of which is crack'd;
Three saucers, each with some defect;
A tea-pot, but the lid is lost;
A beechen bowl, but so emboss'd
With clasps, it can't be understood,
Whether of iron made or wood.
And in a corner by the wall,
We have a bed which cannot fall,
But let this not create surprise -
Securely on the ground it lies;
To furnish it no flocks of geese,
Were plunder'd of their downy fleece,
Plain straw it is ... and o'er this bed,
The ruins of a quilt are spread.
Now nothing else to me belongs,
Except a broken pair of tongs;
And for a shift until they're mended,
We use a branch of willow bended.

Working life

The informal craft activity so widespread in pre-industrial rural life has
already been encountered in Boyle's references to the cadger's making of
domestic plenishings owned by the mill-pout – horn spoons and stave-built
wooden containers for liquids, and to the dishes turned, possibly from
beech wood, by McAfee the turner, in the Gransha area. Huddleston in
1844 in his evocative long poem on Belfast also refers to ladles on sale by
a wood turner, as well as to the tinker's tinwares. Otherwise, Boyle, too,

in his tale of the mill-pout, tells that it was her parents who could make the seats 'o' strae an' briers', an ability to work with materials readily available in any rural area, remnants of which have survived in the museum collections of today, for example straw-work,[8] textiles and some wood-working.

It is possibly not surprising that it was Boyle alone amongst our poets who had much to say about local craftsmen. He was a farmer, so very dependent on craft products for his survival. The weavers seldom reflected in their poetry on their work; rather the nature of their work gave them ample opportunity for reflectiveness in so many other areas: religion, politics, philosophy, love, the masonic brotherhood, and the work of brother bards including Robert Burns. Boyle's poems on the local thatcher, Edward Mills, and on 'Owre Hamely; or, The Famous Basket Maker' have been mentioned.

> Auld Edward was a worthy man,
> A first-rate in the thatchin' clan,
> He co'ert ilk house wi' nimble han'
> An' cam' guid speed,
> Nae wonder now we a' leuk wan,
> Ned Mills is dead!'

Boyle's poem makes it clear that Mills's thatching was with 'scobes' driven through the straw into underlying scraw, or sod, and he explained:

> The guid saugh scobes that ware weel bent,
> He drave their points a' up aslant;
> This hinder't rain to get a vent,
> That through might seep'.[9]

Like his rural contemporaries, Mills turned his hand in season to other activities. Shortly before his death;

> The ither mornin' in a glint,
> Wi' his guid mell as hard as flint,
> Auld Edward bruist twa stooks o' lint,
> Stript to his sark,

and followed that by attending a funeral, and after;

> Ere he had gaen a perch or twa,
> As I do declare,
> He on the frozen groun' did fa'
> An spak nae mair!'

Perhaps his collapse was not too surprising in one past ninety years of age!

In his work on the basket-maker, Boyle tells of the knowledge of local materials essential to the local craftsman:

> He cow't the knowes whar grey saughs grew,
> An' guid aish suckers left but few,
> He down the willow wands did hew,
> An' alders young,
> He snig't the holly souples through,
> An' hazel rung.
> ... Michaelmas moon he looed fu' weel,
> She shone - he saw the rods to steal,
> Guid osiercraft to make a creel,
> About midnight,
> ... O' baskets he made hunners ten,
> Folk far an' near did for them sen',
> What we'll do now I dinna ken.

In his 'On Presenting a Plough to a Clergyman', Boyle is understandably at home in alluding to the details of a good plough, the product of local skills in wood-working and black-smithing.

The plough described by Boyle was wooden framed, but his reference to a two-horse team of 'A fittie-furr an' fittie-lan' suggests that its construction was already influenced by improved ideas which had come mainly from Scotland during Boyle's own lifetime.[10] On the other hand, he was less than complimentary about other incoming improved ploughs:

This pleugh's no made to rin on wheels,
Like them at Hampton town or Sheals;
Or others, made by Scottish chiels,
Poor silly gowks;
Sic pleughs wad never till our fields,
Amang the rocks.

And he went on to complain of the high prices asked for such implements. Francis Davis a generation after Boyle also showed his knowledge of ploughs and their parts in County Down, and his contemporary Robert Young wrote a song for the Ramelton Farming Society in north Donegal 'Success to the Plough', advocating agricultural improvement, nevertheless recording the co-existence of tillage by both plough and spade that was to survive in that part of Ulster long after his own time.

Pre-improvement harvesting, of both hay and corn crops, is recorded by five of our poets. In his list of goods on sale in a country shop in 1825, Thomas Stott refers to 'scythes and sickles, in their seasons'. Seasonality in trading in implements is quite understandable, and, indeed was responsible for seasonal production of them in local manufactories, like the spade mills.[11] When in his long poem on 'The Year's Holidays' Edward Sloan reaches the month of June he sees the mowing of the hay crop with the scythe, and rather romantically, for he was a weaver and not a farmer, he claims that;

The haymakers, with ready will,
Pursue their tasks with lightsome song
Their hours merrily dance along.

It was not long after Sloan's time that the first of the horse-drawn mowing machines became available.

Three of the poets record the reaping of the corn crop with sickles: Francis Davis, a Belfast man by birth but who knew County Down well, and later became a librarian at the Queen's College in Belfast, and Samuel Walker who lived at Shane's Hill in south Antrim, both tell of the use of this hand-tool in the 1840s. Walker did so in the context of a long account of 'The Churn; or The Last Day of Harvest', a theme repeated two decades later by Henry McDonald Flecher of Ballinderry in south Antrim. Both tell of the throwing of their sickles by the reapers at the last of the standing corn, plaited in a ritualistic last sheaf, the shearing of which was seen as bringing good luck. This is romanticised documentation of a seasonal custom which has been commented on in detail elsewhere.[12] However, Davis's poem is published with a long head-note which is invaluable for the account it gives of the organisation in the field of the arduous labour of shearing the corn crop by hand. The poem is entitled 'Low and Clean', which Davis tells us was the farmer's instruction to his reapers how to cut the crop. As technical documentation the poem itself is of little value; but the headnote tells of the competitive spirit instilled into the work by the farmer's careful selection of the best and quickest workers to lead different teams, and to drive them from behind.

He knows that each reaper from the leader to the driver is supposed to keep about the 'making' of the sheaf in the rear of the hook immediately preceding him; that the line thus formed is, under ordinary circumstances, to be kept unbroken; and that, therefore, on the exertions of the 'stubble-hook' and 'corn-land' depend, in a great measure, the amount of labour to be accomplished by the hooks at work between them.

Transport

Thomas Stott, the Dromore, County Down linen bleacher, wrote from personal experience in his 'The Brown Linen-Buyers' of riding on horseback to the brown linen markets to buy webs of cloth from the weavers for bleaching. Horseback was still the common mode of transport for many people then. Slightly later, when John Williamson published his poem on the Ardglass fishing fleet, distribution of goods still relied heavily on animal power. He wrote:

> And there is the cadger, with worn out hack,
> And with panniers of hazel tough,
> With a saddle of straw on his horse's back,
> And a girth of the self-same stuff;
> From his home on the mountain he travels all day,
> His children's lives to preserve,
> And purchases fish at the harbour quay,

To retail them when trudging his homeward way,
And exists where another would starve.

Seven years on, in 1846, Robert Huddleston, a farmer-weaver from Moneyrea south of Belfast, published a remarkable, long poem describing Belfast's 'Lammas Fair'. He sees;

Asses bound between their creels,
Fill'd fu' o' bra' big herrin';
Here, ither beece wi' prataes, meals.

All travelling the market-ward road alongside the solid-wheeled cars and the larger-capacity Scotch carts, and a more elaborate passenger-carrying phaeton.

However, the railway had come to Belfast five years earlier, when the line to Lisburn opened in 1839.

Ohone! 'tis aul' Nick chain'd on wheels,
Wi' reekin' fiery furnace;
Wha's targin' on a train o' hells,
Back, forret tae Lisburnes.

In Belfast harbour a similar contrast was already evident in sea transport, in the contemporaneous docking of square-rigged sailing ships and early steam-driven ones:

A fiery finch on water sweam,
'Gain win' an' tide sae free, ay:
... And 'way she went, O losh! a ship
'Thout sail, like snorin' thun'er,
Right fast that day.

Huddleston sees, too, a sailing ship heading down Belfast Lough, past Black Head, carrying emigrants to America, echoing James Orr's 'The Passengers' which records a ship carrying emigrants away to America in the aftermath of the 1798 Rebellion, as Orr himself had fled after the Battle of Antrim.[13]

....

The value of the local poetry of Ulster in documenting the nature of aspects of the material side of life is quite evident. The dialect terminology is important for what it tells about details of dwellings in particular, and also for its own linguistic significance. However, by bringing together the work of a range of poets, sidelights are thrown on technical and social change occurring in Ulster in the first half of the nineteenth century. We have seen hints of this in relation to the use of slates in roofing, the change from wooden to earthenware containers for liquids amongst ordinary folk, in the suspicion of a countryman about the value of new plough types becoming available about 1810, and thirty years later, the revolution of steam power applied to transport was commencing.

It was in Ulster's economic mainstay of linen production, however, that technical change and its social consequences were being most acutely felt. David Herbison's view of the evils of industrialisation has been quoted from his 'The Auld Wife's Lament for her Teapot' published in 1848. Fourteen years earlier Thomas Beggs published 'The Auld Wife's Fareweel to her Spinning Wheel'. Hand spinning of flax yarn was fast disappearing. He contrasts the lot of young women who had formerly worked at home at their wheels, with now having to work in mills;

In a hot-bed rank wi' vice an' disease.
An' when they speak, it maun be wi' a squeal;
They maun rise an' rin at the toll o' a bell,
An' brook the insult o' a tyrant an' de'il,
An' the jargon they hear is the language o' hell'.

And as for the old widow woman left on her own in the country:

An' now the poke an' the staff I maun tak',
An' wander awa', an awmous to beg,
... For the lords o' the mill and machine ha'e decreed
That bodies like me maun beg their bread'.

171

Poets and Poems Cited

To minimise burdening this article with references to quotations from poems referred to, all of the poets and their poems cited are listed here, in approximate chronological order by the dates of publication of their volumes of poetry:

Samuel Thomson: 'Elegy. The Cottage in Ruins', in *Poems on Different Subjects, partly in the Scottish Dialect* (Belfast, 1793).

John Anketell: 'On Stramore Patron', in *Poems on Several Subjects* (Dublin, 1793).

James Orr: 'The Passengers', 'The Spae-Wife', in *Poems on Various Subjects* (Belfast, 1804).

Andrew McKenzie: 'A Poor Man's Petition to the Right Honourable, and Honourable, the Governors, and Deputy Governors of the County of Down', in *Poems and Songs on Different Subjects* (Belfast, 1810).

Francis Boyle: 'Preface', 'The Mill-Pout. A Tale', 'Owre Hamely; or, The Famous Basket-Maker', 'Elegy on the Death of Edward Mills', 'On Presenting a Plough to a Clergyman', in *Miscellaneous Poems* (Belfast, 1811).

Hugh Porter: 'The Author's Preface', in *Poetical Attempts* (Belfast, 1813).

John McKinley: 'A Winter Night in the North of Ireland', in *Poetic Sketches Descriptive of the Giants' Causeway and the Surrounding Scenery: with some Detached Pieces* (Belfast, 1819).

Thomas Stott: 'A Grocer's List of Goods, for Sale in a Country Town' in *The Songs of Deardra* (London, 1825).

Thomas Beggs: 'The Auld Wife's Fareweel to her Spinning Wheel' in *The Minstrel's Offering. Original Poems and Songs* (Belfast, 1834).

John Williamson: 'The Fishing Fleet', in *Poems on Various Subjects* (Belfast, 1839).

Robert Young: 'Success to the Plough' (referring to a ploughing match in 1843), in *The Poetical Works of Robert Young of Londonderry* (Londonderry, 1863).

172

Francis Davis: 'The County Down', 'Low and Clean: a Harvest Melody', collected in *Earlier and Later Leaves: or, an Autumn Gathering* (Belfast, 1878), but published earlier separately.

Robert Huddleston: 'The Lammas Fair', in *A Collection of Poems and Songs, on Rural Subjects* (Belfast, 1844); 'Epistle to a Friend, on Courtship' in *A Collection of Poems and Songs on Different Subjects*, vol. II (Belfast, 1846).

David Herbison: 'The Auld Wife's Lament for her Teapot', first published in *Midnight Musings; or, Thoughts from the Loom* (1848) and recast and republished by Herbison in *The Children of the Year; with Other Poems and Songs* (1876). Again republished in *The Select Works of David Herbison with Life of the Author by Rev David M'Meekin, Ballymena* (Belfast, 1883).

Edward L. Sloan: 'Mrs. Sleek', 'The Year's Holidays', in *The Bard's Offering: a Collection of Miscellaneous Poems* (Belfast, 1854).

Henry McDonald Flecher: 'The Churn', in *Rhymes and Ravings* (Belfast, 1859); 'Let the Harrows Sough over the Rigs', in *Poems, Songs and Ballads* (Belfast, 1866).

Notes

1   My colleague Dr Philip Robinson tells me that the usual spelling of the family name was Boal, for example on family gravestones, and the title page of the poet's volume of verse is the only recorded spelling as Boyle.

2   Alan Gailey, *Rural Houses of the North of Ireland* (Edinburgh, 1984), p. 94.

3   Alan Gailey, 'A View of Irish Rural Housing in the 1840s' in *Rural Landscapes and Communities*, edited by Colin Thomas (Blackrock, 1986), p. 127.

4   See Gailey, *Rural Houses*, chapters 6 and 8 for a discussion of the features referred to in this paragraph.

5   Gailey, *Rural Houses*, pp. 151-56 for discussion of the bed outshot. The writer examined a house with outshot, in a derelict state in the early 1960s, at Connor, some miles north of Lyles Hill.

6   Gailey, *Rural Houses*, p. 217.

7   Domestic inventories for Ulster homes are few at any social level; the only
     known significant collection is from an eighteenth-century Quaker
     community in County Armagh: see A. Gailey, 'The Ballyhagan
     Inventories, 1716-1740', *Folk Life*, 15(1977), 36-64.

8   K. M. Harris, 'Plaited Straw-work', *Ulster Folklife*, 9(1963), 53-60.

9   Boyle describes the scollop-thatching technique, fully explored in R. H.
     Buchanan, 'Thatch and Thatching in North-East Ireland', *Gwerin*, 1,
     no. 3 (1957), 123-42, and in Gailey, *Rural Houses*, pp. 94-107.

10   J. Bell, and M. Watson, *Irish Farming 1750-1900* (Edinburgh, 1986),
     Chapter 4.

11   Seasonal production in spade mills is discussed in A. Gailey, *Spade-
     making in Ireland* (Holywood, 1983), pp. 105-6, 117-23.

12   A. Gailey, 'The Last Sheaf in the North of Ireland', *Ulster Folklife*,
     18(1972), 1-23.

13   D. H. Akenson and W. H. Crawford, *Local Poets and Social History: James
     Orr, Bard of Ballycarry* (Belfast, 1977), pp. 8, 10-17.

A TALE OF TWO NEWSPAPERS: THE CONTEST BETWEEN THE BELFAST NEWS-LETTER AND THE NORTHERN STAR IN THE 1790S

JOHN GRAY

WHEN, IN SEPTEMBER 1791, leading Belfast radicals set about establishing a new reforming newspaper, the future *Northern Star*, they did so, as befitted their status as leading merchants of the town, in a thoroughly business-like way. The committee of twelve proprietors were probably the first people to manage an Irish newspaper as a board of directors,[1] though in the case of the *Star* such business modernity was tempered by another modernity, that of the political enlightenment, decreeing revolving responsibilities within the committee,[2] and, crucially, the principle that 'where diversity of opinion may arise ... the subscribers shall invariably be governed by the decision of the absolute majority',[3] that is in distinction to government according to weight of shareholding.

In Belfast the committee secured pledges of support from 136 leading citizens, and, thus encouraged, sent a prospectus throughout the province. They were concerned not merely with the political desirability of such a paper, but with its viability. Would those canvassed subscribe and secure other subscribers? Would they advertise, or, provide the *Northern Star* with 'at least an equal share' of the advertising previously monopolised by the *Belfast News-letter*?

Their systematic preparations were well advised. In 1791 it was by no means clear that a new radical newspaper could win sufficient backing; the heady days of 1792 lay ahead. Henry Joy, editor and part owner at the *News-letter*, with his mainstream whiggism which had embraced support for the French Revolution, still served many adequately. Thus the future United Irishman, and Presbyterian minister, Thomas Ledlie Birch remained 'on the most friendly footing with Mr Joy', and, what was more, found that his views received adequate coverage in the *News-letter*.[4]

The new would–be press magnates were indeed up against a formidable rival in Joy,[5] and one fully versed in the wiles of the radical press. When he assumed editorship and part ownership of the *News-letter* in 1782, he was simultaneously Assistant Secretary of the Volunteer Movement, then at the height of its powers. He had helped draft the resolutions at the celebrated Dungannon Volunteer Convention of the same year, and had used his newspaper to the full in the cause. His personal scrapbook of the period, appropriately labelled 'fugitive political pieces',[6] reveals him writing pseudonymously to his own newspaper to support 'more equal representation', and under the *nom de plume* of 'Lucas', thus adopting the mantle of the mid-eighteenth century Dublin patriot and journalist Charles Lucas.[7] He used his press, again in 1782, to run off Henry Flood's broadside address, *To the People*, which was 'given by him to me to have printed and distributed among the Volunteers at the Belfast Review'.[8]

Although Joy's ardour soon cooled, his experience had helped him see off two successive challenges from more radical quarters in the 1780s. *The Belfast Mercury, or Freeman's Chronicle* was launched by John Tisdall on 1 August 1783 to fulfil the need, apparently not served by the *News-letter*, for 'an independent and spirited newspaper'. Tisdall survived denunciation by the Irish House of Commons in February 1784 for publishing Volunteer resolutions, but sold out to William Magee in May 1786.[9]

The Magees had a pedigree as Belfast printers and booksellers stretching back to 1736. They also had an immediate and radical journalistic connection in William's Dublin based brother, John, who, as editor of the *Dublin Evening Post*, was already notorious for the vehemence of his opposition to the government controlled press, and was later to be jailed many times in the cause.[10] William Magee may have followed his brother's Dublin precedent in transforming *The Belfast Mercury* into *The Belfast Evening Post*, but in this guise it survived a bare 30 weeks.

All this experience now became available to the *Northern Star*. William Magee was one of the twelve founding proprietors.[11] John Tisdall, although not a proprietor, printed the first seven issues of the paper from January 1792 and provided the printing equipment with which to do it.[12] When he withdrew from this leading role, one of his own printers, John Rabb, succeeded him.

The funding demands of such a venture were large. The capital of the company was increased to £1,600 in March 1792, and when finally incorporated in June 1792, the twelve shareholders had raised their pledge still further to £2,000. In November, Samuel Neilson, both the principal shareholder and manager, was warning his colleagues that 'at least 25% [was] required to complete [the] capital'.[13]

The costs of purchasing their own press with its 'bourgeois' type,[14] and of furbishing their premises in High Street, were as nothing to the costs of establishing a viable circulation, most of which had to be found outside the still relatively small town of Belfast. In this respect paid agents had to establish the basic distribution networks in the countryside, and recruit the paid carriers who would maintain it.[15] As with the *News-letter*, the agent would make an advertised annual tour to collect subscriptions and advertising revenue due. The *Northern Star* enjoyed an early advantage over the *News-letter* in one respect only in its ability to rely on voluntary representatives in many locations.[16] Nonetheless the *Star* calculated that nearly 20% of its subscription income was expended on distribution costs.[17]

Furthermore, in its first year the *Star* faced an inescapable cash flow problem. The annual subscription for the *Northern Star* ranged from 16s to 19s, depending on location,[18] but many of those anxious to subscribe had already paid an advance subscription to the *News-letter* for the current year, and very few could afford to subscribe to both, thus the *Northern Star* agent reported from Loughgall on 30 January 1792 that 'there will be a good many more subscribers got again their years out with Mr Joy'.[19] Thanks to its sound capital base the *Star* was able to offer the unprecedented terms of subscription in arrears. Meanwhile sales of single issues at two pence undercut the *News-letter* by a half-penny but gave a bare penny of revenue after payment of stamp duty, hardly a profitable margin. Circulation was indeed maximised, probably rising to a peak of 4,200 at a relatively early stage in the life of the paper.[20]

In one respect this strategy paid off. Helped by the still buoyant local

177

economy, the *Star* from the outset secured substantial advertising from the Belfast business community. Meanwhile both newspapers benefited from the torrent of political advertising characteristic of the very brief era of open and public politics in 1792. In that year and in early 1793, the *Star's* financial tactics, though certainly high risk, appeared potentially viable and sufficiently so that the proprietor's agreed to pay the already affluent Samuel Neilson £100 a year for his role as manager and editor.[21]

Both in business and politics there was much duplication of advertising between the *Star* and *News-letter*. This was most clearly illustrated when the proprietors of the *Star* faced their first prosecutions for printing seditious advertisements in December 1792. Six informations were filed against them, but in five of these cases the advertisements had also appeared in the *News-letter*. Two of the cases were eventually brought to trial in 1794, and in one of these trials, a prosecution for publishing the United Irishmen's address to the Volunteers on 19 December 1792, the defence was able to establish, and from a prosecution witness, that the advertisement had first appeared on the preceding day in the *News-letter*.[22]

These prosecutions presaged the government clampdown on the United Irishmen from December 1792 onwards, and with the suppression of the Volunteers and the outbreak of war with France coming in early 1793, the climate in which the *Star* sought to survive, let alone prosper, became dramatically more difficult.

The Attorney General seeking to convict the proprietors in their first trial in May 1794 now made much of the non-economic nature of their venture – they were 'not engaging in such a business as this for fair gain and profit, for they appear to have circulated this paper at a price *far below what was usual*, which evinces that their only object was sedition'.[23] By the end of the year Samuel Neilson and the remaining proprietors could hardly dissent from the economic side of this judgement – 'the circulation of the *Northern Star*' had resulted '(for the last three years) with a constant loss to the proprietors'.[24]

In these circumstances the pressures, both economic and political, to do a deal with government were considerable. As early as April 1793 Thomas Russell in his 'Journal' noted that 'it was in contemplation to sell the *Northern Star* to government' and by July that 'the business was out', that is that the proprietors 'thought they were deserted by the rest of the kingdom and did the best they could' in securing an offer of 'No prosecution. No politicks'.[25] Only the uniquely democratic structure of the paper, with decisions depending on the absolute majority vote of the subscribers held the line for the more encouraging days of late 1794 and early 1795.[26]

The difficulties of the *Star* were not to benefit Henry Joy, for in November 1794 he advertised the sale of the *News-letter*.[27] The ostensible reason was as part of 'a general sale of various partnership properties, pursuant to a devise in trust'. The sale certainly did not arise from a fall in circulation – Joy advertised a 'progressive encrease' in circulation from 2,050 in January 1789 to 3,225 in July 1794, figures broadly confirmed in a letter to the Scotsman, Robert Allan, in January 1795,[28] although in this the figure for 1794 was revised downwards to 'so high as' 2,904. In March 1795, Allan, now actively considering purchase, sent Charles Gordon, soon to be his editor, to check the figures and he found an average circulation over two issues of 2,742.

Although, by then, a slight fall in circulation had occurred, the advent of the *Northern Star* in 1791 had evidently had no adverse effect on *News-letter* circulation, rather the market for newspapers had vastly expanded, indeed increased at least threefold, with potential space for both titles. Here Joy's explanation was certainly correct – 'you'll observe between 1789 and 1794 the effects of peace and war'. Hence again the explanation of exhaustive coverage in both papers of continental events. Joy even suggested that if peace came *News-letter* circulation might fall back to 2,000.

In his letter to Allan, Joy gave a rather different explanation for the desire to give up the business, being 'tired of the duty of editorship, and conceiving that I can do without it'. Indeed he went further than this – Allan had apparently initially offered to go into partnership, but Joy disabused him – 'our intentions seem to have been misunderstood. None of us wish to continue partners in the business but to sell out the copyright entire'.

Joy could not disguise the economic setback which had affected one aspect of operations namely advertising which had begun to be seriously affected by the difficulties of the local economy arising from the war. In his letter to Allan, Joy conceded that the number of advertisements per issue had fallen from an average of 96 in 1790 to 65 in 1794 with a consequent fall in annual revenue after tax from this source from £1,354 in 1790 to £850 in 1794.

Yet by late 1794 the paper was clearly still profitable, indeed Joy suggested that further revenue could be raised by increasing the price of the paper. Why then, beyond the limp excuse of being 'tired', did Joy, ever a calculator, so determinedly decide to give up all interest in the paper? The best explanation lies in political anticipation, that the possibilities of maintaining a 'moderate' or Whig position in the face of the growing polarisation of political opinion in Ulster were rapidly evaporating.

Joy and his political associates had anticipated such a progression as early as January 1793 when as the Friends of a Parliamentary Reform in Belfast they had foreseen a fearful 'dilemma which cannot hold them long in suspense. They must take part with government, or enlist under the banners of the public. They must either co-operate in establishing a tyranny in their country, or rush into the intemperate measures of an indignant multitude'.[29] Again in 1793 the 'Friends' suggested that in such circumstances 'some may seek a remote retreat', as apparently now in 1794 did the 'tired' Joy. And yet, as we shall see, Joy had in no way lost his enthusiasm for political argument, albeit from a stance where he increasingly supported government measures against the United Irishmen. What he really doubted was the economic viability of a newspaper proceeding in such a direction.

Whatever the complexities of motive behind Joy's sale of the *News-letter*, others clearly took a gloomy view of the prospects for the paper as no serious Irish bidder emerged and the original asking price of £4,000 was quickly reduced to £3,000, and eventually, as Joy's personal scrapbook reveals, 'it was sold by my uncle Henry and myself to Robert Allan of Edinburgh for £1,650'.[30]

Meanwhile the strength of the rival *Star's* distribution network was very publicly advertised with a detailed listing of agents in the various towns given on 15 December 1794. In the absence of comprehensive subscription lists,[31] this advertisement, and similar ones in later years,[32] provide the best evidence of the main areas of *Star* distribution. The 1794 advertisement listed agents in 90 locations including Dublin, Edinburgh, Liverpool and London. Otherwise the greatest strength lay in counties

Antrim (28) and Down (25), and then in declining order in Tyrone (13), Armagh (11), Londonderry (10), Monaghan (5), Fermanagh (4), Cavan (1) and Donegal (1).

This is a pattern which broadly fits in with what is otherwise known about the strength of United Irish organisation, but there are significant points of detail. By far the most intensive network of *Star* agents was to be found in south east Antrim just to the north west of Belfast.[33] There was no similar intensity of coverage in County Down, the other area of general radical strength. Two other areas do, however, show some evidence of a village to village network, namely north Armagh[34] and east Tyrone[35] along the western shores of Lough Neagh. Both areas were already cockpits of sectarian conflict, and publicly advertised and detailed organisation here suggests the resilience of the movement in areas of maximum difficulty.

The listing of agents also suggests that despite low prices and high ambitions to do otherwise, the *Star* remained a paper principally sold by Protestants to Protestants, and thus recognisably within the previous experience of the 18th century Irish press. Thus in County Down the *Star* was represented throughout in strongly Protestant Rathfriland but never in the neighbouring and predominately Catholic Hilltown; again it was represented throughout in Protestant Clough but only found an agent in Catholic Castlewellan as late as 1797. Elsewhere the *Star* was represented in Loughgall, soon to be the founding centre of the Orange Order, and in strongly Protestant villages in east Tyrone, but not in Coalisland, which in size merited attention, but had a predominantly Catholic population.

It was almost certainly easier to secure agents in areas where the enthusiastic support of a Presbyterian minister was available, or indeed the Presbyterian minister might himself act as agent. By contrast Catholic priests might subscribe to the *Star*, but more often were actually hostile to the United cause, no doubt a contributory factor in the difficulty of securing agents in Catholic areas.[36] However, mere analysis of the location of agents cannot tell the whole story, as fragmentary information from the *Star* 'journey books' shows; thus the 1795 'journey book' reveals that there were in fact two subscribers in Coalisland listed amongst 18 'who live near to Dungannon', and, elsewhere, speaking of Cookstown, describes how 'the generality of our subscribers lives in the mountains'.[37]

What lies beyond question is the decline in the *News-letter's* fortunes

181

in the same period and following Joy's handover in March 1795 to the new Scottish team with Charles Gordon as editor. Writing in March 1795 to Dublin Castle, Robert Allan claimed that circulation had fallen from 2,742 in March 1795 to 2,000 or by 26.7%.[38] It is a collapse in fortune that can be examined in detail on the ground with the help of the *News-letter* 'Subscribers List' for the period November 1795 to April 1797.[39] This lists 1,822 names, exclusive of duplication arising from transfers of address, but by the end of the period the active subscriptions had fallen to 1,330. The net loss on this basis amounted to 27%, with many cancellations made by letter, and rather fewer arising from non-payment.

Analysis of the full list shows that the *News-letter's* greatest strength lay along the Lagan Valley and into Armagh. Thus Lisburn provided 93 subscribers, and Armagh with 98 provided the greatest number of any single location. In between, the two relatively small villages of Tandragee and Richhill provided no less than 70 names. The fertile ground in this district was reflected by the complexity of the delivery routes. As a whole this region provided 527 names or 29% of the total circulation.

The contrasting extreme to the Lagan Valley lay in Belfast itself and that area of County Antrim to the north and west of the town, also, as already noted, the area with the strongest network of *Star* representatives. In Belfast the subscription list covers 33 copies to be 'called for in shop', and otherwise only 63 copies delivered in High Street (including, by a nice irony, that to be delivered to the *Star*).

The geographical distribution of *News-letter* circulation suggests strength in areas of Church of Ireland dominance within the Protestant community, and weakness in the Presbyterian heartlands. This in turn suggests the rapidity of political polarisation within the Protestant community in the 1790s. After all until 1792 the *News-letter* had served the entire community, and until 1795 had had a prominent Presbyterian editor in Joy.

Geographical analysis of the losses of subscribers by the *News-letter* between November 1795 and April 1797 suggests significant variations. The most severe damage was done in mid and north Antrim with 46% of subscribers defecting in the period covered by the list. In Ballymena the original 29 subscribers fell to 9. By contrast the small villages along the Lagan Valley and into North Armagh remained virtually unscathed.

When Robert Allan wrote to Dublin Castle in March 1797[40] he made it clear that the tale of woe extended beyond circulation. The number of advertisements per issue had fallen from 65 to 20 during his ownership, and a paper which had been making a profit of £1,222 per annum as at March 1795, was now making less than half of that and the position was still worsening.

In yet another respect the *News-letter's* operations were now seriously constrained. In addition to their role as newspaper publishers, the Joy family had had a distinguished role as publishers of books and pamphlets from 1734 right down to 1794[41] and the publication in the latter year of Henry Joy and William Bruce's major compilation, *Belfast Politics*. In this capacity the *News-letter* press was to remain silent right through to August 1796 when Charles Gordon published a broadsheet address *To the People* extolling the 'prosperity' of the north, and 'the advantages of order'.[42] At roughly the same time he had 'printed several thousand copies of the Bishop of Landaff's *Apology for the Bible*, at so low a price as 6d, in opposition to Paine's *Age of Reason*'.[43]

In neither case were these viable publications in themselves. Gordon had incurred 'considerable expense' with his address *To the People*, only defrayed by an order from the Sovereign of Belfast for 1,000 copies, and subsequently one for 2,000 copies from the Earl of Londonderry. As for the Bishop of Landaff's *Apology*, Gordon had acted from 'duty' and not for 'reward'. His only hope in that respect lay in government favours, indeed it was to government that he was relaying this information.[44]

Gordon's supporters assumed that he lacked the resources available to the *Northern Star*, thus John Lees, overseer of the postal services, wrote to Edmund Cooke at Dublin Castle in August 1796 arguing that Gordon 'at his own expense cannot give his paper the general circulation thro[ugh] the Northern Counties which the United purse of the United Irishmen and the turbulent opulent in different places give to the *Northern Star*'.[45]

In fact this was an increasingly mistaken view. As we have already noted, by late 1794 the proprietors of the *Star* were lamenting a steady loss. Accordingly the price was raised from two pence to two and a half pence and at the beginning of 1795 subscribers who wished to continue to pay in arrears were told it would cost them 'three British shillings' extra. Only those who now subscribed in advance could have the paper at the old price.[46]

Even in 1796, a key year in terms of growing United Irish strength, the 'Journey Book' of the *Star* collector is full of tales of woe. In Ballyclare 'Mr Hunter was very angry at being furnished with an account for an advertisement which he never ordered'. In Ballymena he was informed that 'Mr Monaghan['s subscription] is paid by S Barker Stevenson. There is no such person in or about this town'.[47] Signs of consequent financial strain were more than evident by November when the *Star* apologised for the poor quality of its paper – 'the principal cause of it was on account of large sums which were, and continue to be due to us'.[48]

In March 1797, at precisely the moment when Robert Allan was pleading the *News-letter's* case with Dublin Castle, the *Star* was pleading its case with its subscribers, speaking of 'the shameful conduct of many who have given our young men the trouble of a variety of calls for the merest trifles – (trifles to them, but when taken in aggregate of some thousands, no trifles to the proprietors)!' In these circumstances all former notions of liberal credit arrangements went by the board – 'in future no papers will be forwarded to any person whatever, who does not pay in advance!'[49]

Nor were newspaper proprietors the only complainants in the face of prospective financial catastrophe. Their difficulties were merely part of a generalised Irish financial crisis brought on by the pressures of financing the continental war and marked by acute shortages of actual money. General Lake, writing from Belfast, also in March 1797, was heavily pre-occupied with the dangers arising from his own difficulty in paying his troops, but found time to urge upon Thomas Pelham 'the necessity of some expedient being hit upon to supply the manufacturers of this part of the country with cash to pay their labourers', and warned of the risk that 'many thousands will be out of work'.[50]

The *Star* understandably made much of the financial consequences of the successive prosecutions and arrests of its proprietors,[51] but, even if free, they would hardly have escaped the generalised financial blizzard of the time. We can indeed more generally say that the times from 1795 onwards were bad ones for any newspaper and that a marketplace which until then could readily accommodate two newspapers, was now acutely difficult for both.

There is, however, no doubt that the *Northern Star* was in the stronger

184

position, whether as newspaper publisher or in separate publishing ventures, which in complete contrast to the situation at the *News-letter* expanded right up to 1797.[52] There is the shadowy area of the *Star's* role as printer to the United Irish movement which could hardly be expected to be profitable, but even here it appears that the *Star* served as jobbing and hence paid printer. Thus the *Star* agent on tour in 1793 reported that 'Mr [Charles Hamilton] Teeling will pay the Roman Catholic County Meath meeting and handbills, address to the Peep of Day Boys etc.'[53] In relation to more substantial publications, the picture is confused because for no evidently consistent reason, *Northern Star* publications often failed to carry the *Northern Star* imprint,[54] and, indeed it is further confused by the establishment of a separate but closely linked press at the Public Printing Office by Thomas Storey in 1795 which used its imprint with similar inconsistency.[55]

Nonetheless given the increasing financial problems of the newspaper, it is a reasonable assumption that the *Star's* pamphleteering activities were at least economically self–sustaining. The balance in choice of texts for separate publication was also more obviously market driven, particularly in the case of what Ronnie Adams has described as 'the prophecies [which] flooded off the presses'[56] and were clearly angled at a Presbyterian audience; thus William Staveley's introduction to the reprint of Robert Fleming's *A Discourse on the Rise and Fall of Antichrist* (1795) paid no particular attention to the ecumenical political correctness of the time with its reference to 'those chains of slavery that have been forged by hell and Rome'.[57]

In the hard times which now undoubtedly affected both newspapers old courtesies were soon to be forgotten. As late as January 1794 Henry Joy had offered to delay publication of his *Belfast Politics* until court cases affecting the proprietors of the *Star* were over because he did not wish to prejudice their trial and out of a feeling of 'good neighbourhood'.[58] Charles Gordon on assuming control in March 1795 did not immediately abandon the trappings of Joy's moderation and as late as March 1796 admitted that 'by the competition between the various prints error is most likely to be detected',[59] and yet by then aspects of competition between the two papers which had previously been a matter of course became issues of bitter and public contention.

185

This was most evident with regard to days of publication. The *Star* now recounted how it had originally chosen as publication days 'those most remote from those of the *Belfast News-letter*', thus the *News-letter* appeared on Mondays and Thursdays and the *Star* on Wednesdays and Saturdays. Henry Joy had progressively upset this arrangement to his advantage, first switching one of his days of publication from Thursday to Friday, and then, in October 1793, switching his Monday publication to Tuesdays. The effect was that both *News-letter* issues now came out on the days immediately preceding the *Star*. The *Star* found itself 'forced from the original days of its publication [and] adopted those very days *which had been abandoned by the Belfast News-letter*', and in doing so precisely reversed the advantage in its favour.

Jockeying of this kind continued probably to the mutual disadvantage of both papers, and according to the *Star* account, when Gordon took over as editor of the *News-letter* they approached him to suggest a sensible sharing out of the week. This would be one 'whereby the public would be benefited by four different publications in the week'. What is really meant here is that each of the possible four issues of papers in the week would be sufficiently spaced apart to have new news and in particular because 'they would have an equal number of new packets'.[60]

In the event the *Star* proposal for compromise in 1795 was rejected and now in May 1796 the *Star* adopted a 'unilateral' change to the same days as the *News-letter* while Gordon contemptuously 'pledged himself to retain those days which he at present has'.[61] This in turn brought a cry of 'unprovoked attack' from the *Star* and a demand that the editor of the *News-letter* act with 'more patience and consistency'.[62]

Again in May the *Star* attacked what it called 'blank editors – pusillanimous and self–interested men – who would not lose good advertisements for the liberty of mankind'.[63] The implication was that the *News-letter* was taking government advertising, and yet the accusation was as yet premature if prophetic.

For Charles Gordon, faced by falling revenue, it was an obvious route to pursue. The government had after all by this stage bought much of the Dublin press by direct subsidy or through the placing of advertisements,[64] but by maladroit metropolitan oversight had not apparently yet considered doing so in Belfast. It was not until August 1796 that Gordon began systematically to cultivate influential opinion with the aim of securing government assistance. Lord Downshire, one of several who now interceded with Dublin Castle on his behalf, suggested that 'it gives an open to gain attach[ment] to us one of the printers of that damned sink Belfast'.[65]

The first experiment in such a direction was to prove a disaster to all concerned. On 18 November the *News-letter* was, as it put it, 'authorised and desired to' publish an advertisement relating to the murder of a government supporter, John Kingsbury. In fact the advertisement was placed by Colonel Barbour of the garrison and it recounted how Kingsbury had been attacked by 'a set of ruffians from Belfast', and suggested that these were four United Irishmen now in custody at Carrickfergus. The political sensitivity of the matter was made all the greater because one of those under arrest was Thomas Storey currently running the Public Printing Office, as already noted the second United Irish press in the town.

Subsequently Robert Allan was to claim that the *News-letter* was effectively forced to publish the advertisement. Mr Gordon had thought the advertisement 'improper for publication, as prejudicating the trial' of the four arrested men, and because it 'reflected on the whole town of Belfast where he resides'. Colonel Barbour had insisted on insertion on 'the orders of the commander in chief, and threatening him besides with a protest and prosecution or persecution, in case of refusal, he [Mr Gordon] with reluctance complied'.

As Allan also put it, 'fortunate would it have been if it had never appeared', for as a consequence Gordon, his editor, was 'every day threatened with having his throat cut, his house set on fire, and his family ruined ... even the magistrates, principal merchants and friends of government in Belfast complained loudly of this general attack of libel on the whole town'.[66] Gordon was forced to admit publicly that the advertisement 'has given a good deal of offence to many of his readers' and to name Colonel Barbour as the source,[67] the latter a step that in turn angered Dublin Castle.

Subsequently both Gordon and Allan blamed much of their paper's misfortune on this one episode, a singular illustration of the differing effects of government patronage on beneficiaries in Belfast as against Dublin. It should not, however, be assumed that the *Star* was entirely

187

denied law and order proclamations. After all those at whom such proclamations were directed were more likely to read the *Star*. Even when the *Star* was under great threat from government in March 1797 it received a proclamation from General Lake and no doubt published it under implicit duress though countervailing measures could be taken – on that occasion the publication alongside of General Burgoyne's proclamation to the American citizenry in June 1777, on the eve of the British general's catastrophic defeat.[68]

Of course even by late 1796 matters in Ulster were coming to a head. The *Star*'s editor, Samuel Neilson, was amongst those arrested in September.[69] The *Star* moved closer to direct advocacy of revolt, the *News-letter* more openly advocated its rival's suppression. Nor should it be assumed that Charles Gordon at the *News-letter* had moved beyond any position maintained by erstwhile moderates. Annotations to the Linen Hall Library's 1796 volume of the *News-letter* show that Henry Joy was a substantial contributor to the paper,[70] though now, no doubt, mightily relieved to be free of the burdens of ownership.

In this new and venomous atmosphere, and from November 1796 onwards, both newspapers began to suffer attacks on their distribution networks. On occasion disruption was suffered from on high – Lord Downshire had already been instrumental in urging the suppression of the paper and encouraging the September arrests, and it was hardly surprising that two months later, according to the *Star*, he suppressed Hillsborough Book Club and banned his tenants from subscribing to the paper.[71] Still the *Star* persisted in delivering copies in the area, but in March 1797 'our carrier [was] stopped at Hillsborough – taken before a great person – threatened with the tender [i.e. press ganging for the fleet] – confined for a night and discharged upon swearing to carry no more *Northern Stars*'.[72]

More usually, however, attacks were made on the road and were symptomatic of increasing disorder and polarisation of opinion in some areas, notably in County Armagh. Here the *Star* post boy on the road from Banbridge to Armagh was robbed in late November 1796, and further attacks throughout December largely interrupted deliveries right along the line to Monaghan.[73] As late as May 1797 the *Star* was seeking to re-establish a delivery route from Dromore to Armagh.[74] Similar problems, though on a lesser scale, arose on the road to Coleraine.[75]

Attacks of this kind on the *News-letter* started rather later but on a systematic basis in February 1797. The first recorded incident revealed that the Lord Downshire had not after all succeeded in suppressing United Irish support in his neighbourhood. Two miles from Hillsborough, the *News-letter* carrier on the line from Lisburn to Dromore had all his 400 copies of the paper destroyed. Three days later the carrier on the same route was stopped on the Belfast side of Lisburn and had all his papers thrown into the Lagan. It is tribute to the quality of the newsprint that it was possible to rescue them! Four days later a carrier on the Downpatrick road was attacked at Dundonald, as was a carrier on the road to Portaferry.[76]

The *News-letter* concluded that the attacks were indeed systematic – "for some time past the carriers – have been repeatedly stopt [and] the papers taken from them and destroyed', but there was an alternative, albeit an expensive one – 'no other method remains – than to send the papers through the medium of the post office'.[77]

Here the *Star* was at a disadvantage. Officials in the Belfast Post Office had been assiduous in encouraging the suppression of the *Star*,[78] and on 5 December 1796 the *Star* published a presumably only slightly satirical verse entitled 'The Postmaster's Discovery; or a Plot in a Packet'. The first line ran 'trust not your letter by the post' and the poem described the harrowing misfortunes of the recipient of a bill, which had been opened by post office officials and mistaken for seditious literature. It was hardly now possible for the *Star* to use the post.

Star distribution was more directly threatened in another way by actual official intervention. Both papers on occasion used unstamped paper and paid tax retrospectively. By early 1797 the Stamp Office was tightening up on its procedures in any case with a view to controlling seditious publications more effectively,[79] but in proclaimed districts the position was potentially worse still as an anxious Dungannon correspondent told the *Star* on 13 January.

Here 'a military officer' had threatened that if the newspapers's carrier could be found 'he would send him aboard the fleet' under the regulations affecting proclaimed districts which specified the offence of circulating unstamped seditious literature. The paper's correspondent continued, 'if so, I expect that in the future you will not send it to this town, least some of our neighbours might go aloft'. The fact that the *Star* printed such a communication along with re-assurance, suggests that such worries were affecting many *Star* subscribers.

The same was even truer of *Star* agents. One of the great advantages that the *Star* had had over the *News-letter* was its extensive network of mainly voluntary agents, but in early 1797 the normal annual listing of names and places was replaced by the more covert instruction that 'advertising friends and subscribers' were to deal with 'the gentleman in their respective neighbourhoods, *who were formerly* so kind as to transact the business of the *Star*'.[80]

In the meantime the attempted French landing at Bantry Bay at the end of 1796, and the *Star's* response to it – to discount the seriousness of the threat, to oppose the raising of a militia to meet the threat, and yet to sympathise with French intentions, brought a frontal assault on the paper.

It was precipitated by the publication on 27 January of Arthur O'Connor's 'Address to the Free Electors of the County of Antrim' in which he sought 'an advanced post where he may triumph in her [i.e. Ireland's] cause, or fall in her defence'. O'Connor was soon arrested as were the Simms brothers, the last active proprietors at liberty, and on 3 February the *Star* offices were raided. Colonel Barbour, in charge of the raiding party, had as his immediate objective to 'fix on the types belonging to that paper', and he duly 'packed in a box half of the impression of the last intended publication of that paper, and O'Connor's *Address* – ready for striking off'.[81]

Arrests had now finally smashed the original democratic structure of *Star* management, but underlying it Barbour now found another more revolutionary democracy of 'clerks and [printers'] devils that attend there', men with little to lose and a business plan increasingly infused with political and even religious millenniarism. Accordingly Barbour found them 'fully determined' to recommence publication and immune to verbal threats. He sought 'an authenticated document from government' to convince them of the perils of proceeding, but this government could not give, being well aware of O'Connor's original strategy of exposing government oppression to the full view of its Whig opponents in London.[82]

In every practical respect the raid failed. O'Connor's *Address* had in fact already been printed separately by 27 January and was eventually to appear in at least three forms. One of these, a broadsheet version, with the suitably clandestine imprint 'Belfast: Printed by Miles's Boy', recorded the arrest of O'Connor on 2 February in an added line at the foot of the main text.[83]

Somehow, while the press was still occupied by the military, notices were published, first announcing suspension of publication as a result of the raid, and then announcing plans to re-publish.[84] When the government further sought to frustrate this objective by delaying the registration of a new printer, Thomas Corbett, the *Star* operatives called the bluff by proceeding anyway 'under the spirit of the laws of Ireland',[85] and Corbett's registration was eventually grudgingly conceded.

Meanwhile the *News-letter* was little less threatened at the top. As Robert Allan lamented in March 1797, Charles Gordon had had to fly Belfast, and his successor, Mr McKay, was even then leaving 'as [he] is afraid to stay longer'.[86] Nor could the Scottish owner call on any strength in depth as was available to the *Star*. Allan too had abandoned any purely commercial business plan, rather salvation for him lay in government subsidy. In March 1797 there was still a certain diffidence in his approach; something as blatant as 'a pension – seems neither so proper for government to give, or us to receive'.[87] It was a reservation soon to fall by the wayside.

It is well known that the *Star* was finally suppressed by rampaging members of the Monaghan Militia in May 1797 and to 'the extreme satisfaction' of General Lake.[88] What is less well understood is that the pretext for the sacking of the paper stemmed from a miscalculation at the *Star*, an attempt to repeat the coup of 1796 when the *News-letter* had been severely damaged by publishing an unpopular government advertisement.

The circumstances were these. In early May a United Irish conspiracy within the Monaghan Militia had been detected, and the ring leaders had been executed at the army camp at Blaris Moor.[89] The *Star* was suspected as the source of ballads celebrating these Blaris Moor martyrs.[90] The officers and sergeants of the Monaghans now wanted an advertisement offering 'some palliation for our late disgrace'. This was that 'we have been for a considerable time quartered in a town remarkable for its seditious practices, and which has been too successful in corrupting the loyal and well affected'.

The parallel with the 'Kingsbury' advertisement of 1796 was evident, but by May 1797 the times had changed. Non insertion now by the *Star* led

191

to its suppression, still not as a direct result of provable government orders, but with its evident complicity. The era of the democratic contest between the two Belfast papers was at an end. No opposition paper was possible until John Lawless's *Irishman* in 1819,[91] and, on its part, the *News-letter* was to enjoy a government subsidy until 1829.[92]

Acknowledgement

I am grateful to Kevin Whelan for his advice and advance sight of his most valuable essay 'The Republic in the Village: The United Irishmen, the Enlightenment and Popular Culture', which is due to appear in his book of essays, *The Tree of Liberty Radicalism, Catholicism and the Construction of Irish Identity* (Cork: Cork University Press, 1996)

Notes

1   Hugh Oram, *The Newspaper Book: a History of Newspapers in Ireland, 1649-1983* (Dublin, 1984), p.41.

2   Irish National Archives. Rebellion Papers. 620/15/8/1, *Northern Star* Minutes.

3   Ibid. 620/19/26. Meeting of *Northern Star* subscribers 23 September 1791.

4   Ibid. 620/19/25 and 620/19/42, cited in Nancy Curtin, *The United Irishmen* (Clarendon Press, 1994), pp. 202-203.

5   For Joy see Central Library, Belfast. Francis Joseph Biggar papers Q246 for typescript biographical sketch.

6   Linen Hall Library. Henry Joy Manuscripts.

7   For Charles Lucas see the numerous references in Robert Munter, *The History of the Irish Newspaper 1685–1760* (Cambridge, 1967).

8   Linen Hall Library. Henry Joy Manuscripts, 'Fugitive Political Pieces'.

9   A. Albert Campbell, *Belfast Newspapers Past and Present* (Belfast, 1921), pp.2-4.

10 Francis Joseph Biggar, *The Magees of Belfast and Dublin* (Belfast, 1916).

11 The full list of proprietors and their respective shares is given in Richard Madden, *Irish Periodical Literature*, Volume 2 (London, 1867), pp. 225-226.

12 The reason for Tisdall's withdrawal at this early stage is not clear. Perhaps his role as first printer had always been envisaged as a temporary arrangement. The minutes of the *Northern Star* for 24 January 1792 (Rebellion Papers 620/15/8/1) record agreement to compensate Tisdall for use of his equipment. He served as witness to the June 1792 articles of the company. By 1796 he had assumed a much more respectable career as Commissioner for taking Special Bail in the Court of Common Pleas for County Antrim (*Northern Star*, 26 December 1796).

13 Irish National Archives. Rebellion Papers. 620/15/8/1, *Northern Star* Minutes 27 March 1792, and 28 November 1792.

14 Ibid. 650/15/8/3, for *Northern Star* Expenditure Account October 1791 to end January 1792. This includes £13.5.5 'for a press', £10.2.4 for 'hand and press rules', £27.18.0 'for Brevier types', and £75.0.0 for '100 reams of paper'. The minutes for 21 May show a decision for an order 'of bourgeois type immediately'.

15 Ibid. 620/15/8/5, *Northern Star* Journal for 1792.

16 Kevin Whelan, 'The Republic in the Village: the Enlightenment and Popular Culture', in, *The Tree of Liberty Radicalism, Catholicism and the Construction of Irish identity*. (Cork: Cork University Press, 1996 [forthcoming]).

17 *Northern Star*, 15 December 1794.

18 Ibid. 4 January 1792.

19 Irish National Archives. Rebellion Papers. 620/15/8/5, *Northern Star* Journal for 1792. In Cootehill the problem was 'they being at present engaged in the Dublin papers'.

20 *A Sketch of the Life of Samuel Neilson* (New York, 1804), p.8. See also Mary Helen Thuente, *The Harp Re-strung* (New York, 1994), p.89.

21 Irish National Archives. Rebellion Papers. 620/15/8/1, *Northern Star* Minutes 27 March 1792.

22 [William Sampson], *A Faithful Report of the Second Trial of the Proprietors of the Northern Star* (Belfast: [Northern Star], February 1795), pp.14 and 27.

23 [William Sampson], *A Faithful Report of the Trial of the Proprietors of the Northern Star* (Belfast: [Northern Star], June 1794), p.8.

24 *Northern Star*, 15 December 1794.

25   *Journals and Memoirs of Thomas Russell*, edited by C.J. Woods, (Blackrock, 1991), pp. 72 and 80.

26   Possibilities of a more tolerant government approach arose from July 1794 onwards and reached a crescendo during the short-lived Fitzwilliam Viceroyalty in January/February 1795. See Nancy J. Curtin, *The United Irishmen* (Oxford, 1994), pp.61-62.

27   *Northern Star*, 13 November 1794.

28   Irish National Archives. Rebellion Papers. 620/29/122. This includes Robert Allan's account dated 23 March 1797 of the subsequent misfortunes of the paper. To bolster his case for government support he appended Henry Joy's letter of 23 January 1795.

29   *Belfast Politics* [edited by Henry Joy and William Bruce], (Belfast, 1794), p.119 for the 'Declaration and Principles of the Friends of Parliamentary Reform' on 10 January 1793.

30   Linen Hall Library. Henry Joy Manuscripts. 'Fugitive Political Pieces'. The note is appended to a cutting of Joy's last *News-letter* editorial on 15 May 1795. The figure generally cited elsewhere is £3,000.

31   See Kevin Whelan, 'The Republic in the Village' for such detail as is available.

32   For 1796 see *Northern Star*, 22 February, 14 March. For 1797 see 2 and 16 January, 3 and 6 March, 3 and 7 April and 8 May. In 1797 listing was not complete at the time of the suppression of the paper.

33   Ballyclare, Ballynure, Carnmoney, Crumlin, Doagh, Glenavy, Muckamore and Templepatrick.

34   Hamilton's Bawn, Loughgall, Richhill and Tandragee.

35   Coagh, Cookstown, Moneymore, Stewartstown and Tullaghoge.

36   Kevin Whelan, in 'The Republic in the Village', identifies 'half a dozen Catholic priests' on the surviving subscribers list, and yet does not differ from my conclusion on lack of penetration of Catholic areas.

37   Irish National Archives. Rebellion Papers. 620/15/8/9, *Northern Star* Journey Book 1795.

38   Ibid. 620/29/122. Robert Allan to Galbraith, 23 March 1797.

39   Linen Hall Library. Miscellaneous archives.

40   Irish National Archives. Rebellion Papers. 620/29/122, Robert Allan 23 March 1797.

41 John Anderson, *Catalogue of Early Belfast Printed Books, 1694 to 1830*. New and enlarged edition (Belfast, 1890). Appendix 'List of Belfast Printers, 1700 to 1830'.

42 Irish National Archives. Rebellion Papers. 620/25/11.

43 Hugh Warrin, bookseller, advertised R. Watson's *Apology for the Bible* in the *Northern Star* of 16 May at 2s. 8d. Charles Gordon's edition which seems to have lacked his imprint was probably that advertised by William Magee on 8 August as 'a cheap edition'.

44 Irish National Archives. Rebellion Papers. 620/25/11 and 620/26/11. Charles Gordon to Edward Cooke, 3 September 1796 and 5 November 1796.

45 Ibid. 620/24/104. John Lees to Edward Cooke, 18 August 1796.

46 *Northern Star*, 15 December 1794.

47 Irish National Archives. Rebellion Papers. 620/15/8/11. *Northern Star* Journey Book 1796.

48 *Northern Star*, 25 November 1796.

49 Ibid., 6 March 1797.

50 Public Record Office of Northern Ireland. T.755. Pelham Transcripts. vol. iv, pp. 139–142. General Lake to Thomas Pelham, 6 March 1797.

51 *Northern Star*, 25 November 1796.

52 John Anderson's *Catalogue of Early Belfast Printed Books*, and its various supplements identify eight publications with the *Northern Star* imprint between 1792 and 1797. To these may be added a further three with the imprint of John Rabb, the *Star* printer to 1795.

53 Irish National Archives. Rebellion Papers. 620/15/8/6. *Northern Star* Journey Book 1793, entry for 4 March.

54 A relatively uncontentious pamphlet published without *Star* imprint was [William Sampson's], *A Faithful Report of the Trial of the Proprietors of the Northern Star* (Belfast, June 1794). For copy with a stamp duty receipt written on the fly-leaf and made out to 'the Proprietors of the Northern Star' see Irish National Archives. Rebellion Papers. 620/15/8/8

55 See *Northern Star*, 4 August 1794 for Storey's announcement of purchase of the Public Printing Office with the intention to 'print books, pamphlets, poems, handbills etc.' Storey appears to have purchased the press from Daniel Blow. For this see (John Anderson, *Catalogue*

of Early Belfast Printed Books, 1694 to 1830. New and enlarged edition (Belfast, 1890). Appendix 'List of Belfast Printers, 1700 to 1830'. Both John and Thomas Storey were employed as printers on the *Northern Star*, see *Journals and Memoirs of Thomas Russell*, p. 173, footnote 21.

56   J.R.R. Adams, *The Printed Word and the Common Man* (Belfast, 1987), p. 89

57   The imprint is Jno [i.e. John] Rabb, printer of the *Northern Star*.

58   Irish National Archives. Rebellion Papers. 620/21/2. Henry Joy to Robert Calwell, 24 January 1794.

59   *Belfast News-letter*, 25 March 1796.

60   *Northern Star*, 9 and 16 May 1796.

61   *Belfast News-letter*, 12 May 1796.

62   *Northern Star*, 23 May 1796.

63   Ibid., 5 May 1796.

64   See Arthur Aspinall, *Politics and the Press, c.1780–1850* (London, 1949), and Brian Inglis, *The Freedom of the Press in Ireland 1784–1841* (London, 1954).

65   Irish National Archives. Rebellion Papers. 620/25/49. Lord Downshire to Edward Cook, 10 September 1796.

66   Irish National Archives. Rebellion Papers. 620/29/122. Robert Allan, 23 March 1797.

67   *Belfast News-letter*, 21 November 1796.

68   *Northern Star*, 31 March 1797.

69   Neilson was arrested along with Thomas Russell and others on 16 September 1796. See Mrs McTier's account in *The Drennan Letters*, (Belfast, 1931), p. 240 (letter 629).

70   On 7 October a letter by Joy under the pseudonym 'Viator' was published. On 17 October 1796 he contributed 'To the People of Ireland', on 28 October under the pseudonym *X*, 'To my Fellow Citizens', and on 26 December, 'The Farmers Friend or a Word to the Wise'. On 30 December, Gordon described this as a contribution by 'an unknown author' and announced that he had been 'induced to republish [it], to satisfy the solicitations of many of our respectable readers'.

71   *Northern Star*, 25 November 1796.

72   Ibid., 20 March 1797.

73 Ibid., 28 November, 5, 9, and 19 December 1796.

74 Ibid., 1 May 1797.

75 Ibid., 12 December 1796, 20 March 1797.

76 *Belfast News-letter*, 10, 13 and 17 February 1797.

77 Ibid., 17 February 1797.

78 Irish National Archives. Rebellion Papers. 620/25/137 and 620/28/249. Letters from Thomas Whinney, Belfast post master, to Edward Cooke and John Lees demonstrating hostility to the *Northern Star*.

79 *Northern Star*, 30 January 1797.

80 Ibid., 2 January 1797.

81 Irish National Archives. Rebellion Papers. 620/28/221 and 620/28/319. Colonel Barbour to Edward Cooke on 6 and 7 February 1797.

82 See Curtin, *The United Irishmen*, p.210.

83 Broadsheet form is ESTC t187053. Pamphlet versions of 12o (ESTC n005799) and 8o (ESTC t131790).

84 The first was dated 3 February 1797, the actual day on which the *Star* offices were occupied by the military. Others followed on 10 February and 17 February. In addition on 10 February an *Advertisement to the People of Ireland* giving information on the European war from the 'latest packets' appeared. All these items are bound into the Linen Hall Library file of the *Star* after the 19 May 1797 issue. The notice of 10 February with regard to the *Star*'s publication plans, was distributed to those attending market day in Belfast on that day, along with other examples of seditious ephemera all of which were sent to Dublin Castle by Lucius Barbour (Irish National Archives Rebellion Papers. 620/29/122).

85 *Northern Star*, 24 February 1797.

86 Irish National Archives. Rebellion Papers. 620/29/122.

87 National Library of Ireland. Lake MS. Letter 79. Quoted more fully in Inglis, *The Freedom of the Press in Ireland*, p.97.

88 Helen Mary Thuenthe, *The Harp Re-strung*, p.128.

89 See Curtin, *The United Irishmen*, pp.171–173 and 200.

90 *Belfast News-letter* and *Northern Star*, 19 May 1797. For texts see Georges–Denis Zimmerman, *Songs of Irish Rebellion: Political Ballads*

and Rebel Songs, 1780–1900. (Hatboro: Folklore Associates, 1967), p.131. For William Drennan's verse on the same subject see, *The Drennan Letters* p.257. In the same letter Drennan reports that '[William] Sampson has written something on the four soldiers, which I hear is good'.

91   Campbell, *Belfast Newspapers Past and Present*, pp.5–6.
92   Aspinall, *Politics and the Press*, p.121.

JOHN TEMPLETON,
THE LINEN HALL LIBRARY
AND THE PRESERVATION OF IRISH MUSIC

JOHN KILLEN

JOHN TEMPLETON WAS BORN in Bridge Street, Belfast, in 1766, the son of James Templeton, 'merchant of good standing and connections'.[1] A delicate child, he spent most of his time reading and early acquired a taste for natural history. As he grew older, his means and interests were such that he could devote himself to the study of the flora and fauna of his immediate locality. Such was his acknowledged expertise that Sir Joseph Banks, President of the Royal Society, offered him a good salary and a large tract of land in Australia if he would voyage to New Holland on behalf of the Society. Templeton's love of family and his native place caused him to turn down the very lucrative offer: instead, he devoted himself to every movement in the town of Belfast which had as it aim the advancement of knowledge and the betterment of society in general.

Botanist, advocate of Catholic emancipation and parliamentary reform, friend of Thomas Russell and Mary Ann McCracken, founder of the Belfast Academical Institution, Templeton was truly a child of the Enlightenment. He believed that nature, politics and society were amenable to verifiable laws and that man could, by dint of study and application, discover and understand these laws; and by steadfastly adhering to rational principles he could better his lot and that of society. To this end he joined the Belfast Reading Society (later the Linen Hall Library) in 1792 and served on its committee and as curator of its museum from then until his death in 1825. Like many middle class gentlemen of his day his interests were catholic, ranging from meteorology, botany, zoology, horticulture and agriculture to literature, theatre and music. An intimate friend of the McCrackens he mixed freely in their convivial society and knew their lodger Edward Bunting well; delighting in his musical virtuosity.

Templeton was a man of twenty-five when, in December 1791 the following handbill appeared in and around the town of Belfast advertising the opening of a subscription for the preservation of the music and poetry of Ireland:

> Some inhabitants of Belfast, feeling themselves interested in everything which relates to the Honour, as well as the Prosperity of their Country; propose to open a subscription, which they intend to apply in attempting to revive and perpetuate – The Ancient Music and Poetry of Ireland. They are solicitous to preserve from oblivion, the few fragments which have been permitted to remain as monuments of the refined taste and genius of their ancestors.
>
> In order to carry this project into execution, it must appear obvious to those acquainted with the situation of this country, that it will be necessary to assemble the Harpers, those descendants of our ancient lords, who are at present, almost exclusively possessed of all that remains of the Music, Poetry, and Oral Traditions of Ireland.
>
> It is proposed that the Harpers should be induced to assemble at Belfast (I suppose on the 1st July next) by the distribution of such prizes as may seem adequate to the subscribers. And that a person well versed in the Language and Antiquities of this nation, should attend, with a skilful Musician to transcribe and arrange the most beautiful and interesting parts of their knowledge.
>
> An undertaking of this nature will undoubtedly meet the approbation of Men of Refinement and Erudition in every Country: And when it is considered, how intimately the Spirit and Character of a People are connected with this National Poetry and Music, it is presumed, that the Irish Patriot and Politician, will not deem it an object unworthy his patronage and protection.[2]

Early the next year advertisements appeared in the Belfast newspapers reminding the citizens of the proposed 'assemblage of performers on the harp', and requesting a meeting of subscribers to the project. Accordingly, on 23 April 1792 a meeting was held at the Donegall Arms, and a committee of five was elected to;

> Forward and receive subscriptions – to circulate by advertisement in different newspapers, and other ways the period and object of the meeting, and to regulate and conduct the subordinate parts of the scheme.[3]

Among the subscribers that day was John Templeton. The committee which was duly elected comprised: Robert Bradshaw, Robert Simms, Dr James McDonnell, and Mr John Scott,[4] all members of the Belfast Reading Society.[5] In addition to this committee, a further committee was elected to judge the performances of those harpers who would attend the forthcoming festival. Unlike previous festivals where virtuosity of performance was the sole criterion of success, this proposed festival had a more specific aim – the preservation of the national music of Ireland. In this respect it was agreed:

> That the airs to be performed, previous to the adjudication of the premiums, be confined to the native music of the country – the Music of Ireland.
>
> In order to revive obsolete airs, it is an instruction to the judges on this occasion, not to be solely governed in their decisions by the degree of execution or taste of the several performers, but, independently of these circumstances, to consider the person entitled to additional claim, who shall produce airs not to be found in any public collection, and at the same time deserve of preference by their intrinsic excellence.
>
> It is recommended to any Harper who is in possession of such scarce compositions to have them reduced to notes.[6]

Among the judges elected to adjudicate at the harp festival was

Miss Catherine Clarke, the first female member of the Belfast Reading Society.[7] (Both she and John Templeton had been proposed as members of the Society by Dr James McDonnell).[8,9] Edward Bunting was engaged to write down the airs that were played.

In due course, on 11 through 14 July 1792 the Assembly Rooms above the Exchange resounded with the music of the harp. Ten harpers attended:

> Denis Hempson, blind, from County Londonderry, aged 97 years or more, exponent of the old style of playing with long crooked nails: Arthur O'Neill blind, from County Tyrone, aged 58, afterwards instructor to the Belfast Harp Society; Charles Fanning, from County Cavan, aged 56, the most brilliant performer, but in the modernist style; Daniel Black, blind, from County Londonderry, aged 75; Charles Byrne from County Leitrim, aged 80, had the use of his eyes, and as a boy had acted as guide to his blind uncle, a harper contemporary with Carolan: Hugh Higgins, blind, from County Mayo, aged 55; Patrick Quinn, blind, from County Armagh, aged 47; William Carr, from County Armagh, aged 15; Rose Mooney, blind, from County Meath, aged 52; James Duncan, from County Down, aged 45.[10]

That six of the ten performers were blind sparked a train of thought in Templeton's mind that would take sixteen years to come to practical fruition in the establishment of the Belfast Harp Society. In the immediate aftermath of the Harp Festival, however, the organisers and subscribers set about having the airs taken down by Bunting and published to the highest standards of the day: and this despite the less than enthusiastic reception the music received in the contemporary press:

> It appears that the principal reason for assembling them [the harpers] here, originated in a wish to rescue from total oblivion such native airs as were supposed to be in their possession alone, and which might prove an acquisition to the musical world, and an ornament to the Irish nation, but in this they have not succeeded to any great degree, for they played very few tunes, but what were generally known ...[11]

At the first meeting of the newly named Belfast Society for Promoting Knowledge, formerly the Belfast Reading Society, to be held in the house of its first Librarian Robert Cary, with John Templeton in attendance;

> It having been reported to the committee that a collection of old Irish Musick superior to any hitherto published, was made at the late meeting of the Harpers at Belfast,
> *Resolved* that it be recommended to the Society, to take said work under its patronage – To publish it in London under the name of the Society, with a prefatory Discourse, allowing the profits derived therefrom to the person who took down the notes.[12]

In an attempt to prevent plagiarism of this first general collection of Irish Airs the volume was published by subscription, each sub-scriber receiving his book in the order of his subscription. The price was half a guinea, paid on receipt of the book.

Throughout 1793 the most effective way in which to publish the Irish Airs was sought, resulting in December 1793 in a request being made to Mr O'Halloran of Limerick to assist in the matter.[13] Mr O'Halloran wrote a detailed plan for publication, using a Dublin firm but this was rejected in favour of an estimate from London, forwarded by the Society's agent Mr Jameson, which was eventually agreed to. Matters progressed very slowly and 1794 saw further delays and the real possibility of the project coming to nought. Mr Jameson and Mr Bunting obviously did not see eye to eye and in November 1794 Bunting was asked to attend a meeting of the Society to try to find a compromise. A specimen of the Irish Music had been sent over from London by Mr Jameson which Bunting rejected because it was 'not executed with that elegance which the Society had designed'.

Bunting tabled a specimen of the Irish Music which he had himself designed; but this in turn was rejected by the committee.[14] Fearing that the publication would fall by the wayside a special meeting of the Society decided to entrust its completion to a committee of two – the Revd Patrick Vance and Henry Joy. Among the level-headed members who took this decision was John Templeton.[15]

Mr Jameson, in London, was requested to explain the delay in publication and replied 'he was exceedingly mortified that the Irish music should have been so long in finishing, but promised that it shall soon be sent over'.[16] In August 1796 members of the Society were gratified to accept the published volume of Bunting's *Ancient Irish Music*, 'containing sixty-six tunes, adapted for the Harpsichord and Piano Forte, elegantly engraved ... in London, with a preface illustrative of the subject ... published by subscription ... by the most eminent professional men in these kingdoms'.[17]

John Templeton and his intimate friend Thomas Russell (now in prison in Dublin) were delighted. Writing to Templeton in 1797 from prison Russell ends with 'I am told the Irish Music is finished. I have no doubt it will have great success, and raise the reputation of the collectors of the Institute which brought it forward'.[18]

In this, however, Russell was quite wrong. Within months of its publication, Bunting's Irish music had been pirated by a Dublin publisher resulting in pecuniary loss to the compiler and the Society. Writing to her brother, Dr Drennan, Mrs McTier extolled the virtues of Bunting's slim volume of music: 'have you heard Bunting's Irish music well played – no – for you have not heard *him* – to me they are sounds might make Pitt melt for the poor Irish – not a copy is now to be got ...' She went on to lament the unfairness of the publishing trade in the latter part of the eighteenth century 'but I hear they are very unjustly going to reprint them in Dub[lin] ...'[19]

This pirating of Bunting's work, needless to say, annoyed his friends and collaborators who continued to do all they could to promote the volume. Thomas Russell, indeed, had lent his support in the early days when publication still seemed in doubt: 'In the evening a committee at the Library. Tedious. Irish Musick discussed. I think it may go on if well managed'.[20] And again: 'In the evening call at McDonnell's to meet Bunting for whom I promised to write a letter to the society ...'[21] and again: 'A meeting of the society in the evening. By means of the letter ... the Irish musick went down well and was agreed to be done ...'[22]

After its publication Russell continued to promote the work and to add to the airs which Bunting was continuing to collect. He mentioned the project in many of his letters to Templeton during his captivity, enclosing 'a tune for my friend Bunting [which] I do not recollect him to have had',[23] whenever the occasion arose. Templeton, in turn, kept in close contact with Bunting, passing on any new material he received and encouraging him in his work. In one of his last letters to Templeton from his captivity at Fort George in Scotland (dated 5 June 1802) Russell ends a reiteration of his strongly held political views with the words:

> I beg to be affectionately remembered to your family; and believe me to participate in whatever contributes to your happiness ... Remember me, affectionately, to Bunting. I have a copy of his music with me, and will do all I can to introduce it to notice ...'[24]

That the *Ancient Irish Music* was important to both Russell and Templeton is obvious. Russell's interest was patriotic and musical; Templeton's likewise but it also had motives which the hazards of the rigour of his botanical and scientific pursuits suggested. These are best summed up in the words of a contributor to the *Belfast Monthly Magazine*, which Templeton co-founded in 1808: the reasoning is so close to Templeton's own experience that one can be forgiven for believing that the author was Templeton himself. Commenting on a debate on the usefulness or otherwise of music the writer says:

> I have never known or heard of anyone who was not in some degree pleased with music ... much less any who disapproved of it. I rather imagine it impossible to produce a single instance wherein music had lost all its effect, having neither charms to please, nor power to move ... There is nothing more hurtful or dangerous to health than close application, when continued for a long time. [An earlier correspondent] says music is too trifling and unimportant to spend any time with, but I would ask, can time be better employed than in the prolongation of life? Close and intense application to study has hurried many to an untimely grave; whereas perhaps, if they had indulged a little more in so pleasant and innocent an amusement, it might have tended to lengthen their days ...'[25]

205

There was one further impulse in Templeton's liking for the ancient music of Ireland and for the promotion of the Irish harp. Remembering the excellence of the blind harpers of 1792 Templeton saw the possibility of using music, especially the harp, for the purpose of aiding the blind and thus of aiding the society in which they lived. Writing in his diary in 1806 about the ancient civilisation of Greece, Templeton was moved to deplore the almost inevitable loss of the ancient music and airs of his native land, and to suggest how this might be alleviated by the cultivation of the Irish harp amongst those least able to earn their living by other types of employment:

> It is to be regretted that this beautiful fabric [the ancient music of Ireland] raised by our ancestors and preserved for us through so many ages now totters on its foundations and unless speedy support is applied must fall into irreparable decay ... Let a few, a very few, years elapse and this monument of our ancient civilisation will disappear. For a length of time the profession of bard has been confined to a part of the community who generally experience the wretchedness of poverty; a few blind harpers are now the only remains of our numerous bards. While these few are alive it is in our power to revive this nearly extinct art. The greater variety of paths which are prepared for genius, the more easily will each individual be enabled to cultivate those talents with which nature has endowed them. Music has been the principal recource of the blind – for support and amusement ... [Music affords hopes] to many who must otherwise languish in obscurity and spend in poverty and indolence a life which might be agreeable to themselves, useful to their families, and diffuse to all around them the most pleasurable sensations ...'[26]

This well-reasoned argument for the social as well as the cultural benefits of the harp was strongly upheld by Templeton who saw it as a positive factor in benefiting those afflicted with blindness, and consequently benefiting the society in which they lived. In February 1808 the following anonymous letter appeared in the *Belfast News-letter*; that it was written by Templeton is obvious when its wording is compared with the above entry in his diary some fourteen months earlier:

Let a few, a very few years elapse, and this monument of our ancient civilisation, which so often added splendour to the hospitable halls of our ancestors, will disappear. For a length of time the profession of Bard has been confined to a part of the community who generally experience all the wretchedness of poverty; a few blind harpers are now the only remains of our numerous bards. While these few are yet alive it is in our power to revive this nearly extinct art. Music has been the principal recource of the blind, both for support and amusement ... Think that many who now languish in obscurity, and spend in poverty and indolence a life which might be agreeable to themselves and useful to their families, may be taught at small expense, and be the means of diffusing around the most pleasurable sensations ... surely there is not a person in whom the sacred fire of Patriotism is so truly extinct that they do not feel the spirit of their fathers rise up within them at the sound of the harp, and sigh with regret that they have suffered the emblem of their country to remain so long neglected.[27]

On St Patrick's Day 1808 the Irish Harp Society was inaugurated at Linn's Hotel, 1 Castle Street, Belfast, where it was recorded that some 191 subscribers had pledged annual subscriptions to the sum of £300. The minute book of the Society records that the Most Noble the Marquis of Donegall subscribed 20 guineas per annum. The Right Honourable Earl O'Neill subscribed 15 guineas, The Honourable John O'Neill 10 guineas, and the Right Revd Lord Bishop of Dromore 5 guineas. Edward Bunting also subscribed 5 guineas; but most of the subscribers, including Francis, John and Mary Ann McCracken, Robert and William Simms, William and Robert Tennent and John Templeton, all pledged one guinea per annum.[28]

At the first business meeting of the Society on 3 May 1808 at Linn's Hotel a committee was elected to conduct the affairs of the institution.

This committee comprised Robert Tennent as treasurer, Patrick Connor as secretary, with William Magee, Henry Joy, Samuel Bryson, Dr Alexander McDonnell, Edward Bunting, Alexander Scott, John McCracken, John McAdam, Dr James McDonnell, and Joseph Stevenson.[29] That Templeton did not hold office or serve on the committee throughout the life of the Irish Harp Society is in keeping with the man. He was content that the Society had been brought into being by his lobbying behind the scenes; he was pleased that the most effective members of Belfast society were engaged in the execution of its aims – the worth of Bunting, McCracken, Joy and Tennent he knew intimately; and he was prepared to support the enterprise according to his means. There is a further reason which highlights the extreme rigour of Templeton's moral stance. Dr James McDonnell was one of the original movers in the Belfast Harpers Festival of 1792 and had an abiding interest in the promulgation of the Irish Harp. Templeton accepted that McDonnell's participation in the Harp Society was both proper and indeed necessary to its success. But he could not find it in his heart to forgive McDonnell for his treatment of Russell in 1803 when he was induced to subscribe to the reward for Russell's capture after the abortive rising in the North. Accordingly he watched over the progress of the Society from a distance; discussing socially with Bunting, the McCrackens and the Tennents its developments.

Members of the Irish Harp Society met to dine on each St Patrick's Day subsequent to 1808. At their dinner in 1809 they decided to use their influence to promote the teaching of the Irish language in the Harp School. John Templeton was not amongst those who enrolled to learn to speak the Irish language; possibly he had had instruction in the language fifteen years earlier when Patrick Lynch of Loughinisland had taught Thomas Russell among others the rudiments of the language in the Library in Ann Street.

After the first year of the Irish Harp Society's foundation lack of finance plagued its progress. In February 1810 there were only nine pupils. Sponsors of the venture complained in the Belfast press:

> Many have applied, but the state of the funds of the institution,
> which are strained to their full extent to support their present

number, and to enlarge the accommodations for their maintenance and education, are the object of the present address.[30]

To try to raise funds for the Harp School the manager of the Belfast Theatre was applied to for assistance. He organised a benefit performance by the resident company, during which several national airs were performed on the Irish Harp by pupils of the society.[31] Templeton, with his great love of the theatre and his espousal of the cause of the Harp Society, was an enthusiastic member of the audience. During the winter of 1810/11 a series of subscription balls in the Exchange Rooms was held in aid of the Harp School but it seems that the financial burden of employing O'Neill as Harp teacher, renting premises and the up-keep of the pupils proved too much for the coffers of the society. From what little evidence exists, it would seem that the Harp School ceased active work some time in 1814, for in that year the *Belfast Commercial Chronicle* published a poem entitled 'The Last Minstrel' which contains the lines:

T'were better proud Belfast, thou never had striven,
To snatch from oblivion the music of Heaven,
More honour were thine if thou never hads't told,
Thy flattering tale to the Minstrel of old;
More praise-worthy far for thy sons had it been,
If Tyrone's sightless Harper they never had seen;
For thy specious professions were like thy design,
They were false – it has failed – and dishonour is thine.[32]

A copy of this newspaper eventually (five years later) reached a set of ex-patriot Ulstermen in India who wrote to Henry Joy and Robert Williamson offering financial help to revive the Society. As a result of this communication a meeting was held in Belfast on 16 April 1819, to form a society for the management of a fund formed in India to 'Revive the Harp and ancient Music of Ireland'.

Of the fifteen townsmen who attended the meeting, six were the originators of the Irish Harp Society in 1808 (John Templeton among them). The first resolution of the Society was that those attending, plus the donors and annual subscribers in India, upon their return to Ireland, also the surviving members of the Belfast Harp Committee of the year 1792, all be deemed original members of the Society. Edward Bunting was 'requested to order three harps to be made on the most improved construction, in order that an adequate number may be purchased, if those shall be approved of'. He was also asked to ascertain what harpers were to be found, competent to the tuition of a number of pupils, and the terms on which such teacher or teachers could be employed.[33]

And so, the Irish Harp Society was re-constituted, with the six original (1808) members as life members. The India Fund, as it came to be known, breathed new life into the once failing society; and in August 1821 J. Williamson Fulton, Esq., the prime mover of the fund, returned to Belfast. At a meeting of the Society on 20 August 1821 Dr James McDonnell moved the following resolution:

> That the sincere and cordial thanks of the Harp Society be presented to our worthy chairman, whom we are happy to recognise here for the first time since his return from India. It is to his generous and zealous exertions, and those of the distinguished friends of the Harp Society in India, that it is indebted for its origin and present establishment. The Society entreats a continuance of their benevolent exertions, in protection of the blind and helpless pupils – the future minstrels of the land, whose progress and performance on the Irish Harp, have this day been so creditably evinced.[34]

John Templeton fully concurred with these sentiments: sentiments which he had penned in his journal some fourteen months before the original call to form such a society as the Irish Harp Society in 1808. At this same meeting on 20 August 1821 J. Williamson Fulton, Dr McDonnell, John Templeton and Robert Williamson were elected a committee for the purpose of corresponding with Edward Bunting to encourage him to publish 'his remaining collections of the ancient music of Ireland, the publication of which the present juncture is so well, calculated to promote'.[35] No record of this correspondence remains, and it would be another nineteen years before Bunting published his third volume of ancient airs.

By that time John Templeton was dead and the Harp School existed no longer. During his lifetime Templeton had been instrumental in having Bunting's *Music* published (in 1796 and 1809); he had been the originator of the Irish Harp Society (1808); he had encouraged and helped Bunting in his endeavours in the Harp School; and later had remained on the committee of the re-constituted Irish Harp School (1819-25). He was motivated by his love of music, by his love of friends and by his desire to give practical aid to the blind. In all of these he deserved well of his fellow citizens.

Notes

1   This topic, the preservation of the ancient music of Ireland by a dedicated and enthusiastic group of Belfast literati, and the period in which it is set (1788-1825) were well known to Ronnie Adams from his work in the Linen Hall Library and the Ulster Folk and Transport Museum; and from his researches into the publishing history of the north of Ireland. Throughout his life Ronnie was generous with his myriad knowledge of local bibliography and history, and encouraged countless researchers in their often obscure fields of interest. I acknowledge a debt of gratitude to a man with whom I worked, and who was a friend and I dedicate this piece to his memory.

2   LHL. Beath Mss. December 1791.

3   LHL. Beath Mss. 23 April 1792.

4   Ibid.

5   Membership Book of the Belfast Reading Society 1788-1792 .

6   LHL. Beath Mss. 23 April 1792.

7   Membership Book of the Belfast Reading Society 1788-1792.

8   Minutes of the Belfast Reading Society 15 August 1792.

9   Minutes of the Belfast Reading Society 22 August 1792.

10   C. M. Fox, *Annals of the Irish Harpers* (London, 1911) , pp. 102-3.

11   *Northern Star,* 14-18 July 1792.

12   Minutes of the Belfast Society for Promoting Knowledge, 7 March 1793.

13   Minutes of the Belfast Society for Promoting Knowledge, 7 December 1793.

14   Minutes of the Belfast Society for Promoting Knowledge, 4 November 1794.

15 Minutes of the Belfast Society for Promoting Knowledge, 20 November 1794.

16 Minutes of the Belfast Society for Promoting Knowledge, 3 September 1795.

17 *Belfast News-letter*, 12 August 1796. Published as *A General Collection of the Ancient Irish Music* (London, [1796]). Subsequent editions were *A General Collection of the Ancient Music of Ireland* (London, [1809]), and *The Ancient Music of Ireland* (Dublin, 1840).

18 R. R. Madden, *United Irishmen*, series 3 , vol. 2 (1846), p. 194.

19 PRONI. Drennan Letters, No 685. 12/12/1797.

20 *Journals and Memoirs of Thomas Russell*, edited by C. J. Woods (Dublin, 1991), p. 174

21 Ibid.

22 Ibid., p. 176

23 R. R. Madden, *United Irishmen*, series 3, vol. 2 (1846), p. 199.

24 Ibid., p. 202.

25 *Belfast Monthly Magazine*, vol.12, no. 66 (January 1814).

26 Ulster Museum Mss. Templeton's Journal. 9 December 1806.

27 *Belfast News-letter*, 26 February 1808.

28 Minutes of the Irish Harp Society, 17 March 1808.

29 Minutes of the Irish Harp Society, 3 May 1808.

30 *Belfast News-letter*, 7 February 1810.

31 *Belfast Commercial Chronicle*, 13 June 1810.

32 *Belfast Commercial Chronicle*, 8 June 1814.

33 LHL. Beath Mss. Irish Harp Society, 16 April 1810.

34 QUB. Bunting Manuscripts. MS 37/12.

35 Ibid.

THE REVEREND ROBERT MAGILL: A BIBLIOGRAPHICAL VIEW, 1827-1828

JOHN ERSKINE

It was late in the October of 1813 that a 25 year old student set out from his native Braid Valley to take up his studies at the University of Glasgow.

Robert Magill was born in County Antrim, in the village of Broughshane, on 7 September 1788. He was educated locally and became a teacher before deciding to enter the ministry of the Presbyterian Church. In preparation for his theological education he studied for a period under the Rev. John Paul, the Covenanter minister of Loughmorne, a man who was to remain a friend and colleague during Magill's own ministry.[1]

Presbyterians, being dissenters, were prevented from attending the only university in Ireland, Trinity College in Dublin. Ulster Presbyterians, therefore, had to look elsewhere for their higher education, chiefly to the Scottish universities and in particular to the University of Glasgow. For most of them the only way to reach Glasgow was to walk. 'The long road from Portpatrick to Glasgow', observed T.W. Moody, 'was familiar to generations of foot-slogging scholars from Ulster'.[2] Magill duly followed in their footsteps. He set out from Broughshane on Friday 22 October and walked to Donaghadee, breaking his journey at Belfast; on the Sunday he made the crossing to Portpatrick, a difficult crossing of some twelve hours during which, Magill records, the passengers were 'as sick and as tired with the journey as Jonah was with the whale's belly'. He spent the night at Portpatrick and on Monday set out, again on foot, for Glasgow, sleeping at Ballantrae and Ayr – pausing at Alloway to visit Robert Burns's house, then an inn, to pay his respects to the bard and 'to drink his memory' – before reaching his destination on the evening of Wednesday 27 October.

213

Of his journey he notes, 'I experienced much kindness since I left my native country – nor was there a drop of rain from I left Broughshane till I reached Glasgow'.[3] He had walked a distance of some 140 miles. This journey he was to repeat at least annually throughout his university career.

In 1820, following the completion of his university education and his presbytery 'trials', Magill was ordained and installed as minister of Mill Row (now First) congregation in Antrim. The ordination dinner was attended by many members of the local presbyteries whose meals, wine and whiskey cost the far from wealthy congregation the sum of £39.15s.1d. The cost of the dinner, and the particularly healthy appetites of the ministers present, led the understandably dismayed congregational secretary, Alexander McMaster, to conclude: 'If the clergy had been as numerous in the days of Pharaoh, the sovereign governor of the Universe might have commissioned them, instead of the Locusts, to destroy the land of Egypt'.[4]

Magill ministered in Mill Row until his death in 1839. For almost all of his ministry he kept a diary from which the entries for two years, 1827 and 1828, have recently been published.[5] These entries are in brief note form and are overwhelmingly factual, Magill rarely allowing himself to comment or to express an opinion. He is assiduous in recording his daily journeyings, the names of the people he visits, and those with whom he dines or drinks tea although he never records what he actually ate. He carefully notes the names of his correspondents although, frustratingly, with the exception of the details of preaching engagements, he rarely records the content of their, or his, letters. He is particularly scrupulous in noting, Sunday by Sunday, the biblical texts which he has explained and on which he has preached and he invariably records the amount of the collection. His diaries record his involvement with the Kildare Place Society on behalf of a number of local schools, notably the Bush School, and his involvement with the local Mendicity Committee of which he was an active member. The diaries also provide brief details of the work, employees and expenses involved in running the manse farm which was an important source of income for any minister. Despite their factual nature, however, the diaries make it clear that Magill took great pleasure in the natural world around him and in particular in his garden which contained a wide range of soft fruit in addition to its shrubs and flowers.

One unexpected feature of the diaries is the detail with which Magill records the state of health of many of the people he visits, often noting whether their condition has improved or worsened since his last visit. At first reading, such an interest in his fellow men and women appears at best curious and at worst prurient until it is realised that Magill had included medicine in his studies at Glasgow. In effect the pastor doubles as physician and is to be found writing 'recipes' (prescriptions) for many of his flock – including simpler remedies such as blackcurrant jam or port wine! – apparently with the concurrence of the local doctor. Indeed, at the beginning of 1828 Magill is to be found 'cutting' many local children with 'cow pock', a common practice at the time to prevent the spread of smallpox. Magill clearly enjoyed both the medical and pastoral confidence of his flock.

One incidental feature that emerges from a reading of the diaries is what appears to be a most un-Presbyterian attitude to drink: Magill thinks nothing of laying in a gallon of spirits for his harvest workers[6] or of entertaining some clergymen, passing through the town of Antrim, to several tumblers of punch.[7] The Temperance Movement would radically alter such an attitude.

However, this paper is concerned with an examination of one particular aspect of the diaries: the books and periodicals noted by Magill for the two years under review. We know little of the reading and book ownership of Presbyterian ministers so Magill provides us with a useful glimpse of the reading of one, if perhaps not a typical, early nineteenth-century minister. What is presented here does not pretend in any way to be a definitive study: it is no more than an initial exploration of Magill's bibliographical environment. Such an examination can be divided into four main areas: Magill's reading of newspapers and journals; his general reading; the preparation and publication of his poem, *The Thinking Few*; and his own part in the distribution of local publications. However, one caveat should be entered immediately. We should not assume that the diaries offer an entire inventory of Magill's reading, for a diary records not so much the usual as the exceptional and the different. It seems likely that, just as he fails to record what he ate at meal times, so Magill also omits reference to a number of books and other items which he may have used on a regular basis. One obvious example may serve to illustrate the point: Magill explained, and preached on, biblical texts every Sunday yet at no point in the diaries does he ever mention reading the Bible in English.

Newspapers and journals

Newspapers and journals appear to have formed a regular and important part of Magill's reading: he records some 19 different titles in his diaries for the two years in question. Again, however, caution needs to be exercised in drawing conclusions from the references Magill makes to the publications which he reads for he was clearly not a regular subscriber to all of them. He is likely to mention a newspaper or journal in his diary precisely because it was not part of his regular reading; he will mention a newspaper because it contains a report which attracts his attention; and he will list the titles of several newspapers simply because on one particular day he has read an unusual number of them: for example, he notes in one day's entry that he has read some five different newspapers and lists them.[8]

The number of times a title is noted, therefore, is not necessarily an indication of the frequency with which the newspaper came to him. However, given this caveat, the newspaper title which Magill notes most commonly is the *Dublin Evening Mail*, partly for the number of reports of conversions to Protestantism that it contains; however, these reports were also carried, with due acknowledgement to the original source, by the *Belfast News-letter*. Clearly, however, copies of the *Mail* came regularly to hand for in June 1827 Magill is able to record that he gave the teacher of the Bush School some 22 copies of the paper for use by the scholars.[9]

Magill also makes mention of a number of other Dublin-published newspapers, though none is mentioned more often than a couple of times: these are the *Freeman's Journal*, the *Patriot*, the *Warder* and the *Watchman*. The latter two, with the subtitles of the 'Constitutional Observer' and 'Protestant Guardian' respectively, indicate the political and religious stance that each of them adopted, their general outlook being shared by the *Dublin Evening Mail*.

Not surprisingly, however, the group of newspaper titles most frequently recorded in the diary is a series of Belfast-published papers: the *Belfast Commercial Chronicle*, the *Guardian* (recently established by the former editor of the *Belfast News-letter*), the *Belfast News-letter* itself, the

Northern Whig, and somewhat enigmatically, the *Irishman*.[10] None of these is mentioned as often as the *Dublin Evening Mail* though some of them, or possibly all of them, are likely to have been an equally regular part of Magill's reading: we know, for example, that he was a subscriber to the *Chronicle* for in June 1827 he renews his annual subscription with a Mrs Clark, a subscription costing him £1.11s.6d.[11] He was also invited to subscribe to the newly established *Guardian* by a Mr or Mrs Greg, but unfortunately he does not record whether he did so or not.[12]

Other newspapers recorded by Magill include the *Drogheda Journal*, copies of which were lent to him by Lord Ferrard, and a series of London titles: the *Morning Herald*, the *Observer*, the *Record* and, almost inevitably, the *Times*, although each of these is noted on no more than a couple of occasions. In a rare comment on his newspaper reading, Magill remarks of the *Record* (merged over a century later with the *Church of England Newspaper*) that it is 'talented and of a highly evangelical character'.[13]

Magill was not only a reader of newspapers but also a contributor. His diary records a couple of murders in the district including that of Alexander Kernoghan Brownlees in May 1828.[14] Shortly afterwards the proprietor of the *Belfast News-letter*, Alexander Mackay, wrote to Magill asking him to prepare an account of the murder for the paper: Magill agreed and his account appeared in the issue of 16 May, the same issue which also carried a notice of the death of his own father, a coincidence on which Magill himself remarks.

A vast range of Irish Presbyterian periodicals became established during the nineteenth century but these postdate the two years in which the diaries under review were being written. Consequently the periodical literature which Magill does mention is not specifically Presbyterian in character. He borrows copies of the *Christian Moderator* and also the *Pioneer*, probably to be identified as the *Christian Pioneer*, the latter being a journal of which he strongly disapproves: it is 'a Unitarian publication and advocates Socinianism'[15] and 'a very prophane work'.[16] He mentions, only once, the *Dublin Christian Instructor* but also notes receipt, apparently on a regular basis, of the London 'Missionary Chronicle'.[17]

General reading

The books and pamphlets which, according to the diaries, Magill reads, lends or borrows, are overwhelmingly theological and ecclesiastical in character. However, he does have some time for the reading of more general literature: confined to his study one day in early March 1827 by the dreadful weather which left the roads impassable, Magill records that he sat down and read 'Moore's *Melodies*, Shakespeare's *Macbeth* and *Der Freischütz* by Weber', though in what form this last would be available is unclear.[18] Poetry also interested Magill: two weeks previously Magill had returned a copy of Byron's *Don Juan*;[19] he lent a parishioner a copy of Edward Young's *Night Thoughts*, an item of enduring popularity since its first publication in the middle of the eighteenth century;[20] and he seems to have read some of the poetry of James Grahame.[21] He also enjoyed a compilation entitled 'Select Poetry' and makes an extract in his diary of one of the poems:

> The bridal is over, the guests are all gone,
> The bride's only sister sits weeping alone...[22]

He makes reference to two novels: at the beginning of 1827 he reads part of James McHenry's *O'Halloran; or, The Insurgent Chief*, first published in 1824,[23] and in September 1828 he notes that he 'read part of the 1st volume of Waverly', adding, in an interesting if elusive comment, 'I have not read any of the works of Walter Scot except extracts'.[24] Scott's prose works had been published anonymously and although his authorship was widely known it was not acknowledged publicly until 1827.

It might be expected that the reading of an Ulster Presbyterian minister in the nineteenth century would be overwhelmingly a diet of Scottish theology and church history. However, in Magill's case this is not so.[25] While there are clearly some items by Scottish writers, Magill refers to only two works of specifically Scottish church history in his diaries for these years: Thomas McCrie's *Life of John Knox*,[26] and the 'Scotch Worthies', almost certainly John Howie's *Biographia Scoticana*, a work of Scottish Presbyterian hagiography popularly known as the *Scots Worthies*, a title under which it has long since been published.[27]

Magill clearly also sought to keep up his Hebrew: he refers on one occasion to reading part of Parkhurst's Hebrew lexicon[28] and some days later records that he has read the first chapter of the Old Testament in Hebrew.[29]

As indicated above, Magill regularly lent and borrowed books, his own study being a source of many items for friends, parishioners and fellow ministers. At the time these diaries were being written there was a vogue for formal debates on the doctrinal differences between Protestantism and Roman Catholicism. Such debates were conducted over a period of several days before paying audiences. An advertisement for the debate in Dublin between Pope and Maguire (Mr Pope, somewhat confusingly, taking the side of the Reformation) appeared in the *Belfast News-letter* and laid down what might best be described as the rules of engagement:[30] among the conditions, for example, was an undertaking that an agreed text of the debate would be published, a text to which Magill later refers on several occasions.[31] When, in July 1827, his friend Robert Stewart, the minister of Broughshane, was about to engage in a similar debate with the local parish priest, Bernard McAuley – a debate lasting three days and which Magill attended – Magill called at Broughshane with a manuscript and three or four books to assist his friend:

> called at Mr Stewart's and left him Eusebius, Anderson's defence of Presbyterianism, The Vaudois – a book of chronology.[32]

An authorised account of the Stewart-McAuley debate was published,[33] but increasingly personal sparring between the two men continued in the local press until the editor of the *Belfast News-letter*, tiring of the whole business, called a halt and threatened to charge the protagonists for the inclusion of further articles.[34] Magill also kept well abreast of other local theological controversies, noting many of the pamphlets that were published during the two years under review.

However, lending books, then as now, was a hazardous business: it was not until the July of the following year that the books Magill had lent to Stewart were returned and then only because Magill himself called to collect them.[35] Almost immediately he again lent the book on the Vaudois, this time to the Rev. William Ellison who took the opportunity to borrow it when he returned the second volume of Mosheim's *Ecclesiastical History*.[36] Magill, indeed, had an interest not only in church history – Josephus[37] and Neal's *History of the Puritans*[38] figure in his reading in addition to the items already mentioned – but also in history generally: his reading includes Antommarchi's *Last Days of ... Napoleon*[39] and Benn's *History of Belfast*.[40]

The diaries, however, do not always make it possible to identify Magill's reading accurately: the more familiar Magill is with a work the more truncated and elusive does the citation in the diaries become: items such as 'Witsius Body of Divinity',[41] 'McEwen on the types',[42] and 'Dwight's Theology'[43] are not always immediately identifiable. Similarly, when an acquaintance, William Molyneaux, was involved in a shooting accident, Magill records that he 'read Couper on gunshot wounds', possibly a standard text from his university days.[44] One initially elusive item in this respect is what Magill refers to on several occasions as 'my Sacramental Catechism', a work which he distributes liberally but which goes unrecorded in the usual printed sources.[45] In some cases, owing to either the brevity or imprecision of a reference, it has simply not been possible to identify the item in question.

The Thinking Few

At the time these diaries were being written, the most contentious issue within the Synod of Ulster – the major Presbyterian body of the day – was the matter of subscription to the Westminster Confession of Faith. Controversy over this issue had arisen in the Synod a century before but on this second occasion the debate centred not so much on the validity of man-made confessions as on the Arian theology of the non-subscribers. The leaders of the opposing parties were Henry Cooke and Henry Montgomery, two of the most eminent men in the Synod.[46]

Cooke championed the orthodox, and ultimately triumphant, party and was strongly supported by the Rev. Robert Stewart, minister of Broughshane, and by Magill himself. The controversy occasioned many publications, among them Robert Magill's poem *The Thinking Few*, a satire of some 1,000 lines.[47] That Magill should make his contribution in verse is no surprise: he was no newcomer to poetry having won a poetry prize while a student at Glasgow[48] and later, in 1834, was to publish a selection of his other poems.[49]

The poem – an unashamedly satirical romp through ancient and modern history, biblical reference, theology, philosophy and politics – was intended as a polemical contribution to the publications arising from the controversy. Its full title mocks William Porter's remark that Arianism was making progress among 'the thinking few' in the Synod of' Ulster, and incorporates allusions to the Book of Revelation, secret societies and a canting use of the term non-subscriber. Thomas Hamilton described the piece as 'a satirical poem of considerable power'.[50] Modern judgements vary: in his biography of Henry Cooke, Finlay Holmes, writing as a historian, dismisses it as a 'jingle' although he does remark that it may well have been more influential than many of the more 'serious contributions to the debate'.[51] John Hewitt, from a literary rather than a religious point of view, remarks:

> The best verses on the controversy, in fact, came from clergymen, with *The Ulster Synod* (1817) of William Heron of Ballyclare and *The Thinking Few* (1828) of Robert Magill, another County Antrim man. It is a nice coincidence that both were from the territory of the rhyming weavers.[52]

Magill first mentions his poem by name on 13 February 1828 when he records in his diary that he 'spent the greater part of the day writing out The Thinking Few – a poem'. It is not clear when he first began to compose the poem nor precisely what prompted him to write it. The *DNB* entry for Magill states that he wrote *The Thinking Few* at the instigation of the Rev. Henry Cooke:[53] this may well have been the case although it is not attested by the diary. However, in January 1828, Magill had received a letter which was 'a poetic answer to a piece of satire poetry written against Mr Stewart'[54] and it may well be that this also prompted him to put pen to paper.

Magill worked on the poem throughout March and had it ready for the press by early April. Travelling to Belfast in the 'Champion Coach' towards the end of March, Magill found himself in the company of the Rev. Andrew McCaldin, the minister of First Coleraine, and his daughter.

Having the manuscript with him and taking advantage of his captive audience, Magill proceeded to read the poem to his ministerial colleague. The reaction of the McCaldins – and the other passengers – to this in-coach entertainment goes unrecorded.[55]

Magill delivered the manuscript of the poem to Alexander Mackay at the *News-letter* Office on 18 April and ordered a printing of 1,000 copies, to be sold at 6d. per copy, 'the printing paper etc., etc. to cost £11.10s.0d.'[56] The topicality of the piece clearly demanded some urgency and Magill was in receipt of 'the proof sheet of the 1st 8 pages' by 25 April and the second proof sheet by 30 April. Proofs and corrections were delivered and returned by a series of intermediaries so that Magill was able to record on 6 June that he 'received a letter from Alexander Mackay stating that the poem (The Thinking Few) is printed'. Magill makes no mention of it in his diaries, but at some point in this period it appears that the decision was made to double the printing to 2,000 copies. On 9 June, Magill travelled to Belfast to arrange for the stitching and sale of the poem:

> Bought from Mr Blow, 1 Ream and 1 quire of blue cover paper at 17s.6d. per ream – engaged Winnington of Chapel Lane to stitch 2,000 copies of my poem at 2s. per hundred copies – M. Jellet and Harrison engaged to sell them.[57]

Three days later Magill is back in Belfast collecting some 200 stitched copies of the poem from Winnington and paying him £1.0s.0d., half of the account.[58] He returned again to Belfast on 18 June to collect a further 400 copies, leaving the remainder of the account for Winnington with Mackay. Mackay's own account, for £21.17s.6d., reached Magill on 12 September and a week later he records that he paid Mackay £21.0s.0d.[59] What happened to the outstanding 17s.6d. is unclear.

As agreed, the booksellers added the book, a generously printed octavo, to their stock. On 19 September Magill records that he received 9s. from Harrison for the sale of 24 copies (total selling cost 12s.), Harrison apparently taking 25% commission. This rate appears to be confirmed by the account with Morgan Jellet: Jellet sold some 98 copies of the poem and paid Magill part of the sum due on 9 October. Magill sets out the account in his diary for that date:

222

	£2.	9.	0.
Commission ¼		12.	3.
	£1.	16.	9.
recd.		16.	9.
Due	£1.	0.	0.

Jellet paid the balance on 6 November.

The distribution of local publications

It might appear from the meagre sales by Harrison and Jellet – 122 copies in all – that the decision to print 2,000 copies had been an unmitigated disaster. However, this fails to take account of another, and highly effective, network of distribution: the ministers themselves. It is clear from many instances in the diaries that such a network, albeit informal, existed within the ministerial brotherhood and their congregations. Magill mentions some ten sellers, mainly ministers, who between them sold over 300 copies of the poem. By far the most assiduous and successful of these was the Rev. John Paul, Magill's former teacher and long-time friend, who sold 104 copies. Some other colleagues, on the basis of the very specific numbers of copies involved, had clearly taken orders for the poem from the members of their congregations, while in other cases quantities of the poem were left with a minister in the hope that he would sell some or all of them. In some congregations sales were disappointing: an optimistic Magill left 100 copies with the Rev. John Hall of Clough only to have 80 of them returned.[60] Magill himself was an enthusiastic salesman: on the day following publication he attended a meeting of the local Mendicity Committee and records that he 'sold' – he may mean took orders for – some 48 copies;[61] and throughout the diary he notes that he 'bestowed' copies on a considerable number of individuals.

Magill's enthusiasm as a salesman and distributor extended to the publications of his fellow ministers. When he received a printed prospectus for the publication of two sermons by the Rev. Robert Stewart he gathered up orders from 32 members of his congregation and later lists the names of those to whom he gave them.[62] Some 100 copies of John Paul's 'Review of the speech of the Rev. Henry Montgomery',[63] 100 copies of the 'Discussion between Messrs. Stewart and McCauley',[64] 50 copies of Mark Cassidy's 'Address to the Newtownards congregation',[65] 25 copies of James Elder's 'Sermon on Justification'[66] and numbers of various other pamphlets are noted in the diaries as being left with or obtained by him for sale or distribution. One interesting item among these is James Seaton Reid's synodical sermon, *The History of the Presbyterian Church in Ireland ... Reviewed ...*, the first publication on the subject by the man who remains the father of Irish Presbyterian historiography. Curiously, Magill 'bestowed' many pamphlets on those who were emigrating and indeed sent copies overseas to former residents of the district. When Charles Lyness was about to board ship for Barbados, Magill 'bestowed him Cassidy's pamphlet, also Mr Paul's: Rev. James Reid's Synodical Sermon and a copy of "The Thinking Few"'.[67] How Lyness reacted to this beneficence we do not know but he may have consoled himself with the thought that at least the reading would help to pass the time on the long boat journey.

One final contribution which the diaries make to our knowledge of the book trade in Ulster, to be found in an entry for April 1828, may be noted here:

Recd. a letter from the Revd. James Morgan, Lisburn stating that several Clergymen wished to establish Mr William M'Comb, Belfast in the book trade and requesting to know if I would cooperate – each is to subscribe 10£ to be repaid in books.[68]

Magill replied to Morgan the following day but, once again, his diary fails to record whether or not he agreed to support the venture; he did however receive a letter from McComb some four months later, although its contents too go unrecorded.[69] McComb, 'the poet-laureate of Presbyterianism', had entered the book trade, as a bookseller and publisher, in 1828 after a period as a teacher in the Brown Street School.[70] The question as to how, if not why, he made that transition now appears to be answered.

....

224

This paper has attempted to offer an introduction to Robert Magill's world of books, a world which appears busier than we might perhaps expect of the minister of Mill Row congregation in the late 1820s. Clearly, many issues remain to be explored; and it must be emphasised again that the diaries offer us not a complete inventory of Magill's library, but simply a glimpse at his shelves. It has not been possible, even if it were desirable, to discuss here all the publications that Magill mentions; indeed, not all of them can be identified. Therefore, in order to offer a more complete picture, a preliminary trial list of publications, with possible identifications, is appended to this paper.

At first sight the diary of an early nineteenth-century Presbyterian minister seems an unlikely starting point for a tribute to Ronnie Adams. Yet this exploration of Magill's diary touches upon several areas of local bibliographical research – newspapers, reading, literacy, printing, publishing, book-selling and book distribution – which Ronnie pioneered and to which he contributed so ably. His encouragement, scholarship, friendship and generosity in many ways suggested this study, one to which he would himself have brought much greater knowledge and insight.

APPENDIX

A preliminary trial list of publications noted by Magill, 1827-1828.

An initial attempt is made here to list and to identify briefly the publications noted by Magill in his diaries. For each of the items listed Magill's wording is given first and is followed by a fuller citation of the item in question. Since Magill often cites the same item in several ways – for example he describes the report of the Stewart-McAuley debate in eight different ways – usually only his fullest citation is reproduced here.

I am indebted to colleagues in the Presbyterian Historical Society, Union Theological College, the Linen Hall Library, the Royal Irish Academy, and Trinity College Dublin for their help in locating certain items. Of necessity, most citations have been derived from secondary sources. I should, of course, be grateful for information on items not fully identified or identified incorrectly.

1. Newspapers and journals

Many of the newspapers and journals cited by Magill are discussed above. Only a summary list is given here.

Belfast	*Belfast Commercial Chronicle*
	Belfast News-letter
	Guardian and Constitutional Advocate
	[*Irishman* ?]
	Northern Whig
Drogheda	*Drogheda Journal*
Dublin	*Dublin Christian Instructor*
	Dublin Evening Mail
	Freeman's Journal
	Patriot
	Warder
	Watchman
Glasgow	*Christian Pioneer*
London	*Christian Moderator*
	[London/Missionary Chronicle?]
	Morning Herald
	Observer
	Record
	Times

2. Biblical texts

A Bible; a testament, 6 testaments, a New Testament; Douay testament, Douay Bible; Bible in Hebrew

It has not been possible, nor probably necessary, to identify specifically the editions of biblical texts mentioned by Magill. Bibles and New Testaments would have been ubiquitous and a Bible in Hebrew not uncommon for a minister with any scholarly ability. What is perhaps of interest is that Magill possessed a Douai Bible, and possibly also a Douai New Testament, which other ministers borrowed: Jamison, for example, borrowed it and this may be the 'Rhemish Version' to which he refers in his pamphlet.

3. Specific publications: probable and possible identifications

Anderson's defence of Presbyterianism
> ANDERSON, John. *A Defence of the Church-government, Faith, Worship & Spirit of the Presbyterian. In Answer to ... An Apology for Mr Thomas Rhind.* Glasgow: Brown, 1714.

Antomarchi's "Last Days of Napoleon"/ 2nd vol. ...
> ANTOMMARCHI, C. Francesco. *The Last Days of the Emperor Napoleon.* 2 vols., London: Colbourn, 1825.

History of Belfast
> BENN, George. *The History of the Town of Belfast with an Accurate Account of its Former & Present State: to which are added a Statistical Survey of the Parish of Belfast and a Description of Some Remarkable Antiquities in its Neighbourhood.* Belfast: Mackay, 1823.

Blair's preceptor
> BLAIR, David [i.e. Sir Richard Phillips]. *The Universal Preceptor, being an easy Grammar of Arts, Sciences and General Knowledge.* First pub. ? 2nd ed., 1811. 20th ed., London: Whittaker, 1825.

Brown's dictionary of the Bible
> BROWN, John. *A Dictionary of the Holy Bible.* First pub. Edinburgh, 1769. 7 further editions, 1778-1819.

Byron's Don Juan
> BYRON, George Gordon, Baron Byron. *Don Juan.* First part pub. 1819. First complete ed., 1824.

Mark Cassidy's address/Cassidy's pamphlet
> CASSIDY, Mark. *An Address to the Arian, Unitarian or New Light Congregation of Newtownards.* Belfast: Gregg, 1827.

2nd edition address to the Newtownards congregation
CASSIDY, Mark. *An Address to the Arian, Unitarian or New Light Congregation of Newtownards.* 2nd ed. Belfast: Stuart & Gregg, 1828.

Dr. Chalmers' sermon preached in Belfast
CHALMERS, Thomas. *The Effect of Man's Wrath in the Agitation of Religious Controversies: a Sermon Preached at the Opening of the new Presbyterian Chapel in Belfast on Sabbath, September 27, 1827.* Glasgow: Collins, 1827.

Dr. Samuel Clark's Sermons on the attributes of God
CLARKE, Samuel. *A Demonstration of the Being and Attributes of God: more Particularly in Answer to Mr Hobbs, Spinoza and their Followers* ... First pub. 1704? 2nd ed., 1706. 4th ed., 1716.

Mr Curoe's reply to Mr Jamison
CUROE, Daniel. *Strictures on 'An Appeal Addressed to the Members of his Congregation'.* Belfast: Smyth, 1827.

Dr. Drummond's essay
DRUMMOND, William Hamilton. *The Doctrine of the Trinity Founded neither on Scripture, nor on Reason and Common Sense, but on Tradition and the Infallible Church: an Essay Occasioned by a late Controversy between the Rev. Richard Pope and the Rev. Thomas Maguire.* Belfast: Dublin, 1827. 2nd ed., Dublin, 1827.

Drummond's 5 letters to Lord Mountcashel
DRUMMOND, William Hamilton. *Unitarian Christianity the Religion of the Gospel; and the New Reformation a Chimera; in five Letters to the Earl of Mountcashel.* London: Hunter; Belfast: Hodgson, 1828.

228

Dwights Theology 6 Volumes
DWIGHT, Timothy Dwight. *Theology Explained and Defended in a series of Sermons ...* 5 vols. 1818-19. London, repr. 1819. Abridged ed., 4 vols., London, 1823.

The Rev. James Elder's Sermon on Justification
ELDER, James. *A Sermon Preached in the Meeting-house of Drumacose* [sic] *on the Arian Controversy on 13th January 1828 in Defence of the Doctrine of Justification by the Imputed Righteousness of Christ.* Londonderry: Londonderry Journal, 1828.

The Vaudois/Gilly's Waldenses
GILLY, William Stephen. *Narrative of an Excursion to the Mountains of Piemont in the Year MDCCCXXIII, and Researches among the Vaudois, or Waldenses ...* London, 1824. 3rd ed., London: Rivington, 1826.

Minutes of the General Synod of Ulster [1827]
GENERAL Synod of Ulster. *Minutes of a General Synod at Strabane.* Belfast: Finlay, [1827].

Minutes of the General Synod [1828]
GENERAL Synod of Ulster. *Minutes of a General Synod at Cookstown.* Belfast: Finlay, [1828].

Unitarianism unmasked by Philip Dixon Hardy
HARDY, Philip Dixon. *Unitarianism Unmasked; or, the Unitarian's Creed, as Given in a Pamphlet recently Published by W.H. Drummond, D.D., Proved to be Inconsistent with itself, and Opposed to Reason.* Dublin: Curry; Tims, 1827.

[1st-9th] report of the Commissioners of Education Enquiry

HIS Majesty's Commission of Irish Education Inquiry

First report	H.C., 1825	(400) xii
Second report	H.C., 1826-7	(12) xii
Third report	H.C., 1826-7	(13) xiii
Fourth report	H.C., 1826-7	(89) xiii
Fifth report	H.C., 1826-7	(441) xiii
Sixth report	H.C., 1826-7	(442) xiii
Seventh report	H.C., 1826-7	(443) xiii
Eighth report	H.C., 1826-7	(509) xlii
Ninth report	H.C., 1826-7	(510) xiii

Scotch Worthies

HOWIE, John. *Biographia Scoticana; or, a brief Historical Account of the Lives ... of the Most Eminent Scots Worthies ...* First pub. 1775 (?). 2 vols., ed. McGavin, 1828.

Mr Jamison's address to the Catholics/Jamison's appeal

JAMISON, Archibald. *An Appeal to the Members of the Church of Rome Residing in Randalstown and its Vicinity.* Belfast: Mairs, 1827. 2nd ed., 1827.

Jamison's reply to Curoe

JAMISON, Archibald. *A Second Appeal to the Members of the Church of Rome Residing in Randalstown and its Vicinity.* Belfast: Mairs, 1827.

Minutes of a discussion of the question ... between the Rev. Abner Kneeland and Rev. W.L. McCalla at Philadelphia ...

KNEELAND, Abner and W.L. McCalla. *Minutes of a Discussion on the Question 'Is the Punishment of the Wicked Absolutely Eternal?': between Rev. Abner Kneeland and Rev. W.L. McCalla, which Commenced at the First Independent Church of Christ called Universalist, in Lombards Street, Philadelphia, July 13th and Concluded on the Friday following.* Taken in shorthand by R.L. Jennings. [s.l.], 1824.

1st Volume of McCrie's life of Knox/2nd volume ...
McCRIE. Thomas H. *The Life of John Knox*. First pub. 1811.
2nd ed., 2 vols, 1813. 4th ed., 2 vols, 1818.

McEwen on the types
MacEWEN, William. *Grace and Truth; or, The Glory and Fulness of the Redeemer Displayed in an Attempt to Explain ... the Types, Figures and Allegories of the Old Testament.* First pub. Edinburgh, 1763.

The O'Halloran family or the insurgent chief
McHENRY, James McHenry. *O'Halloran; or, The Insurgent Chief.* First pub. Philadelphia, 1824. Republished London, 1824.

"Theory of the World" by Mr McNab
McNAB, Francis Maximus. *A Theory of the Moral and Physical System of the Universe, Demonstrated by Analogy in which the Elements of General Science are Explained upon a Principle entirely new.* Edinburgh, 1817.

My Sacramental Catechism
MAGILL, Robert. *A Sacramental Catechism for the use of Young Intending Communicants.* Belfast: Mairs, 1826.

The Thinking Few
MAGILL, Robert. *The Thinking Few: a Poem, dedicated to the Right Worshipful Grand Masters of the New Arian Lodge, No. 666, under the Patronage of the incorporated Joint Stock Company of Thinkers in Ireland commonly known by the Name of the Free and Fearless Thinking Few*, by a non-subscriber to Arian plate. Belfast: Mackay, 1828.

Mitchels Sermons of Newry
MITCHEL, John. *The Scripture Doctrine of the Divinity of our Lord Jesus Christ and other Subjects Connected therewith ... In a Series of Sermons ...* Belfast: Mairs [?], 1828.

231

Montgomery's Psalmist
MONTGOMERY, James. *The Christian Psalmist; or, Hymns Selected and Original.* First pub. Glasgow, 1825. Many editions.

Moore's melodies
MOORE, Thomas. *Irish Melodies.* First 2 vols. Dublin, 1808. First complete ed., Dublin: Power, 1820.

1st Volume ... /2nd Volume of Mosheim's Ecclesiastical History
MOSHEIM, Johann Lorenz von. *An Ecclesiastical History, Ancient and Modern, from the Birth of Christ to the Beginning of the Present Century* ... First pub., 2 vols., London, 1765. Various eds. 1781, 1812, 1815, 1822 (2 vols.).

Neals History of the Puritans 2 Volumes
NEAL, Daniel. *The History of the Puritans or Protestant Non-Conformists from the Reformation in 1517, to the Revolution in 1688* ... First pub. 1732-1748. Abridged ed., 2 vols., London; Leeds, 1811. 5 vols., London, 1822.

Dr. Owen on the 130th Psalm
OWEN, John. *A Practical Exposition on the 130th Psalm wherein the Nature of the Forgiveness of Sin is Declared.* First pub. London, 1669. New ed., Edinburgh, 1819.

Parkhurst's Hebrew Lexicon
PARKHURST, John. *A Hebrew and English Lexicon, without Points in which the Hebrew and Chaldee Words* ... First pub. 1762. 5th ed., 1801. New ed., 1823.

Pauls reply to Dr. Bruce
PAUL, John. *A Refutation of Arianism; or, a Defence of the Plenary Inspiration of the Holy Scriptures, the supreme Deity of the Son and Holy Ghost, the Atonement, Original Sin, Predestination, the Perseverance of the Saints &c. In Reply to the Sermons of the Rev. William Bruce D.D.* Belfast: Mackay, 1826.

Review of the Rev. Henry Montgomery's Speech
PAUL, John. *The Speech of the Rev. Henry Montgomery Reviewed, and the Sentiments of the most Celebrated Antitrinitarian Divines Examined.* Belfast: Mackay, 1828.

Address of the People of England to the Catholics of Ireland
The People of England to the Roman Catholics of Ireland, in Answer to their Address ... London: Seeley; Dublin: Curry, 1827.

Authentic report of the discussion between Pope and Maguire
POPE, Richard T.P. and Thomas Maguire. *Authenticated Report of the Discussion which took place between the Rev. Richard T.P. Pope and the Rev. Thomas Maguire, in the Lecture Room of the Dublin Institution, on the 19th, 20th, 21st, 23d, 24th, and 25th of April, 1827.* Dublin: Coyne, 1827.

The Bee hive, relative to Popery
RABBOTENU, Isaac [i.e. Philips Von Marnix]. *The Bee Hive of the Romishe Churche, wherein the authour (Isaac Rabbotenu) a Zealous Protestant, under the Person of a Superstitious Papist, doth so driely refell [?] the Grose Opinions of Popery and so Divinely Defend the Articles of Christianitie, that ... there is not a Booke to be Founde ... Sweeter for thy Comforte.* Trans. by George Gilpin. First pub. London 1579; later editions 1623, 1636.

Rev. James Reids Synodical Sermon
REID, James Seaton. *The History of the Presbyterian Church in Ireland, briefly Reviewed and Practically Improved. A Sermon Preached at the Opening of the General Synod of Ulster, Assembled at Cookstown, June 24, 1828.* Belfast: Greer, 1828.

1st Volume of Waverly ... Scot
SCOTT, Walter. *Waverley; or, 'Tis sixty Years since.* First
pub. Edinburgh, 1814.

Shakespeare's Macbeth
SHAKESPEARE, William. *The Tragedy of Macbeth.*

Mr Stewart's 2 sermons/Mr Stewart's Sermon against Papal supremacy
STEWART, Robert. *Papal Supremacy Examined: a Sermon
upon Matthew, XVI, 18,19 ... whether our Lord did in these
Verses invest Peter with a Visible and Local Supremacy.*
Belfast: Smyth, 1827.

STEWART, Robert. *The Essential Divinity of the Lord Jesus
Christ; Illustrated in a Brief Examination of the Socinian and
Arian Systems: a Sermon Preached at Lismore, in County
Waterford, January 1, 1825.* Belfast: Smyth, 1827.

The controversial discussion between Messrs Stewart and McCauley
STEWART, Robert and Bernard McAuley. *Authenticated
Report of the Controversial Discussion upon the Supremacy
of St. Peter which took Place between the Rev. Bernard
McAuley, P.P., and the Rev. Robert Stewart, A.M., ... on the
24th, 25th and 26th July, 1827, at Ballymena.* Belfast:
Smyth, 1827.

Samuel Tucker's reply to Mr Paul
TUCKER, Samuel. *A Refutation of Certain Calvinistic
Principles Advocated by the Rev. John Paul in his late Reply
to the Sermons of Dr. Bruce. In four Letters Addressed to a
Friend.* Belfast: Mairs, 1826.

Der Freischütz by Weber
WEBER, Carl Maria von. *Der Freischütz. Romantische Oper.*
Vocal score first pub. Berlin, 1822.

6 Shorter Catechisms
  WESTMINSTER Assembly of Divines. *The Shorter Catechism Agreed upon by the Assembly of Divines at Westminster with the Assistance of Commissioners from the Church of Scotland.* First pub. 1648. Numerous editions, including Belfast.

Witsius Body of Divinity
  WITS, Herman. *The Oeconomy of the Covenants between God and Man, Comprehending a Complete Body of Divinity ...* Faithfully translated ... by William Crookshank ... First pub. London: Dilly, 1763. Edinburgh eds. 1771, 1803.

Night thoughts
  YOUNG, Edward. *The Complaint; or, Night Thoughts on Life, Death, and Immortality ...* First complete ed., 1750. Numerous editions.

4. More general references

2 reports of the Bible Society [1827]/report of the Bible Society for 1828. Magill was involved with a Bible Society; the reports are possibly the annual reports of the Belfast Auxiliary Bible Society, issued by Finlay.

Cranmers Martyrdom
  Several volumes with similar titles were published e.g. *The Life, Martyrdom, and Selections from the Writings of Thomas Cranmer* (London, 1809) and *The Life and Martyrdom of Thomas Cranmer* (Church of England Tract Society, 1815; 1824).

Speeches of Curran
  Several editions of speeches by John Philpot Curran (1750-1817), the lawyer and parliamentarian, appeared in the early years of the 19th century.

Eusebius

Eusebius of Caesarea (c.265-c.339) the 'Father of Church History' and the author of many works is best known for his *Historia Ecclesiastica*, the most important of the histories of the Early Church.

Graham's poetry

James Grahame (1765-1811) was born in Glasgow and was the author of several books of poetry which appeared between 1794 and 1809. His long poem, *The Sabbath*, appeared in 1804 and two volumes of collected poems in 1807.

Harvey's Sermons/Harvey's Letters

James Hervey (1714-1758), an English Calvinist, was a popular devotional writer. His work included meditations, sermons and letters. His complete works were published in 1769.

1st Volume of Hurreon's Sermons

John Hurrion (1675?-1731) published several collections of sermons. The three volumes of *The Whole Works of ... John Hurrion*, edited by Rev. A. Taylor, were published in 1823.

Jenks on prayer/Jenks prayers

Benjamin Jenks (1646-1724) wrote several devotional works on prayer. His *Prayers and Offices of Devotion for Families and for Particular Persons upon most Occasions* ran through many editions.

2nd vol. of Josephus

The historian Josephus Flavius (AD 37-??) is best known as the author of *The Jewish War* and *Antiquities of the Jews*. Many editions exist.

Printed address of ... the Presbyterian Society for Ireland
The Presbyterian Society was an orthodox pressure group within the Synod of Ulster. Several writers refer to its addresses.

The Munster Synod against Mr Cooks testimony before Parliament
'Observations of the Presbyterian Synod of Munster on the Testimony of the Rev. Henry Cooke before the Committee of Parliament etc.' appeared in the *Belfast News-letter* of 28 Aug. 1827. It may also have been independently printed as Magill received a copy by post shortly before this.

5. Unidentified items

Arianism displayed
A biographical dictionary
A book of chronology
A book of prayer
Couper on gunshot wounds
A French book on Transubstantiation
Historical Recollections
Minutes of a discussion on Universal Redemption [Kneeland & McCalla?]
Missionary reports
An old exposition of the Bible
The Pocket Encyclopedia
Printed observations relative to a New Jail
Select poetry

Notes

I am grateful to the Very Rev. Professor Finlay Holmes and the Rev. Dr W.D. Bailie for their comments on an earlier draft of this paper.

1   *Dictionary of National Biography* (Oxford, 1921), vol. 12, p. 763.
2   T.W. Moody, Higher Education, in *Ulster Since 1800. Second Series: a Social Survey* (London, 1957), p. 192.

3   This account of the journey is derived from W.D. Bailie, 'Two Tired Feet: a Trek to Glasgow', *Presbyterian Herald*, 373, Nov. 1975, p. 4. Dr Bailie's article is based on Magill's own unpublished account. Magill had been familiar with the works of Robert Burns from an early age and knew several of his poems by heart.

4   Ms in the Presbyterian Historical Society of Ireland, Belfast. I am indebted to Dr W.D. Bailie for drawing it to my attention.

5   The transcript of the diaries for these two years is contained in James G. Kenny, *As the Crow Flies over Rough Terrain, Incorporating the Diary 1827/28 and More of a Divine* (Glengormley, 1988) pp. 283-399. Hereafter, Diary. I am indebted to Mr Kenny for a presentation copy. The original diary is now in the possession of the Presbyterian Historical Society of Ireland.

6   Diary 7.9.1827.

7   Diary 18.11.1828.

8   Diary 22.6.1827. The newspapers are: *The Times, Dublin Evening Mail, Guardian, Belfast News-letter* and *Northern Whig*.

9   Diary 16.6.1827.

10   Diary 9.1.1827. This is a curious reference: most sources date the demise of the *Irishman* to 1826. Magill's entry ties the reference to a specific event, the death of Frederick, Duke of York, which occurred on 5 January 1827. It is, of course, quite possible that Magill simply made a mistake.

11   Diary 15.6.1827.

12   Diary 16.10.1827.

13   Diary 26.12.1828.

14   Diary 12.5.1828.

15   Diary 24.9.1827.

16   Diary 11.10.1827.

17   I have been unable to trace a journal with the title 'Missionary Chronicle' or 'London Missionary Chronicle' for the years in question. Earlier and later journals carried this title and it may be that the title used by Magill is a common or popular title for the journal of one of the London missionary societies of the time.

18 Diary 8.3.1827. There was apparently a piano in the manse as on 4
October 1827 Magill records that he 'paid Mr Reid of Belfast 5s. for
tuning Piano Forte'. The manuscript music book of Magill's wife, Anne
Jane (née Skelton), is held in the library of the Presbyterian Historical
Society of Ireland.

19 Diary 20.2.1827.

20 Diary 16.7.1828.

21 Diary 29.8.1827. Magill spells the author 'Graham'. I suggest the
Scottish-born poet James Grahame (1765-1811) as a possible
interpretation.

22 Diary 24.10.1828. I have been unable to identify this compilation.

23 Diary 13.1.1827. McHenry was born in Larne. He became a doctor and
later emigrated to the United States. A poet and novelist, he was one
of the first to take the '98 rebellion as a topic for fictional treatment.

24 Diary 22.9.1828.

25 In a conversation some years ago Ronnie Adams suggested precisely this
to me: his research indicated that Presbyterian ministers read much
more widely than simply Scottish publications. Magill, for one,
confirms his view.

26 Diary 4.2.1828.

27 Diary 30.10.1828. John Howie's book was first published in 1775 as
*Biographia Scoticana; or, a Brief Historical Account of the Lives ... of
the Most Eminent Scots Worthies ...* An enlarged edition followed
shortly afterwards. McGavin's two-volume edition was advertised in
the *Belfast News-letter* of October 1828.

28 Diary 18.9.1827.

29 Diary 28.9.1827.

30 *Belfast News-letter*, 17.4.1827.

31 *Authenticated Report of the Discussion ... between the Rev. Richard T.
Pope, and the Rev. Thomas Maguire ...* (Dublin: Coyne, 1827). Reports
of the debate were carried in supplements to the *Belfast News-letter*
of 27.4.1827, 1.5.1827, and 4.5.1827.

32 Diary 16.7.1827.

33 *Authenticated Report of the Controversial Discussion ... between the Rev.
Bernard McAuley, P.P., and the Rev. Robert Stewart, A.M. ...* (Belfast:
Smyth, 1827).

34   *Belfast News-letter*, 25.12.1827.

35   Diary 10.7.1828.

36   Diary 15.7.1828. Ellison had borrowed the first volume on 28 July 1827 and the second volume on 5 January 1828.

37   Diary 13.2.1827.

38   Diary 23.8.1828 ff.

39   Diary 9.2.1827 ff.

40   Diary 21.7.1828 and 24.7.1828.

41   Diary 14.12.1827. Kenny transcribes this name as 'Wilsins'. I suggest that the Ms may be read as 'Witsius'.

42   Diary 21.1.1827.

43   Diary 8.12.1828.

44   Diary 29.1.1827.

45   Diary e.g. 1.3.1828. Magill's pamphlet, *A Sacramental Catechism for the Use of Young Intending Communicants*, was published by Mairs in 1826. I am indebted to Mr Robert Bonar of the Presbyterian Historical Society for his assistance in locating a copy in the Society's library.

46   For accounts of the two Controversies within the context of Irish Presbyterian history see Finlay Holmes, *Our Irish Presbyterian Heritage* (Belfast, 1985). For particular studies of each of the controversies see *Challenge and Conflict: Essays in Irish Presbyterian History and Doctrine*, edited by J.L.M. Haire (Antrim, 1981) especially the essays by A.W.G. Brown, pp. 28-45, R.G. Crawford, pp. 96-115, and Finlay Holmes, pp. 116-133.

47   The poem was published anonymously under the full title: *The Thinking Few, a Poem: Dedicated to the Right Worshipful Grand Masters of the New Arian Lodge, no. 666, under the Patronage of the Incorporated Joint Stock Company of Thinkers in Ireland, Commonly Known by the Name of the Free and Fearless Thinking Few*, by a Non-Subscriber to Arian Plate (Belfast: Mackay, 1828). 38p.

48   Magill's Glasgow poem was published as *The Race: a Prize Poem, Composed at Glasgow College* (Glasgow, 1815).

49   *Poems on Various Subjects, Chiefly Religious: Particularly Designed for the Young* (Belfast, 1834).

50   *Dictionary of National Biography* (Oxford, 1921), vol. 12, p. 763.

51   Finlay Holmes, *Henry Cooke* (Belfast, 1981) p. 55.

52 John Hewitt, *Rhyming Weavers and Other Country Poets of Antrim and Down* (Belfast, 1974) p. 35. Indeed Magill, like the rhyming weavers, may also have written poetry in Ulster-Scots. In 1865 the Rev. R.J. Bryce read a paper to the Belfast Literary Society under the title 'Specimens of Unpublished Poetry in the Scoto-Hibernian Dialect of the North of Ireland, with Notices of their Author, the Rev. R. Magill, and of the Character and Habits of the People'. *Belfast Literary Society, 1801-1901: Historical Sketch* (Belfast, 1902) p. 158.

53 *Dictionary of National Biography* (Oxford, 1921), vol. 12, p. 763.

54 Diary 17.1.1828.

55 Diary 27.3.1828.

56 Diary 18.4.1828.

57 Diary 9.6.1828.

58 Diary 12.6.1828.

59 Diary 19.9.1828.

60 Diary 6.8.1828 and 20.10.1828.

61 Diary 10.6.1828.

62 Diary 31.1.1827 and 5.4.1827.

63 Diary 9.6.1828.

64 Diary 16.11.1827.

65 Diary 19.2.1828.

66 Diary 4.6.1828 and 18.7.1828.

67 Diary 27.11.1828.

68 Diary 22.4.1828. Magill had visited McComb in Belfast four days earlier, on 18 April, the day, he notes, on which McComb's two year old son had died.

69 Diary 9.8.1828.

70 For an account of the Brown Street School and some details of McComb's tenure and resignation see Aiken McClelland, The Early History of Brown Street Primary School, *Ulster Folklife*, 17 (1971), 52-60.

CONTRIBUTORS

Dr W.H. Crawford is Development Officer of the Ulster Federation of Local Studies.

Roger Dixon is Librarian of the Ulster Folk and Transport Museum.

John Erskine is an Assistant Librarian at Stranmillis College, Belfast.

Sir Peter Froggatt is a former Vice-Chancellor of the Queen's University Belfast and is Secretary of the Belfast Literary Society.

Dr Alan Gailey is Director of the Ulster Folk and Transport Museum.

John A Gamble is an antiquarian bookseller in Belfast.

John Gray is Librarian of the Linen Hall Library.

John Killen is Deputy Librarian of the Linen Hall Library.

Dr W.A. Maguire is Head of Human History at the Ulster Museum.

Trevor Parkhill is Keeper of History at the Ulster Museum.

Dr Barbara Traxier Brown is a Lecturer in the Department of Library and Information Studies, University College Dublin.

Dr Brian Walker is Director of the Institute of Irish Studies at the Queen's University Belfast.

Gordon Wheeler is a Governor and former President of the Linen Hall Library.

TABULA AMICORUM

Adams, Mrs A.F., Holywood, Co. Down

Adams, Miss Alexandra M., Holywood, Co. Down

Adams, Mrs Amber M., Holywood, Co. Down

Adams, Ms Peace, Cavan

Aiken, Sydney, Spa, Co. Down

Association of Assistant Librarians (NI)

Ballantine, Ms C., University of Ulster

Ballard, Ms Linda-May, Ulster Folk and Transport Museum

Barnard, Dr Toby, Hertford College, Oxford

Belfast Central Library, Royal Avenue

Benson, Charles, Trinity College Library, Dublin

Blaney, Dr Roger, Holywood, Co. Down

Brennan, M., Holywood, Co. Down

Brown, Dr Barbara Traxier, University College Dublin

Brown, Tom, Belfast

Buchanan, Malcolm, Belfast

Buchanan, Prof. R.H., Institute of Irish Studies, Queen's University, Belfast

Buckley, Dr Anthony D., Ulster Folk and Transport Museum

Chambers, Dr George, Ulster Historical Foundation

Clarke, Prof, and Mrs R.S.J., Belfast

Cochrane, Clive, Queen's University, Belfast

Connolly, A.L., Dundalk

County Masonic Lodge No. 381, Holywood, Co. Down

Craddock, Peter, Castlerock

Craig, Lt/Cdr Andrew M.A., R.N., Southsea

Craig, Andrew M.A., Lib., Stonehaven

Craig, Mrs Catherine, Aberdeen

Craig, Grace, Aberdeen

Crawford, Dr Bill, Federation For Ulster Local Studies

Dallat, Dr Cahal, J.P., Ulster Local History Trust

Dallat, Michael, Belfast

Day, Angelique, Institute of Irish Studies, Queen's University, Belfast

Deeny, Donnell, QC, Belfast

Delargy, Mary, Linen Hall Library

Department of Irish Folklore, University College Dublin

Dickinson, C.W., Belfast

Drennan, Anthony S., Belfast

Duffy, Dr Seamus, Armagh

Dunlop, A.J., Holywood, Co. Down

Dunlop, Dr Eull, Mid-Antrim Historical Group, Ballymena

Dunlop, F., Carryduff

Eagleson, D., Belfast

Elliott, Prof. M., University of Liverpool

Fennessy, Richard, City Library, Waterford

Finegan, Ms Joanna, Ardee, Co. Louth

Fitzpatrick, Olivia, University of Ulster

Fox, Patrick O'D, Bangor

Gailey, Alan, Ulster Folk and Transport Museum

Garner, Mrs Margaret A.K., Helen's Bay

Given, Mrs S., Stranorlar, Co. Donegal

Gordon, Angus, The Linen Hall Library

Gordon, W.D., Holywood, Co. Down

Gormley, Kathleen, North West Archaeological and Historical Society

Gracey, Jim and Diane, Cambridge

Greene, Muriel, Brontë Society (Irish Section)

Gribbon, Dr H.D., Castlerock, Co. Londonderry

Gribbon, Jane, University of Limerick

Haensel, A, Irdning, Austria

Hamil, Cormac, Belfast

Hamilton, Victor, Holywood

Haworth, Richard, Trinity College, Dublin

Heatley, Fred, Belfast

Hoare, Peter, Nottingham

Hobart, Ann, Belfast

Humphreys, John J., Belfast/Ballycastle

Irvine, Elizabeth, South Eastern Education and Library Board, Library and
    Information Service

Irwin, Harry, Belfast

Johnston, Jack, Clogher

Johnston, Roy, Belfast

Johnston, Wilson, Co. Armagh

Kee, Arthur and Claire, Kee's Hotel, Stranorlar, Co. Donegal

Kelly, Mrs Marion, Belfast

Kennedy, Maire, Dublin Public Libraries

Kerr, William, Derriaghy

Kimber, Richard, Holywood

Kinane, Vincent, Trinity College Library, Dublin

Kingston, Ms Irene, Holywood

Lambkin, Brian, Lagan College, Belfast

Lancaster, Mrs P.A., Carrickfergus

Larkin, John F., Bar Library, Royal Courts Of Justice

Library and Information Services Council (NI)

Linnell, J.M., University of Keele

Longwell, Sarah and David, Congleton

Loughbrough, Brian, Museums and Galleries Commission

McAlister, Colette, Prospect House Books, Donaghadee

MacAulay, Rev. Ambrose, St Brigid's Presbytery, Belfast

McCleery, Dr Alistair, Napier University, Edinburgh

McCormick, T.J., Bangor

McCullough, Catherine, Armagh County Museum

McCullough, Des, Comber

McDowell, Doreen E., Belfast

McFaul, Michael, North Eastern Education and Library Board, Carrickfergus

McGonagle, J and Co., Belfast

McGovern, Gabriel J., Churchtown, Dublin

McGroarty, Antoinette, Stranorlar, Co. Donegal

McIvor, Mrs Jill, Ombudsman, Belfast

McKee, Maureen, Belfast

McKendry, Dr E., St Mary's College, Belfast

McKinney, Ms Dorothy, Belfast

MacMonagle, Patrick, Muckross House, Killarney

McNeill, D.B., Newtownards

Mallon, Jim, Colin Glen Trust, Belfast

Maume, Patrick, Cork

Mawhinney, Graham, Draperstown

Merrick, Anthony C.W., Holywood

Mid-Glamorgan County Libraries, Bridgend

Millar, Mr D.H., Belfast

Montgomery, Michael, University of South Carolina, USA

Moore, John S., Holywood

Morgan-Binney, Jane, Prospect House Books, Donaghadee

Murphy, Grace, Belfast

Murphy, Seán, Newtown School, Waterford

Nelson, E. Charles, National Botanic Gardens, Glasnevin

Nesbitt, Noel, Belfast

Newall, Dr Venetia, University of London

Nicholls, N.A.G., Papua New Guinea

Nicholson, Ciaran P., Dublin

Ni Fhloinn, Bairbre, Department of Irish Folklore, University College Dublin

Nolan, Sean, Belfast

O'Dwyer, Michael, Kilkenny

Ó Lúing, Gearóid, National Library of Ireland

O'Malley, Prof. William T., University of Rhode Island, USA

O'Sullivan, John C., Dublin

Parker, Liam, Belfast

Patterson, Ella, Queen's University, Belfast

Pitt, Linda and Dennis, Derby

Pitt, Michael, Oxford

Pollard, Mary Paul, Dublin

Prenter, Eddie and Jennifer, Whitehead, Co. Antrim

Prospect House Books, Donaghadee, Co. Down

Rankin, Peter, Saintfield

Rankin, Alastair and Gillian, Lisburn

Rankin, Fred, Belfast

Reid, Horace, Ballynahinch

Robinson, Fred, NI Prison Service Sports Association

Ross, Noel, Dundalk

Royal Irish Academy, Dublin

Russell, Norman J., Queen's University, Belfast

Rutherford, J.G.T., Ballycarry

Ryan, Eddie, Newtownards

Scott, Sam, Ulster Folk and Transport Museum

Simms, John, Linen Hall Library

Slater, Dr Gerry, Public Record Office of Northern Ireland

Sloan, David, Downtown Radio, Cool FM

Sloan, Noel, Belfast

Smith, Ms Deborah A., Bureau of Historic Sites, Waterford, NY, USA

Southern Education and Library Board, Armagh

Speers, Sheela, Ulster Museum, Belfast

Stewart, Mr and Mrs William, Northolt

Tennis, D., Bangor

Todd, Martin, Saintfield

Towers, Robert, Monkstown, Co. Dublin

Turkington, David, Belfast

Turner, Brian S., Saul, Co. Down

Tynan, P.J., Courtwood Books, Co. Laois

Tyrrall, Mrs Mary, Newtownabbey

Ulster-American Folk Park Library, Omagh

Valentine, Barry, Linen Hall Library

Vowles, Margaret, Portstewart

Warde, Martin and Alice, Belfast

Webb, Patricia, Belfast

Weatherup, Roger, Armagh

Welch, David, South Eastern Education and Library Board, Belfast

Western Education and Library Board, Library Service

Western Education and Library Board, Omagh, Co. Tyrone

Wheeler, Gordon, Downpatrick

Wilson, Tony, Belfast

Wilson, Philip B., Craigavon Museum

Wilson, Wm. C., Belfast

Woodman, George, NI Assembly Library, Stormont, Belfast

Workman, Ian, Belfast

Worthington, Miss V., Dublin